Sensory Theatre

Sensory Theatre: How to Make Interactive, Inclusive, Immersive Theatre for Diverse Audiences by a Founder of Oily Cart is an accessible step-by-step guide to creating theatre for inclusive audiences, such as young people on the autism spectrum or affected by other neuro-divergent conditions and children under two.

Conventional theatre relies on seeing and hearing to involve its audience; sensory theatre harnesses the power of five or more senses to address its participants who have different ways of relating to the world around them. This book is an insightful history of Oily Cart and its pioneering development of work for the very young, including Baby Theatre, and for neuro-divergent audiences including those on the autism spectrum. It gives a clear introduction to the fundamental concepts of this theatre, suggests a host of practical techniques drawn from over 40 years of experience, and describes some of Oily Cart's most radical innovations, including theatre on trampolines, in hydrotherapy pools and with flying audiences in the company of aerial artists. The book also includes copious photos from the Oily Cart's archives and links to video examples of the company's work. Readers will learn how to:

- Research the intended audience while not being led astray by labels.
- Create a welcoming, immersive sensory space in classrooms, nurseries, school halls and playgrounds.
- Devise sensory stories that can be adapted to suit different audiences.
- Recruit, audition, cast and run rehearsals.
- Ensure that the production is truly sensory and interactive.

Written for Theatre for Young Audiences, Drama in Education and specialised Applied Theatre courses, as well as educators and theatre practitioners interested in creating inclusive, interactive productions, *Sensory Theatre* offers a goldmine of ideas for making work that connects with audiences who can be the hardest to reach.

Tim Webb is one of the three co-founders of the Oily Cart theatre company producing inclusive shows for young people of all ages and abilities. He was the Artistic Director and chief writer of the company from 1981 to his retirement in 2018. During this time, he led a team that created more than 85 productions for young people including those labelled as having Profound and Multiple Learning Disabilities or other complex disabilities. An honorary fellow of Rose Bruford College, he has taught and directed sensory, immersive and interactive theatre in Abu Dhabi, Belgium, Canada, China, Ireland, Russia, Sweden and the USA, as well as throughout the UK. In 2011, he was honoured to be appointed MBE by Her Majesty Queen Elizabeth II for his work for young people with disabilities. To find out more about Oily Cart, visit www.oilycart.org.uk.

Sensory Theatre

How to Make Interactive, Inclusive,
Immersive Theatre for Diverse Audiences
by a Founder of Oily Cart

Tim Webb

for Menrat, I appreciated
your book launch very much.
I hope you will enjoy
mine

Routledge
Taylor & Francis Group

NEW YORK AND LONDON

Cover image: Blue 2006 Oily Cart. A starry, starry night. Ace, played by
Mark Foster, opens his Blues Bag full of stars. Design: Claire de Loon. Photo:
Patrick Baldwin.

First published 2023
by Routledge
605 Third Avenue, New York, NY 10158

and by Routledge
4 Park Square, Milton Park, Abingdon, Oxon, OX14 4RN

Routledge is an imprint of the Taylor & Francis Group, an informa business

© 2023 Tim Webb

Library of Congress Cataloging-in-Publication Data
A catalog record for this book has been requested

ISBN: 978-0-367-54863-6 (hbk)
ISBN: 978-0-367-54947-3 (pbk)
ISBN: 978-1-003-09128-8 (ebk)

DOI: 10.4324/9781003091288

Typeset in Goudy
by Apex CoVantage, LLC

For my grandchildren: Émil and Etta

Contents

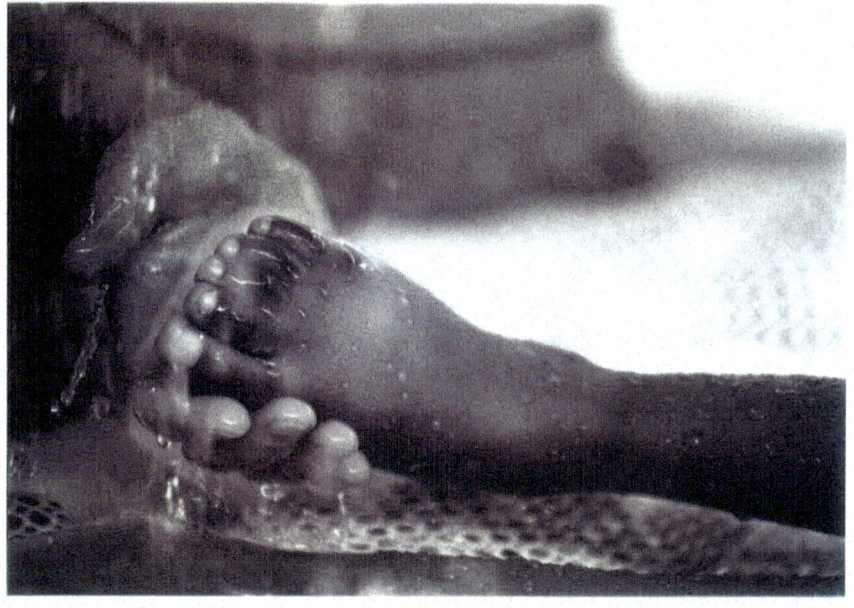

Bubbles 1997 Oily Cart. Design: Claire de Loon.
Photo: Paul Harris

Foreword

Up and Away premiere in 2015. The Fogg Family Balloon Society lift off through the clouds. Commissioned by Lincoln Center and created by Trusty Sidekick Theater Company. Environment Design by Nic Benacerraf, Lighting Design by Simon Harding, Costume Design by Natalie Loveland.

Photo by Alexis Buatti-Ramos. www.trustysidekick.org

I'm seated on the floor, on a carpet of grass. I feel a breeze, brimming with the scent of lavender. The air is filled with the sound of beautiful music. I'm completely lost in the immersive environment. And I see a child, usually defined by their complex disability, engaged in a moment of pure and uninhibited delight with a performer dressed as a sheep. I see the child's carer, tears streaming down their face, surely witnessing a moment that is far from typical in the day-to-day life of that child. And we know, the lucky few who find themselves seated in this *pasture*, that we are experiencing a moment of transcendent beauty together in community. We are experiencing the magic of the Oily Cart.

It is a rare and remarkable gift to encounter a true artistic pioneer in one's lifetime. According to the Merriam-Webster dictionary, the word *pioneer* describes someone who *originates or helps open up a new line of thought or activity*. Tim Webb, along with his visionary band of artists who created the Oily Cart, embodies this title more than any artist I've had the honor to work with and learn from in my career. Tim paved the way for generations of young people with complex disabilities to experience joy, wonder, connection and awe through the power of live performance. In the 80s, Oily Cart had the audacity to create immersive, sensory theatrical experiences for audiences deemed "impossible" to serve – children under five and audiences with complex and multiple disabilities. Utilising and refining the techniques outlined in this book, he proved that sensory theatre artists could unlock new doors of experience for young people with complex disabilities that surprised parents, carers, schools and therapists.

The key to Oily Cart's success may seem like an obvious technique for theatre makers, but it is far more rare than it should be – they actually *listened* to their audience and drew artistic inspiration directly from the audience's needs. They approached their audiences with a sense of wonder and openness, rather than viewing them only through the lens of their diagnoses or limitations. They created a lab for artistic experimentation embedded within schools and care centers, partnering with children and teachers by building trust through creative play and authentic relationships. The audience became part of the creative team, driving the process through play, sensory engagement and one-to-one interaction. And they fervently believed that these audiences deserved the highest quality, small-scale, intimate, meticulously designed theatre created especially for them.

In 2015, Trusty Sidekick Theater Company was commissioned by Lincoln Center Education to create its first show for audiences on the autism spectrum, and I had the honor of helming the production. I was nervous. The stakes felt high, and the ensemble of artists on the project wanted to ensure that the audience had an incredible experience. As we researched best practices in this emerging field of multisensory performance, all roads led back to Oily Cart. I was surprised to find how many companies and artists across the world were trained by Tim Webb before launching their own practice in this type of work. It is no exaggeration to say that Tim Webb and Oily Cart cat-alysed a global artistic movement by nurturing a generation of artists to cre-ate. My company was honored to join the ranks of these disciples under the guidance of Oily Cart, which led to the creation of our show *Up and Away*.

As a generous and supportive mentor, Tim Webb offered three lessons that have stayed with me, far beyond the time we spent in the rehearsal room together. **First, the audience is the most important ingredient.** We are there for them, in service of them. Use what they offer to guide and feed the cre-ative process. **Second, embrace the role of artist rather than trying to be a therapist or an "expert" on disability.** Our innate curiosity and creativ-ity was exactly what we needed to reach these young people in new and unexpected ways that their traditional carers might not, and that's why we already possessed the tools necessary to be successful. **Finally, make it your own.** Tim humbly offered a set of techniques and principles learned over decades of creating sensory theatre, but he was the first to say that his way wasn't the only way. He encouraged us to use these techniques as a starting point for further discovery, forging our own path forward in expanding this art form.

And now, he offers them to you. Throughout these pages, you'll find a treasure trove full of concepts, techniques and methodologies developed over thou-sands of experiences in theatres, schools and community centers. Become inspired, discover their power and then experiment with your own path for-ward by making your unique brand of sensory performance. Together, we can continue to expand the canon of work created for and with audiences of all abilities. Now more than ever, at a time when live gathering is on pause and our interpersonal interactions are more limited than ever before, I have an even greater understanding of the true power of sensory human connection and shared imaginative experience. May the seeds planted through these pages grow into a lush *pasture* of wonder, experimentation and connection for generations of artists and audiences to come.

Jonathan Shmidt Chapman
October 2020

Preface

I have written this book during a terrifying pandemic that is raging around the world. Sometimes it seems to die down in one country only to erupt the next day somewhere else. One moment we are told that we must retreat into our family *bubbles* to stop the virus spreading. We should stay at home, not go to work, not use public transport and not travel abroad.

Then in the blink of an eye, the advice changes, the law changes and we are told that we have totally new priorities. We must leave home, we must go to work, go on holiday, go to a nightclub, to save the economy. We no longer need to worry about the virus because now we have the vaccines, we will be safe – except that the majority of people worldwide have not been vaccinated. Indeed in many countries no vaccine is available.

But for some groups nothing changes, those who are vulnerable for medical reasons, or the fragility that comes with age or because they are classified as having complex learning disabilities. Since early in the pandemic, not always early enough but still . . . these groups have been in lockdown, shielded, issued with personal protective equipment, because they are the most threatened by Covid.

Many of the fragile aged, or those who are vulnerable for medical reasons, or those that have learning disabilities will remain socially distanced and shielding. For the most part they will not have been consulted. Most decisions will be made for them – *for their own good* – and the social distancing that comes and goes as the pandemic waxes and wanes will only remain or even intensify for the threatened groups.

Because of physical, sensory, cognitive or emotional disabilities they will remain cut off, hard for us to reach, and hard for them to reach us. To counter this kind of alienation we need, not social distancing, we need social proximity. We need to make use of all the senses: taste, smell, touch, temperature, and the kinaesthetic sense, the sense that the body has of its own position and volition in space. These are all senses that work better at close range. Even those senses that work well at longer range, like seeing and hearing, will be more effective close up. If you want to help someone with impaired vision to see something, show it to them close up where it fills their field of vision. If you want to help someone with impaired hearing to hear something, present it to them close where it can have a chance to be heard above all the other sounds competing for the listener's attention.

Another consideration. If you are a performer and you find yourself working with an audience of 50 or more, can you really be aware of the reactions of each audience member, so aware you can sense their responses and interact with them? That awareness is not generally required in most forms of theatre.

In a West End or Broadway-style show, if it is a "straight" play, you will still often find the performance tucked away behind a proscenium arch, the architectural frame in front of the stage that forms the so-called fourth wall. Many productions are content to remain cut off behind this wall. The performers do not look at the audience members, who observe everything as from afar. There may be surtitles, subtitles and audio-description to aid understanding, but basically the dramatic action is in a world of its own, unaffected by the presence of the audience until the applause at the end.

There are many productions, much musical theatre for example, which even though they are played on a raised stage and with a proscenium arch do acknowledge that there is an audience in the room with them. But with audience numbers ranging from the low hundreds to more than a thousand, any attempts for a performer to connect with an individual audience member is doomed to fail except in the most dilute way.

Yes, over the past decade we have seen the introduction of relaxed performances that accept that not everyone wants to sit nice 'n' still in a dark room and keep quiet. This is not sufficient to truly engage the many people in our society who could be considered hard-to-reach, for example people who are defined as having Profound and Multiple Learning Disabilities (PMLD), people with dementia, people on the autism spectrum.

For those groups and many others like them theatre needs to change radically. It needs to become a much more Sensory Theatre, a theatre that is multisensory and interactive, that is it is directly responsive to the reactions of its audiences and builds up a relationship with them as individuals. Crucially to be truly interactive it has to be theatre that works close up to its audience.

I have spent the past 35-odd years, with the Oily Cart and numerous other companies in the UK and abroad, making theatre for audiences which are the hardest-to-reach and in this time I believe that I have come to see why a Sensory Theatre is essential and some of the factors that are key to its success.

In **Part One**, the Beginnings of Sensory Theatre, I begin this story with an analysis of some of the shows with which I have been involved that made some significant steps in the growth of the sector.

In **Part Two**, How Sensory Theatre Works, I split Sensory Theatre into its component parts, the nature of its audience, design, music, scripting, pre-show preparation, performance style and so on and devote a chapter to analysis of each of these topics.

Part Three traces the Growth of Sensory Theatre around the world and features contributions from Sensory Theatre makers in Canada, Ireland, Japan, Russia, Sweden, the UK and the USA.

Part Four contains a list of the books that I have found extremely useful in my work, a summary of the Sensory Theatre shows with which I have been involved as writer and/or director and an extract from an inspiring blog by Professor John Vorhaus of University College London. Finally Appendix 4 is a list of clips of video of Oily Cart shows to be found on YouTube.

Tim Webb

Acknowledgements

Many thanks to my colleagues, the pioneers of the Oily Cart and Sensory Theatre, Claire de Loon and Max Reinhardt – without whom none of this would have happened.

To the True Colours Trust who have helped so much over the years and specifically in the writing of this book.

To Arts Council England for their support over three decades and encouragement of our most adventurous work.

My gratitude particularly to Professor David Mongomery, NYU, Jeremy Harrison, Rose Bruford College, Jonathan Shmidt Chapman Exec Director, TYA/USA, to all the other contributors to this book including Ellie Griffiths, Kim Selody, Paul Brewster McGinley, Christopher Davies, Lucy Garland and Amber Onat Gregory, Francis Italiano, Kaori Nakayama, Francesca Pickard, Jacqueline Russell, Viktoria Violleau-Avdeeva, Eva von Hofsten, John Vorhaus and Joanna Williams.

In the early years of the Oily Cart things did not always run so smoothly and I remain thankful to those *early adopters* of the company like Lyn Gardner, Simon Mellor, Steven Hoggett, Scott Graham, Georgina Lamb, Natasha Chivers, Charlotte Jones, Jackie Elliman, Rachel Clare, Sarah Holmes, the late Jeff Teare, William James, Liz Moran and Tony Graham. Thank you to the late Dave Mann who designed the fabulous Oily Cart logo.

Many of the wonderful artists and technicians with whom I have had the honour and delight of working over the years are mentioned in the text but there is one group, the General Managers, the Administrators (more recently metamorphosing into Producers of various kinds) who never get a fraction of the credit they are due for getting this business of art on the road and keeping it there. I should particularly like to thank Sharon Parr, Joanna Ridout, Rebecca Farrar, Kevin Walsh, Kathy Everett, Sarah Crompton, Roger Lang, Alison Garratt, Flossie Waite and Sharon (Zhang Xiaohong).

A final and heartfelt thank you to our auditors, Jon Catty and Bridget Kalloushi who have supported the Oily Cart so well over many years.

Part One
The Beginnings of Sensory Theatre

Big Splash 1999 Oily Cart. Marigold, played by Yasmine Maya welcomes participants to the pool.

Photo: Don McPhee.

DOI: 10.4324/9781003091288-1

1
Sensory Theatre

The Beginnings

People sometimes ask where did my interest in Sensory Theatre originate. Why did I want to make theatre for people with impairments? I have usually answered, *Why not?* After all, this is an area that continually presents great artistic challenges but, when it works, when we engage and communicate with people, who for a great variety of sensory, cognitive, emotional, physical reasons, are initially hard to reach, when we overcome those barriers, there is a wonderful sense of achievement.

But I believe that some who ask these questions are searching for a more personal reason. *Is there someone in your family who . . . ?* It can be irritating. Why should I need a personal reason? – and yet there is one. It isn't someone in the family. It's me. Mid-way through primary school I had an accident that caused third degree burns to both my legs.

I had been running round a bonfire in some sort of a plastic cowboy outfit when the trousers caught fire. I spent the next ten months in the burns unit of the local hospital. When they finally sent me home, it was in a wheelchair – quite unable to walk. It took me another year before I was back on my feet and able to return to school.

The memory of the months spent in hospital and in the wheelchair stayed with me and gave me some insight into the lives of the young people I was later to work with in special schools. Although I still do not believe that you need a personal reason to make Sensory Theatre, this one certainly had an effect on me.

Afterwards my life was unexceptional. I spent five years studying English and Theatre at university and then wrote to every theatre in the UK asking for a job.

One replied – and I became an Acting Stage Manager at the Citizen's Theatre Glasgow where I was a virtually useless ASM but was soon promoted

DOI: 10.4324/9781003091288-2

to being a performer in the Citizen's Theatre for Youth, a TIE (Theatre in Education) company where I was a little more useful. From there, I progressed onto another TIE team, the Greenwich Young People's Theatre (GYPT). Both these companies had a powerful formative influence on me and on the early years of the Oily Cart.

From their beginnings in mid 1960s, TIE companies thrived, with several UK repertory theatres having teams attached to them. The TIE teams had close links with the educational sector and often tackled social issues. They created theatre productions that toured to schools and colleges and additionally ran training workshops for young people.

Nowadays the teams are fewer and the profile lower but I believe that the TIE movement was a powerful influence on the development of Applied Theatre training.

In both of the TIE teams in which I worked, a production very often began with the identification of a particular social issue or a strand in the educational curriculum followed by discussion, sometimes a lot of discussion, and research involving the whole team. Only then would the work of devising, writing, rehearsing and previewing begin.

My time in Glasgow was most significant as the place where I met Claire de Loon who was then working as Assistant Designer to the great Philip Prowse. Claire went on to design more than 80 shows for the Oily Cart and took charge of all the audience preparation resources.

After Greenwich YPT, I spent two years working as assistant director to Peter Cheeseman at the New Victoria Theatre, Stoke-on-Trent. Under Cheeseman's artistic directorship, the Vic had built a huge reputation for pioneering work with the theatre-in-the-round/arena theatre form and for his documentary dramas, now better known as Verbatim Theatre. These productions dramatised local themes and used the actual words of the people involved, recorded in interviews by the actors, as the basis of the scripts. The Vic clearly made a massive impression on me in terms of the development of theatre for specific audiences and experimental staging.

By the end of the 1970s, I was a member of the resident company at the Albany Empire in Deptford with Jenny Harris, John Turner and Noel Greig. This again was a company deeply embedded in its community. Marcel Steiner was also a member of that team and a highlight of my career there, came in a show called *Shadow of the Guillotine* when I was fired by Marcel from a cannon. I was also part of Marcel's Smallest Theatre in the

World where the auditorium was fitted into the sidecar of a motorbike and seated no more than two people. The rest of the audience stood around the motorbike and were entertained by a behind-the-scenes view of whatever was being inflicted on the two people in the stalls. In the Smallest Theatre production *The Complete History of World War Two*, I played the part of the entire German armed forces and the Siege of Stalingrad was evoked by several bucketfuls of torn up paper much of which went down the collars of the two spectators.

In 1979, I met Max Reinhardt when we were both working at Battersea Arts Centre where I was director of the youth theatre. Max was Head of the ILEA Family Workshop unit, a pioneering outfit dedicated to education for the family unit, parents and pre-school children working together. Max suggested that we should work together and write a hit musical. I liked the sound of that. However, we both had young families at the time and needed day jobs.

It so happened that about that time, stirred by childhood memories, I had begun to perform a version of the traditional Punch and Judy show with added pyrotechnics, *The Exploding Punch and Judy Show*. I persuaded Max to join the act as musician and head of security – my solo performances were forever being interrupted by kids intent on backstage invasion. We would do puppet shows by day and write by night.

Now I believe a good Punch and Judy is a wonderful entertainment, but not really one for the very young. It is more suited to an intoxicated rabble outside a pub during a time of social unrest.

Nowadays Punch, performed outdoors as it should be, pulls a decidedly mixed audience. On the one hand there is the mob outside the pub (see previous), on the other there are very young children, including toddlers. The parents always choose to put the little children right on the front row so they can see the puppets better – but that means there is a scrum of grown-ups yelling at the children's back. Not the best seats in the house if you are three years old.

Max and I began to see that there was an audience of very young children out there, who might be better served by a different kind of show. As well as the Punch, we had both worked for a pioneering company, Theatre Kit, run by an Australian couple, Katherine Ukleja and Chris Speyer, who had created four plays for the under-fives at the end of the 70s.

Our own children were, of course, another significant inspiration. We decided that perhaps the time had come for us to make theatre that really was appropriate for the very young with a story that began in an everyday world but spiraled off into fantasy, and that included beautiful design and music, and plenty of asking the children what to do and then acting on their suggestions.

In the autumn of 1981 with the help of a small grant from Greater London Arts, we made *Out of Their Tree*, our first show for the under-fives and the first show by the Oily Cart.

2
Theatre for Two to Five Year Olds

There was an Old Woman 2015 Oily Cart. Griff Fender as the Dancing Bear samples some porridge. The tree in the forest is made of shoes. Design: Claire de Loon.

Photo: Patrick Baldwin.

DOI: 10.4324/9781003091288-3

Unfortunately, *Out of Their Tree* (1981) was not an overnight success. The Punch and Judy theatre had been replaced by a foam rubber tree with knot holes in its trunk from which a number of glove puppet birds and a squirrel would pop. The tree was in an urban park and Max played the hapless park keeper. We shared the challenges experienced by the local wildlife, as he accompanied the songs on his guitar.

We played the show in schools and nurseries where it was generally well received by audiences of three to five year olds and their accompanying adults. For financial reasons, we also performed at birthday parties where the reception was usually chaotic. In *Out of Their Tree*, we thought we were creating material that was appropriate for under-fives. But at the parties, there were often children of seven, eight and nine in the room with the three to fives and this older group tended to take the line that our show was childish and beneath them. They could be quite rude about it, but that only made us more determined to explore age-appropriate forms of theatre.

Between 1981 and 1987, our pattern was to create a three to fives' show each year and then, in alternate years, create either a five to sevens' show or a production for seven to elevens. The strategy was to have two shows in the van and perform them both in the course of a day in one primary school if possible.

We also made a point of hiring experienced directors for all of our early shows. Now this was an area in which most start-up companies, then and now, definitely thought they could save money. I still believe that having an expert external eye around was worth it even if we could only afford to rehearse for a week or two. We learned a lot working with directors like Christine Eccles, Chris Speyer, Roland Jaquarello and Peter Rowe. They were all very patient.

Theatre for under-fives is quite common these days but when we began, it had a very low status in the theatre world, considered little better than augmented baby-sitting for children who had the concentration span of a goldfish. But Max and I, from the experience of *Punch and Judy* and *Out of Their Tree*, plus the observation of our own children, had concluded that if we applied a few basic principles, we could engage and focus an audience of three year olds or even younger. Those principles included:

- comical characters.
- telling the story using a range of media, including puppetry and not sticking to any one of them, especially not talking, for too long.
- the right sort of participation where the audience helps and suggests rather than shouts and also has opportunities to be physically involved.

- live music that could be responsive to the audiences.
- fascinating visuals including costumes.
- the highest production values we could afford.
- beginning our stories in an everyday reality before spiraling off into fantasy.

Putting our shows together along these lines, we produced performances for under-fives that were 45 to 50 minutes long. It was curious how much concern we met with about the length of show. We were often told that these children did not have the attention span to cope with such long running times – usually just after we had finished a show where the children had sat in rapt attention throughout.

As well as the performances in nurseries and reception classes, we also began to take our early years' shows into art centres and studio theatres where a touring circuit developed during the 1980s. Sometimes they even put us on a main stage, but in many ways this was not so satisfactory. We had become used to tucking ourselves into corners in a day nursery and performing on the same level as the young people as a kind of extension to the story carpet. And of course when we performed to a nursery group or a reception class, we rarely performed to more than 30 children. Working with these relatively small audiences seemed to suit the children who relaxed more quickly than when they arrived to see a show in a theatre. In the theatre, young people were often experiencing not the performance but a mob of people in a strange place, that is, the rest of the audience.

We began to consciously create productions in a more intimate style. It obviously suited the younger children to enjoy the show in the company of people they knew. And it was a treat for us to see the close-up audience relax and play with us.

Take for example the show *Jumpin' Beans* (2002) in a version for two to four year olds. An audience of 30 including children and adults, sitting together on the floor of an inflatable, met a little pink bird, operated and voiced by Ruth Calkin using a Punch and Judy man's swazzle (the gadget which gives Mr. Punch his distinctive sound). Ruth used it to make the Baby Bird's voice. The Bird was right there on the floor with the children and the adults. There were no sophisticated controls on the puppet and the swazzle was clearly held between Ruth's lips, yet the belief of the children in the reality of the character was intense.

Largely by asking the children what they thought the Baby Bird was saying, or squawking, we developed the narrative. The rule of the game was that every suggestion from a child should be acknowledged and acted on as far as possible. To get started, the other performer, Patrick Lynch, would ask the children if the Baby Bird looked happy or sad. The Bird moved slowly and without confidence so the answer was almost always "sad." The audience was then asked why was the Baby Bird sad? There were many responses. He was lost, hungry, thirsty, wanted his mummy and so on. If he was hungry, Patrick would ask: "What do birds like to eat?" If he was lost, then: "Where does he live?" If he wanted his mummy: "How could we find her?" These open questions all proved very effective in enlisting the children to help us create the story.

We often came round to the need to find the Baby Bird's nest. But where was it? There was a rather abstract-looking tree in a corner of the inflatable, with a very crude nest in it. Patrick would suggest that perhaps we could build a comfortable nest, pointing out that there was plenty of comfy nest-type material – wool, fur and the like, on the floor around the inflatable that the children could tuck between the tree branches to make the nest cosy and warm.

When the hunt for materials began to slow, Patrick would introduce another sensory category. "What else would be good in a nest? What about some shiny things?" Of course there were little mirrors and shiny paper and tinsel scattered about the space that were hunted down and added to the nest.

After that, the question might be "What sort of sounds might the Baby Bird like in the nest?" and a treasure hunt would discover plenty of tiny bells to be hung from the branches.

The treasure hunt and the nest building provided a good opportunity for the children to let off some steam while also using their creativity and imagination. By switching between the modes (from dialogue to music to active participation to problem solving, for example) it is possible to maintain the engagement of a very young audience over quite a considerable period.

The next conundrum for the *Jumpin' Beans* audience to tackle was how to get the Baby Bird into the lovely new nest. Most often the children told us he could fly up. But you could see this Bird had no wings. One boy told us we should *hurl it*.

A more orthodox suggestion was that the Baby Bird should jump in the nest. We would always try this one out because it could be more easily staged with the puppet than the hurling. On one occasion we had the puppet jumping but making a bad landing. The Baby Bird began to limp around the stage.

Three little girls rushed out of the inflatable. Were they upset that the Bird appeared to be in pain?

They returned a moment later with a Scotch Tape dispenser, grabbed the Baby Bird and wrapped tape round and round the injured leg. The puppet made a rapid recovery and managed a second leap that landed him safely in the nest.

One suggestion of genius was that we should put the Baby Bird in a bowl in the classroom sink. Then put in the plug and turn on the taps. The water would fill up the sink and fill up the room then the Baby Bird would float up in the bowl to the top of the tree.

No matter how long you sit at your laptop, you will never come up with an idea as good as that.

My argument is that the intimate relationship of the performers to the participants in the performance space was crucial in getting the audience members to relax and engage with the show.

It also helped that the young people had opportunities to get up, move around and have a physical, visceral relationship with the space and the characters. This close-up and interactive style is something that I have continued to develop whatever the audience, always looking for ways to get the participants as close to the action as possible.

In *Ring A Ding Ding* (2011), the audience of three to six year olds and their adult companions were seated around a four-meter diameter turntable made up of two concentric rings on which the puppets would circle. At the very centre of these rings was a space for the performers to operate the puppets and address the participants.

There were two concentric rows of seating for the audience wrapped around the stage area. While the adults and the less confident children were seated on the back row, the majority of the children sat on the front row from where they could actually touch the stage. Not only could they touch it, they would actually make the stage revolve backwards and forwards propelling the puppets through the story on an assortment of up-cycled toy vehicles including a milk float, a tricycle, a motorbike, a paddle steamer, a hot air balloon and a speedboat. Trusting the children to operate a moving stage with plenty of stop/go cues sometimes provided almost too much kinaesthetic excitement. There was the odd occasion when the smaller ones forgot to let go of the moving stage in time and barely avoided being shot into Earth orbit.

I believe that an even richer physical involvement of the audience was achieved with the show *In a Pickle* (2012). This was a co-production between the Royal Shakespeare Company and the Oily Cart, loosely based on Shakespeare's *The Winter's Tale* and made for an audience of 60 two to five year olds and their families.

The setting for this was two lines of tables with benches behind. The tables faced one another forming a long narrow (traverse) performance space. The tables were covered with various different cloths: the first of these, the one that greeted the audience when they first sat on the benches, was a silky green carpet begging to be stroked and ruffled. This was a thoroughly tactile way of establishing that we were in the countryside.

I realise that *The Winter's Tale* usually begins at the court in Sicily with some very serious business, but in an effort to make the adaptation more suitable for under-fives, I decided to tell the story from the point of view of characters neglected in all previous adaptations, namely the sheep. So my version began with the sheep-shearing scene that in Shakespeare's original had been left to the second half. The participants were asked to wear sheep dress-ups, learn to baa, find the lost baby, Perdita, and go on a quest to reunite her with her parents.

At this point the grass table covers were removed to reveal the actual table-tops. Down the centre of these were metal troughs filled with shells, shingle and sand. Jugs of water scented with seaweed were poured into the troughs. Now we began the sea voyage during which each child was given a piece of carrot (readily accepted as a "carrot fish"). The audience swam these fish in and out of the water to the music of our sailing song.

In Sicily, the King believed that the Queen was dead. All that was left of her was a statue. This was a moment revealing Shakespeare as the master theatre artist. The two, three, four and five year olds in the audience were absolutely gripped as we waited to see if the statue would come to life. Of course it did and King, Queen and baby Perdita were reunited at last.

For this happy ending, the tables were covered again, this time with pies and pizzas, tarts and cakes, all part of a richly quilted and embroidered table covering that the children squeezed and prodded – a highly tactile feast.

I was happy with *In a Pickle* and I can only hope that Shakespeare might have said the same. But there was another side of my work that was advancing more quickly and that involved a rather different audience.

Here is a YouTube link to video of **In a Pickle (2012) in the Swan Room** at the Royal Shakespeare Company.

https://youtu.be/kJ0rHc-vId8

3
All Sorts of Shows
for All Sorts of Kids

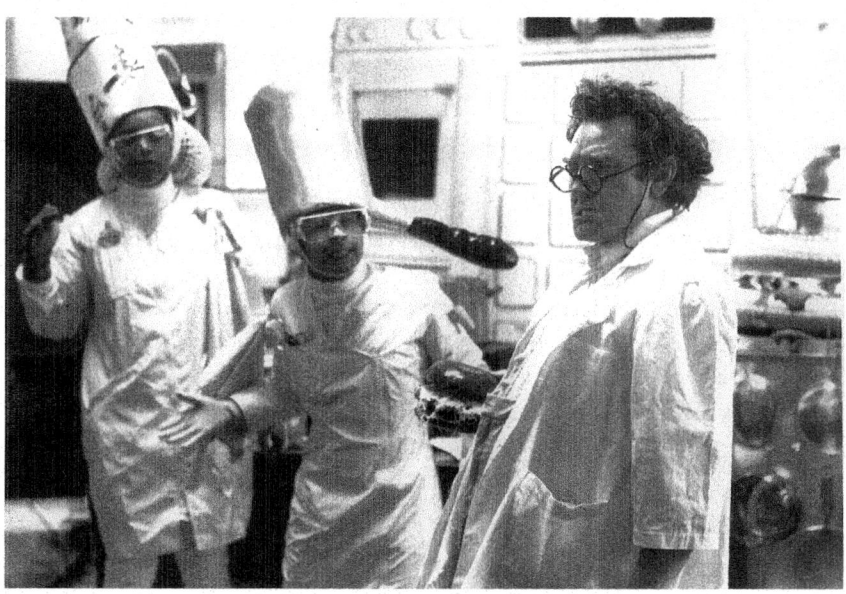

Dinner Ladies from Outer Space 1992 Oily Cart. Cast: Nicky McCrae, Paulette Brown, Geoff Bowyer. Design: Claire de Loon.

Photo: Amrando Atkinson.

In 1988, Oily Cart first became involved in theatre for young people with Special Educational Needs with a week's research in a Severe Learning Disability school where ages ranged from five to nineteen. The Deputy Head of a West London SEND (Special Education Needs and Disability) School invited us to perform one of our under-fives shows for his students. I had a distant memory of performances for SEND audiences around Glasgow when I was part of the Glasgow Citizens' Theatre for Youth company. What

DOI: 10.4324/9781003091288-4

I recalled from that Scottish experience was that the audiences in those SEND Schools were very different from the two to five nursery and early years children with whom we had been working as the Oily Cart.

I asked the Deputy the ages of the students in his school. When he replied that that they ranged from five to nineteen years I thought we might be out of our depth. We had done no work for young people over eleven years, and my experience with SEND schools had been limited to Glasgow.

The Deputy's response was to invite us to spend a week in his school meeting the students and staff and observing the school day. It turned out to be the most amazing, mind-expanding experience.

Three things impressed themselves on us in the course of that short visit. Those three things have stayed with me to this day.

First: The Enormous Range and Variety of Different Personalities in the School

Back in 1988 in fact the range of abilities and personalities in a SEND school was much wider than it is now. In the 90s, there was a determined effort to integrate students with disabilities into the mainstream wherever that was possible. In this school there were senior students, eighteen to nineteen years old, who were articulate, mobile and likely to find work and live independent lives after school and college.

On the other hand, there were small classes of students, then called "special care," people with the most complex sensory, physical and cognitive disabilities often in association with high medical support needs. These were people who required assistance with most everyday activities and were likely to remain in this condition into adulthood.

And then there were all these other individuals in between. We quickly saw that it would present a formidable artistic challenge to make theatre relevant to such a wide range of people. But we were young (ish) full of energy and believed that having found a way of successfully engaging under-fives audiences, we had a chance of breaking through to an audience which, on the face of it, would be far harder to reach. Could we find what all these young people had in common? Was this one audience or a hundred different audiences?

Second: The Question – How Long Should a Show Be?

Several of the staff told us it was pointless if we came into a school like theirs and did one of our 45 to 60 minute long shows. They said that we would need much longer to get to know the young people and that they, equally, would need longer to get to know us. In the years to come and over many productions we were to discover the great value of this advice. Although for sound practical reasons (mostly financial ones) we have done more than our fair share of 50 to 60 minute shows in SEND schools over the years, but whenever we have managed to break through the theatre time barrier, with day-long performances or one or even two week-long character embeddings and residencies, the effects have been revelatory.

Third: Hammocking and the Kinaesthetic Sense

One afternoon during that first school visit, we saw young people sitting around an old navy-issue hammock laid out in the middle of the school hall. One after another they took a turn lying on the hammock that was then lifted off the ground with a teacher holding the rope from one end and one of the senior students holding the other. These two began to swing the hammock quite gently, checking the reactions of the person in the hammock and increasing or decreasing the energy of the swing to get the best response. Some people preferred the most gentle and relaxing sway while others laughed and whooped as the hammock went higher and higher. The action of the hammock could respond to and enhance every mood.

This was the first time that I became aware of the importance of the kinaesthetic sense as a way to engage and establish two-way communication with people who for a variety of sensory, physical, cognitive and emotional factors might be described as hard-to-reach. Once you begin to look for it, the evidence is everywhere. Very many people enjoy fairground or theme park rides and I have yet to meet a toddler who did not enjoy going on the swings. Fairground rides and swinging on swings are definitely kinaesthetic experiences.

There is considerable evidence that many people on the autism spectrum are hyposensitive to kinaesthetic stimulation, that is, that they display low sensitivity to their bodies' position and volition. This is why people on the spectrum can enjoy high levels of this stimulation. It is a fact that a visit at playtime to a school for pupils on the autism spectrum will usually reveal intense activity around swings and self-propelled roundabouts.

A particularly valuable aspect of the kinaesthetic sense is that it is accessible to people who have impaired vision and hearing.

The conclusions that I drew after those few days in the West London School have been reinforced by similar experiences on numerous occasions and have remained a strong influence on my work over the next three decades.

We imported hammocking into our work continuing to use it until a Mencap Conference in Blackpool. Here we spent a whole day hammocking adults (there were no children), an experience that encouraged us to search for alternative ways of stimulating the kinaesthetic sense and saving our backs. First, hand-held hammocks were replaced by hammocks on stands, garden swing seats and by leaf chairs, but this was only the start of a trail that led us to work on trampolines and in hydropools.

As soon as we found a space in our schedule, we set to work making our first show for Special Schools, which was *Box of Socks* (1988). By this time the Oily Cart had grown to three performers courtesy of a grant from the late and still lamented Greater London Council to help us expand the company. Max and I were aware that two balding white guys were not representative of the culturally diverse audiences with whom we worked in London. Since that time the Oily Cart has always been diverse, once or twice all female, but never all white.

The performer we invited to join us for *Box of Socks* was the resourceful Maureen Hibbert. She had been a nurse working on both cardiac and psychiatric teams and was very funny at audition. We thought she would be perfect – and she was.

The title of the show came from a donation from The Sock Shop in the form of a large box containing . . . you guessed it. Many thanks Sock Shop.

The show began when the students and staff assembled in the school hall first thing in the morning and found a crashed spaceship smoking slightly. There was a note asking the finders to play a VHS on the school's television by way of explanation. The video showed a spaceship travelling through space in order to bring friendly greetings from the other side of the universe. A voice asked the audience if they would like to meet the space people. The participants readily agreed.

Out came the aliens with their baldy blue heads (including Maureen) waving their long, striped tails, meerkat-style and singing a song of greeting. One of the aliens carried four babies (sock glove puppets) at all times.

The aim of the visitors was to find out about life on this planet about which, it became clear, they knew absolutely nothing. They wandered all over the school observing and misunderstanding.

ALIEN ONE: (*Friendly Dalek voice*) Why are you making black marks on white surface?
STUDENT: I'm writing.

ALIEN ONE: Oh. Writing. On my planet we have no "writing."
Or, later, in a dining hall.
ALIEN TWO: Why are you sticking solid material in hole in face?
STUDENT: I'm eating.
ALIEN TWO: Can I do it – this eating with this stuff? What is it called?
STUDENT: Pudding.
ALIEN TWO: Pudding? Ah.

The aliens did not understand anything. Not computers, not doors, not paint, not pudding, not teachers – all were equally baffling and equally marvelous. The students found the aliens funny, mostly, though some thought they were too silly sometimes. For the young people in the school who were often being told what they did not know and what they should not do, to meet the space characters who treated them as great authorities, just as likely to answer questions as any of the teachers, was very empowering.

The morning of each school performance involved visits to every classroom with every department generating a fabulous carnival atmosphere, a holiday from the usual school timetables and rules. One of the aliens (played by me, actually) announced that in the afternoon there would be goodbye party for our visitors and that I would need some of the senior students (sixteen to eighteen year olds) to come shopping with me for drinks and snacks.

Naturally I would rush into the dry cleaners demanding cake and buns before the students had time to tell me that the baker's shop was next door and that Halfords bike shop was not the best place to buy soft drinks and sweeties. It took time but we got there in the end.

The party itself was relatively conventional with a magician from another galaxy but with a lot of tricks from the same old magic catalogue and a disco that revealed that Kylie Minogue was as popular beyond the stars as she was down here on earth. (This was 1988.)

Box of Socks worked well largely because of the original research and how the cast in performance reacted and responded to the audiences. Yes, we did our best to work with our audiences as individuals and not as representatives of this or that categories. Yes, we did not do a typical 50 to 60 minute show. We took a whole day over it. But what the tour really confirmed was that what made the difference in the schools was the sense of play and fun and carnival that we conjured up. We were welcomed in each of the SEND schools we played, and, very importantly, we were often asked if we could come back again at Christmas. We assumed we must be doing something right although it turned out there was a great deal more to do.

4
How Long Is a Piece of Theatre?

Georgie goes to Hollywood 1994 Oily Cart. Cast: Carol Walton, Sue Eves, Geoff Bowyer, Jonny Quick, Brent Clark. Design: Claire de Loon.

DOI: 10.4324/9781003091288-5

The English Special School system changed considerably during the 1990s and the first two decades of the new century. In response to the Warnock Report of 1978, there was a sustained effort to integrate young people with disabilities into a mainstream educational setting while the Special Schools retained only those students needing more individual care. But the change was gradual and I continued to write shows for the whole school right up to 1996.

The highlight of this period for me were the George shows (five shows in all over five years). Each show had the same rather dubious hero called George Broadbent, played by a brilliantly funny actor, Geoff Bowyer.

George was a sort of benign conman who would appear in Special Schools and announce at an assembly that he had a grand scheme that would make everyone famous except that he had lost either:

a. key members of his team
    or
b. the van with all his stuff in it
    or
c. both of the above

so he was sorry but everyone would be disappointed . . . unless the students and staff of the school could help with his latest project. Each year there was a different theme, as can be guessed at from the titles:

1991   *Funky Philharmonic*
1993   *Eurobroadbent* (a tribute to Disneyland Paris)
1994   *Georgie Goes to Hollywood*
1995   *George After a Fashion*
1996   *George Sells Out*

In *Funky Philharmonic*, the first in this series, we spent one day in each school that we visited, but after that, we moved to a different format in which the school visits lasted two days. The reasons for this stem from the original development period back in 1988 when many of the teachers had been keen to tell us that one day-long visits to many in the SEND school audiences were too abrupt because they needed a longer period to get used to the theatre company, and that equally we needed longer to get used to them.

Once we began to find the opportunities to challenge the accepted time limits of performance from under an hour to over two school days (in the case of *George* shows) we found the results were remarkable. Young participants who might find the arrival of a theatre company a bit much on the morning of the first day, *new people! new sights, new sounds!* were more comfortable on the afternoon of that day, but positively at ease with us on the morning of day two.

The format remained pretty similar. On the first morning, there was an assembly for the whole school, featuring the introduction of George and the rest of the cast. This was followed by outlining of this year's theme and how everything had gone wrong again but could be put right if the students would help.

After this opening session the students returned into their usual classes, classes which were usually based on ability levels. Each of the classes, usually with between five and ten students in them, would receive two 30- to 40-minute long visits from two or three members of George's team. The visits involved interactive performance introducing the characters and themes of the show, then going on to get the class creating puppets, props or other performance elements that would be featured in a performance for the whole school in the afternoon of the second day.

To make things a little clearer, I would like to spotlight *Georgie Goes to Hollywood* from 1994, a production that introduced a significant innovation, video, to our work for Severe Learning Disability Schools. *Georgie Goes to Hollywood*, as the title suggests, was based on a vision of the Golden Age of the Movies. This time George was the boss of a film company and had come to the school because it was such a perfect location. But – wouldn't you just know it? – the van had gone missing with many of the actors and most of the equipment. Would the people in the school mind helping out?

George was accompanied by the "designer," Jonny Quick, the star, Sue Eves, and the stagehand, Carol Walton. Geoff, Carol and Sue all played musical instruments.

The story of the film concerned a sea voyage to a number of very different islands. Fortunately, some parts of the film, the titles and the sea voyage, had already been shot, but that left six island scenes still to be filmed. These scenes were each pitched to different ages and abilities and it was planned so that each of the students would find a role in at least one of the scenes.

The scene for the PMLD students (a.k.a. Butterfly Island) was a multisensory idyll in which the young people relaxed on scented bean bags, serenaded by gentle music and wafted by the wings of giant butterflies. As the scene was played, it was filmed and then edited into the final film shown at the world premiere.

At the end of the first day, the company serenaded the buses and taxis as they waited to take the young people home. The phenomenon became known as the Bus Busk. This was another key moment in the school day when the whole school came together, and all the young people and staff had the opportunity to see more of the performers. This always generated a great deal of carnival-style fun and a real sense of occasion.

The filming and editing were a high-pressure job undertaken by our cameraman, Brent Clark, who after filming a scene with the pupils on VHS tape, would race off to edit it into the main body of the film. This usually took place in the medical room or a broom cupboard. Nowadays it is fairly straightforward to edit video on a laptop. Spare a thought for the heroic Brent clutching a sandwich, working through his lunch hour, editing VHS in a cupboard.

Sometimes it was touch and go. The sense of urgency was quite genuine. On the second day, after lunch, the whole school would assemble in the hall ready for the premiere of the movie. Would Brent be finished in time? The hall was decorated. Students and staff dressed up as their film star favourites: Superman, Wonder Woman, Batman, James Bond, the Hulk. Then, at last, Brent rushed from the broom cupboard clutching the VHS. The lights were dimmed.

Sometimes that did not make much difference because the blackout in the hall was no good anyway. But the atmosphere, that carnival atmosphere, was everywhere in the school. Everyone was posing, in groups, getting their photos taken. Then there was the movie itself and the excitement when it was your turn to be seen on the silver screen.

After the movie, there was an awards ceremony – at which each class received an award. It was a small cardboard figure, not so much gold as yellowish. Not so much an Oscar – a Georgie.

We used video for the first time in *Georgie Goes to Hollywood* and found that it enabled many of the young participants to get a clearer idea of what was going on. Video projected on to the big screen made facial expressions and other details much clearer. One of the small class scenes involved table-top puppetry, that would not have been viable for many in our audiences, especially anyone with a vision impairment.

We also found that many of our young participants gained a much clearer sense of the interactive adventures in which they were involved and of their central role in the performance. It certainly made things much clearer to parents and school staff who were watching from a distance.

I have often wondered what made George Broadbent so popular apart from Geoff Bowyer's wonderful performance. Many of the older school students and the staff were delighted to welcome him back each year. They clearly remembered his foibles. He was forever losing things, particularly his temper and with it, his control over language. For young people with disabilities who are forever being told what they should and should not do, watching an "authority" figure, even one like George, lose the plot, was a source of much laughter. This was another benefit of long-form theatre, the knowledge that could be built of a character over appearances recurring over a number of years.

5
Close up on PMLD

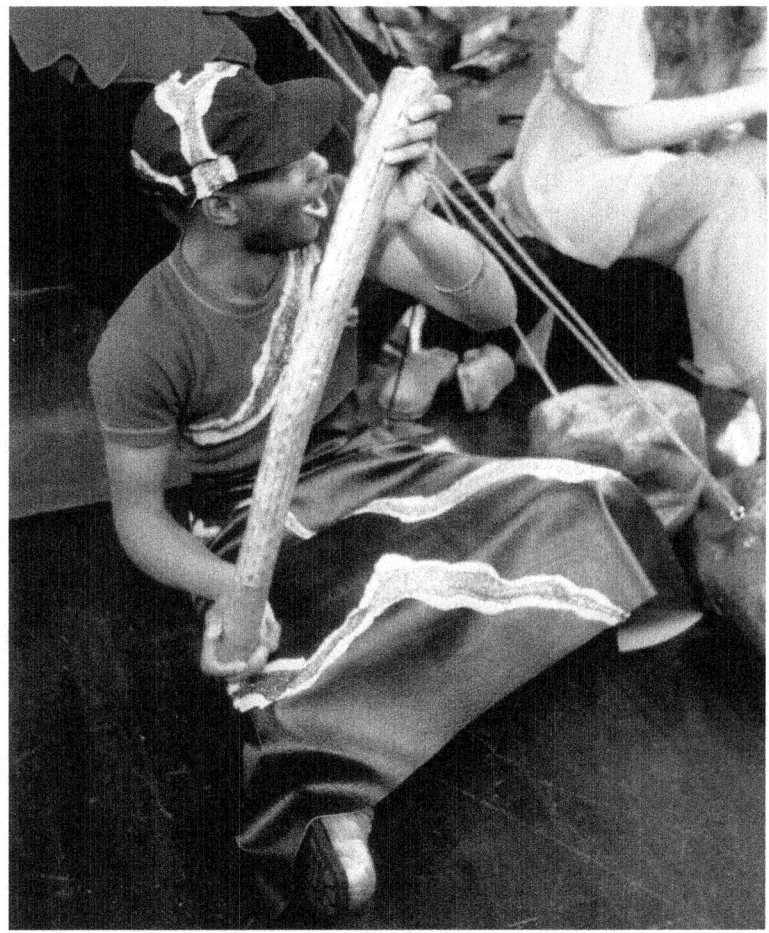

Hunky Dory 1998 Oily Cart. Mark Foster as Rock playing the rain stick. Design: Claire de Loon.

DOI: 10.4324/9781003091288-6

While the George Two-Day Shows were generally very well received, the feedback from school staff frequently made an important point; that the sessions specifically for the classes categorised as having Profound and Multiple Learning Disabilities (PMLD) were particularly welcome. They told us that there was very little alternative provision for this group of young people. The Oily Cart creative team decided to change course for a while to see how shows exclusively created for the PMLD units would be received.

This resulted in a large step towards a much more Sensory Theatre as we gradually discovered what strategies were really effective. We were unaware of any precedents for a stand-alone performance specifically for the PMLD but we tried our best by building on what we had developed in the two day-long whole-school shows.

One of the great advantages of being part of the Oily Cart was that the creative team were able to spend years together, experimenting and learning through making new shows. Not many artists have the means to develop their own style over such a long period. The Arts Council actively encouraged us to constantly try new approaches and enabled us to maintain high production standards. The shows for young people with complex disabilities also attracted funding from interested trusts and foundations.

The Sensory Audit

From our experience with the PMLD sessions in the George series, we had found that if we included a selection of material that addressed the senses of touch, smell and the kinaesthetic sense as well as seeing and hearing then there was a good chance that there would be something to engage almost anyone labeled PMLD – or, in fact, almost anyone. If your sight or hearing was severely impaired, then there were other sensory channels via which we might engage. We decided that from then on, everything we created should be subject to a sensory audit, just to make sure that we were examining as many ways as possible to engage our participants.

The Use of Verbal Language

Questioning the use of the languages of the senses led to an evaluation of how much we should rely on verbal language. Should we rely on it at all? It was clear that the families, the friends, the people who worked in the PMLD units, spoke to the young people all the time but without necessarily assuming that they were being understood in the usual sense. In this context, the words may often be friendly sounds that say you care rather than anything more specific. I came to think that it was important that we make these companionable noises in performance too. What they mean is things like, *I'm a friend, Everything's OK*. But I concluded that in a performance for young people with PMLD, we should not *rely* on words to explain things, because many who fall into that category do not primarily use verbal language to communicate. We should at least offer other ways of making things clear. Unlike the neuro-typical majority, neuro-divergent people do not necessarily use verbal language to make sense of, or to control, the world around them.

Structure

Similarly, we found problems with constructs like narrative and plot, that many would say are at the heart of conventional theatre. These things may seem essential to neurotypicals but they present some difficulties when considered from the point of view of people who have different ways of relating to the world.

Many people labeled as having Profound and Multiple Learning Disabilities have challenging memory issues. In the past I cooperated with Mencap on producing a DVD about arts work for people with PMLD. The title was *In the Moment*. The assumption underlying the title was that many PMLD people have little memory of what came before and little anticipation of what is to come. They are, in a sense, fixed in the present. So I began to wonder if it was appropriate to insert twists and turns in a story or set up conflicts in the plot to be resolved at the end.

I would suggest that what works best in a production for many people categorised as PMLD is a sequence of varied and strong atmospheres, each of which makes a powerful impression as you experience it but which neither depends on knowledge of what went before to affect the audience, nor does it necessarily have to raise questions or issues that can be sorted out in later scenes.

This does not mean that there is no underlying structure to a show for PMLD people. On the contrary. Any show benefits from a firm underlying emotional arc, but the structure in these shows for people with complex disabilities is not primarily concerned with the development of characters or the resolution of conflicts in the course of the performance. Those are common features of TV soaps, of novels and of multi-volume DVD box sets, whereas I believe the models that should guide us in making PMLD theatre are perhaps a piece of music, a poem, a painting or a music video. What I am looking for is more like a multi-facetted jewel which may engage many different people via many different languages (sensory languages, sounds, images, textures, tastes, movements, body language and yes – even spoken languages). My hope is that each participant who is involved in an experience like this will take away something that is quite specifically personal to them and may differ radically from what other participants perceive. The job of the performer is to provide worlds of opportunities.

Sometimes great inspiration for this kind of work comes from a quite straightforward concept, as with our productions *Drum* (2010) or *Tube* (2013). As we made *Drum*, we played with the visuals, the sounds, the textures, the smells, the movements, the heat, the cold that could be produced from or by drum sounds or drum shapes. We would not admit that there was any sense that could not be associated with some kind of drum or drumming and so many a fascinating idea was unearthed and explored. The making of *Tube* followed this productive pattern.

Another kind of inspiration might be the feelings evoked by a poem. We certainly found this with Matthew Arnold's *Dover Beach* (translated into Swedish as *Stranden*, 2019) or S. T. Coleridge's *Kubla Khan* (2017). Could not our inspiration be the sound of the waves on a shingle-strewn beach or a river voyage that disappears into a mysterious underworld? These are experienced using many senses, not just something that can be reduced to a straightforward message to be spelled out in words.

Hunky Dory

I would like to take as a more detailed example *Hunky Dory* (1998). It was the third piece that I created with Oily Cart specifically for the PMLD groups and although it had its flaws, there was quite a lot right with it.

It had been preceded by *Tickled Pink* (1996) and *Over the Moon* (1997). Each of these lasted all day with two sessions in the morning and two in the afternoon. The cast of four performed the morning session twice to two different groups of around 20 young people with about eight carers. Then they performed the second part of the show to the same groups in the afternoon.

Hunky Dory was a radical innovation in that it was performed to a group of only five participants accompanied by at least three carers. Although it was shorter, it was very intense with much **one-to-one interaction**. The performance was repeated for new groups, several times over the course of the day.

Mark Foster

An even more significant development was the inclusion in the *Hunky Dory* cast of performer Mark Foster. Mark was the first person in the company to have spent his entire educational career in SEND schools. I believe that in many ways it is essential to include people in our theatre with whom our audiences can identify. On stage, we always need both men and women of different ages and who are black or brown as well as white – because that is what the society out there looks like. Just as a multitude of diverse groups make up our world so they must be represented on our stages. Because our society includes people who see the world in 100 different ways and who use 100 different languages to express themselves, I believe that these people with different ways of being in the world should all be made welcome to our theatres.

Mark has made a tremendous impression on the company and the participants, as a charismatic performer with a rich bass voice and as a role model for many in our audiences. Two decades after first joining us Mark is still involved in Oily Cart productions.

The inspiration for *Hunky Dory* was the world underground. When the audience first encountered the set, it looked like a heap of out-sized leaves in the middle of the performance space. (This heap was in fact based on a converted family-size tent.) An entrance tunnel led into the heart of the leaf pile, where samples of subterranean wonders were to be found. There was a huge, glowing chunk of rock salt, glowing on top of a light source. There was a pool with a bubbling fountain and piles of root vegetables illuminated by transparent stalactites stuffed with fairy lights. It was a magical immersive space.

The characters introduced themselves outside the mound. One of the deep bass instruments featured in *Hunky Dory* was the Australian aboriginal instrument, the didgeridoo. It not only produces wonderful drones that can be felt as much as heard but is also a powerful tactile experience in itself. Didgeridoo Massage is an experience everyone should try.

Each of the characters in the production was fascinated with a particular totemic underground element: water, clay, sand, crystals and pungent roots would each have their moment in the spotlight. Each participant had the opportunity to handle and explore these natural objects for themselves with all their different sensory aspects: appearance, smell, taste, sound and texture.

The flaws with this show that I referred to earlier concerned anxieties some people had with entering the space. These were particularly apparent when we found ourselves working with young people with a dual PMLD/Autistic diagnosis. At this time (1998), we were only beginning to be aware of the requirements of people on the spectrum. In retrospect, it is not at all surprising that over the course of a couple of shows, we would struggle to lead people on the spectrum down tunnels into confined spaces, with only one exit, even when accompanied by family members or teachers.

After *Hunky Dory*, we devised simple tactics like widening the entrance and putting a beanbag just inside the hall where the performance was taking place. A reluctant participant could sit there throughout the show if necessary, but at intervals we would ask if we could move the beanbag forward and by this means edge the participant closer to the action. There were times when this process would last the length of the show.

We would make no more igloo-shaped structures with only one exit. We also realised that we had to be thinking more seriously about an audience we were encountering more and more frequently – people said to be on the autism spectrum.

There was another issue with *Hunky Dory*. Once the audience was inside the space, there was almost nothing that was kinaesthetically stimulating: no hammocks, not even a rocking chair and we were to learn that kinaesthetic experiences were particularly appreciated by many individuals on the spectrum.

6
Truly Immersive – Theatre in Hydropools

Pool Piece 2009 by Oily Cart in collaboration with Theatre Is . . . and Apples & Snakes. The cast, participants and carers explore the watery delights to be found in the pool. Sam Alty, Jumoke Oke, Mark Foster at Linden Lodge School, Wimbledon. Design: Claire de Loon.

Photo: J. Gamon.

Our work with hammocks was fine but surely there was another way to harness the kinaesthetic sense.

One lunchtime, Claire de Loon and I went for a swim in our local pool where, off in a corner, an aqua-aerobics class was taking place. An instructor stood on the side while his class followed him closely and splashed along to some disco beats.

DOI: 10.4324/9781003091288-7

Did we not know another audience who would enjoy something like this? During our many visits to Special Educational Needs Schools, we had seen that many schools had hydrotherapy pools. When we investigated further, we were told by many staff members that the pools were particularly enjoyed by the wheelchair users and others with restricted mobility where the support of the warm water (I still feel that being in a hydropool is a bit like swimming in a cup of tea) relieved some of the effects of gravity and facilitated a much greater range of movement than was possible, in, say, a wheelchair. In a wheelchair there is a great deal of sitting still, and backwards and forwards movement but not so much movement side to side or up and down.

Several teachers told us that they needed more ideas of things to do in the pools. Some of them had organised movement sessions in the water accompanied by recorded music but wondered if a theatre company might be able to suggest other directions.

In 1997, thanks to a small grant from Greater London Arts Association, we embarked on a short period of R&D. This developed into a small-scale tour of a show called *Bubbles* inspired by the design of a Turkish Hammam.

We thought there were at least three big questions to answer:

One. What exactly could we add to the young people's usual pool experience? Many of the hydropools in schools already had disco-style lighting and sound systems.

Two. How many young people would we be able to work with in the water? Most of the pools we had visited were considerably smaller than conventional swimming pools. The work we saw in them commonly involved two young people with two accompanying adults and not much space left over.

Three. How long should each performance last?

We calculated that we had to allow for plenty of time for the participants to be changed into their bathing costumes and get in and out of the water. We realised that if we kept the young people in the pool for too long then they might end up both cold and exhausted.

We decided would try a hydro show with a primary audience of two people from the PMLD classes each accompanied by an adult carer.

We were further concerned that our emphasis on close-up, one-to-one work might present financial problems for some schools. Nearly every school we approached could see the point of working in this way with very complex people. But the cost per head, even when the price was subsidised, gave many schools pause.

Always bearing this quality versus cost debate in mind, we pressed on and up until the time of writing I have created seven hydropool productions that have toured successfully. Once the more sceptical schools had seen the feedback and viewed the video, they tended to be convinced by the high production values and obvious engagement of our audiences. We were told that not only were these shows valuable in themselves but that they had a significant training function in schools, especially where staff were new to water-based work.

In *Bubbles*, we spent one day each in nine schools, doing eight performances per day with two young people per show each accompanied by an adult companion. The size and composition of the hydropool audiences has stayed the same to this day, but we found it necessary (because of performers losing the will to live) to limit the number of performances each day to a maximum of four, each approximately 20 to 30 minutes in length.

When we came out of the R&D phase, we began to make *Big Splash* (1999), a hydropool show for a full tour of 30 schools. We were lucky to find Eddy Anderson as a trainer. Eddy had been the Head of a Special School and as a physiotherapist, had created a number of methods for making both the hydropool and the trampoline more accessible to people with complex disabilities.

Eddy's most noteworthy invention was the Floatsation Mat. This mat was similar to a floating Li-lo in shape and size but made up of a hundred ball-pool balls sewn up into a netting bag. The mat could be folded in a variety of ways to provide different kinds of support for people with disabilities in a hydropool. We decided we were going to use the mats to take our audiences, two at a time, on voyages of discovery around the pool. This would be no ordinary trip – each of the pools we visited was converted into a fantasy laundry with the pool apparently filled by a giant overflowing washing machine that created a small waterfall. We collaborated with the sculptor and fountain designer Daniel Lobb to create several such pieces. We invested in scuba divers' torches to provide underwater lighting effects and adapted a bathroom jacuzzi to create columns of bubbles bobbing from the depths.

On the surface floated two chime buoys created by a discovery of Max Reinhardt's, musical instrument maker, Jamie Linwood. Jamie would go on to create a host of amazing-looking and beautiful sounding instruments for shows over the years. The chime buoys floated on top of regular life preserver rings. They each had a xylophone-like mechanism with its keys rising vertically around a central mast. A golf ball on a string dangled inside the xylophone. As the water – or the young people – rocked the chime buoys, the balls swung around hitting the inside of the xylophones that were tuned pentatonically so that they always made a pleasing sound.

Also floating on the surface were two water puppets with long arms and spongy hands, who would pat your hands or feet as you drifted by.

As Claire de Loon began to design the show, she realised that the shoulders and heads, the bits that showed above the water, were the most visible parts of the performers and so concentrated on head gear and neck pieces for the characters. These included Peg, whose collar and headdress were composed largely of plastic clothes pegs, Sponge, with her totally squeezy ruff and hairdo and Marigold, who had yellow rubber gloves everywhere except her hands.

Working in chlorinated water is a challenge. Much experimentation was needed to find materials that floated and would not be ruined by the water. Plastazote proved to be a great material, and all sorts of fittings from plumbers' suppliers to ships chandlers. All the electrical equipment used anywhere near the water was powered by batteries or a low voltage, 12 Volt, system to ensure safety.

As the participants might be spending most of the performance looking up at the ceiling, it was important to find a way of incorporating the inaccessible area above the pool. In *Dreams and Secrets* helium filled balloons were tethered to plastic bottles that floated on the surface. In *Pool Piece*, dozens of mirror balls were suspended by magnets attached to the ceiling in the way that Point-of-Sale notices are hung up in supermarkets. This was a trick that Claire de Loon picked up at a balloon decorators' convention in Belgium.

Effective innovations included some huge, shiny and delightfully pierced Bangladeshi colanders that we transformed into portable and effective showers. After filling the colander with water from the pool, the performers would hold it over the participants to create a shower. As the water poured down, we would light it with the divers' torches from above and below. When we lowered the general lighting in the pool area, it created a magical effect – a truly immersive experience. The pure sound of the shower hitting the surface was particularly evocative.

In later years on our revisits to schools, we would often find colanders, amongst the poolside props, though none perhaps as beautiful as our Bangladeshi originals. We also found that some schools had treasured old audiocassettes of the music from our earlier shows. The staff were still leading Oily Cart musical multi-sensory sessions until the C90s were worn out and had to be replaced by CDs (and now by material on-line.)

There was a story of sorts underpinning *Big Splash*. We reasoned that because what we had created was a laundry then the story should have something to do with washing clothes. So the problem that we introduced when we first met the participants was that one of a pair of socks had gone missing. The cast's motivation then was to explore all parts of the pool/laundry in order to find the missing sock.

This storyline survived all the rehearsals and the opening weeks of the tour right up to the point when one of the teachers pointed out that the idea of putting together a matching pair of anything was not something that an audience described as having Profound and Multiple Learning Disabilities was likely to understand. I supposed it was debatable whether no-one in these audiences would understand. The levels of understanding of many people categorised as PMLD have continually surprised me. But I took the point. If we were relying on someone to match a pair of socks in order to make sense of this performance, then we were going astray. Surely, we should be concentrating on material that would engage people **living in the moment** or who would benefit from a multi-sensory approach, rather than hoping that one or two in our audiences might understand intellectually what was going on.

In later hydropool shows to extend and enhance the experience in the water, we added an introductory *dry* scene to the show. Before entering the water, the participants were guided through a contrasting set of themed experiences. In *Dreams and Secrets* (2000), the participants started off in a cosy and welcoming bedchamber. They then passed on into the sparkling dreamlike pool. In *Waving* (2001) the experience began in the *Windy City* pavilion, the walls of which were made up of bamboo wind chimes activated by scented fans. The pool was a shimmering playground animated by water drumming and the music of the balafon.

One of the most remarkable features of any hydro show is the one that is impossible to replicate in any other medium. This is the relationship between participant and performer that total immersion in the water makes possible. The young people are floating in water and on the same (eye-to-eye) level with the performers. It can be so difficult not to tower over and look down on the audiences when working on dry land, but in the pool performer and participant naturally drift into a very equitable proximity.

Of course, there are always important issues of touch to be negotiated with the participants, their companions and carers, but if you have the necessary agreements, it can be wonderful to work with the feet, the arms, the shoulders of someone in the warm waters of the pool, parts of the body that would be inaccessible on the land – if only because they would be covered by clothing. Another possibility is that even if touching a particular area is felt not to be appropriate by the adult companion, if that companion is the mother or father, then the performer can suggest that mum or dad take over.

The important question of what Sensory Theatre has added to the usual pool visit is hard to describe. Words like magic, wonder and joy come to mind. Some of the most marvelous performances have been the ones where the young participants were accompanied by a parent. The parents are often moved to tears by the beauty of the shared experience. To see the young person being lavished with sometimes gentle, sometimes exciting sensory delights is a deep pleasure for everyone involved. The water shows require an immense effort on the part of the company in terms of logistics and considerable physical and emotional strain, but the rewards are a powerful incentive to do more. It is the shortage of school hydro pools that presents the biggest problem.

Eddy Anderson had always argued that his work with trampolines was just as effective as what he taught in the hydropool, and in 2002, we began trampoline further training with him as we made a piece called, inevitably, *Boing!*

7
Magic Carpet Ride

Boing! 2002 Oily Cart. Twirl (Ruth Calkin) strikes a pose like a film star for her portrait in the Teachers' Handbook. Design: Claire de Loon.

There is a difficulty with performances in hydropools; far from every school in the UK has one.

Back in 1999, many schools were keen to have an Oily Cart water-show but when asked if their pool was big enough would reveal that their "pool" might be better described as a hot tub or jacuzzi. Some wondered if we brought a hydropool with us.

DOI: 10.4324/9781003091288-8

Well – in *Boing!* (1999), we did bring our own trampoline with us and it was a relatively inexpensive 12 feet diameter garden trampoline. It is important to maintain any trampoline properly and to supervise it with the utmost care whenever young people might have access. But compared with a hydropool, it is easy to manage and the effects of working on a trampoline with people with the most complex impairments can be truly amazing.

Oily Cart first began using trampolines in SEND schools under the supervision of Eddy Anderson who taught us his method known as Rebound Therapy. Eddy's focus was on physiotherapy, so I had to adapt his approach to suit our Sensory Theatre needs.

For several years, Oily Cart had consulted a visionary teacher, Sue Hewitt, from William Morris School in Walthamstow. Sue was an expert in both PE and provision for young people with PMLD. We added a trampoline artist to the touring team, Stacey Willmer. Stacey already had experience of working on trampolines with young people with learning disabilities. Together these two experts enabled us to work creatively but most importantly safely.

When I first met young people labeled PMLD, I felt something close to helplessness. I have seen so many young people, slumped in their seats or in their wheelchairs, chin on chest, staring blankly at the floor, apparently oblivious of the world around them. However, when we laid one of these participants onto the bed of the trampoline with one performer or carer supporting their head and another performer creating a gentle bounce, we often witnessed a sort of miracle take place. I remain amazed at the transformations brought about by the trampoline.

As the music began, traces of perfume drifted across the surface of the trampoline. We were in a different world, a world that responded to the participant's sounds, movements and reactions. During each 15 to 20 minute-long trampoline session, the performer and carer on the trampoline would start off very gently, but then adapting to any growing confidence from the participant, would gradually increase the energy of the bounce. The carer/adult companion has a particularly important part to play. With their knowledge of the participant, they could suggest a change of energy or style of movement. The performer or the carer might make the Makaton sign for *more* which could lead the performers and the participants into a dialogue in which, wherever possible, the participant would take the lead.

A session could quickly assume its own identity as the eyes of the participants opened, their muscle tone changed and they opened up like a flower unfolding, growing to engage with the world around them.

The chief delights of the trampoline were similar to those of the hydropool. Firstly, the trampoline offered a vast range of kinaesthetic experiences from the serene through to the joyously energetic. The trampoline responded to and amplified the movements of the young participant and the performers who were with them on-board. What is more, the rhythm of live music complemented and reinforced the rhythm of the trampoline bounces. Of course, there are some people who needed to be handled with extra care on the trampoline. If a firmer surface like a gym mat were placed between the participant and the trampoline bed, this would remove a good deal of the energy from the bounces and remove the risk of physical harm.

The work on the trampoline was done very close-up, one-to-one or even two-to-one. The majority of the senses are most evocative at close range. This close-up work is particularly valuable for participants who have little or no sight or hearing. Anything that needs to be seen or heard will be seen or heard more clearly when it is close by.

The setting for *Boing!* was a middle eastern fantasy in a luxurious nightspot where the chief attraction was a flying carpet ride. As each of the guests waited for their ride on the carpet (in fact the trampoline), they lolled on cushions and beanbags, and were fanned and hand-massaged to the accompaniment of reed and percussion music with an appropriately Maghrebi feel.

During the run of *Boing!* we began to experiment with adding live video to the mix and in 2003, *Boing!* transformed into *Moving Pictures*. The new show looked and sounded a lot like *Boing!* but featured a large video screen above the trampoline. The participants could see themselves in the midst of their great adventure, their flying carpet ride. By using live, close-up images of the participants on the screen, we hoped to help them (at least those of our guests who were sighted) to a greater awareness of the scene in which they were the central characters. The carpet ride was not only a kinaesthetic and an auditory experience; it could also bring powerful visual feedback to the participants. *See, hear, feel what you are doing now!*

What is more, all the others around the trampoline, the adult companions and anyone who was apprehensive about a forthcoming trampoline ride, could see for themselves what the experience was going to be like by looking up at the screen. In *Boing!*, the feel of the flying carpet ride was essentially private, shared only by the three people actually on the trampoline. But the addition of video in *Moving Pictures* opened the doorway into another dimension, a dimension shared by everyone in the room, the dimension of a shared experience.

I don't believe that this kind of shared experience is the key goal in Sensory Theatre. I would argue that the first priority in Sensory Theatre is to break through the barriers to communication between individuals, between, in my terms, the performer and the participant. But it is a wonderful bonus if we can also involve the participant in a shared group experience.

During many of the *Moving Pictures'* video feedback moments, I have seen teachers, administrative staff, dinner ladies, school keepers and the bus drivers gazing in wonder at the screen. They are seeing the young person they know in an astonishing new light.

Both in *Boing!* and *Moving Pictures*, the attention of performer, companion and our musician away to the side of the trampoline were focused on one participant and this allowed them to mould the experience to the requirements of that one person. The whole event could be serenely relaxed, or high energy or some enchanting ever-changing mixture. There was one difficulty. If you were on the trampoline, you were at the centre of the universe, but otherwise you were waiting your turn.

The latest trampoline production we were to make, *The Bounce* in 2014, involved **two trampolines** (plus a specific version for people on the spectrum). Having two simultaneous trampoline sessions introduced a joyful shared, social element and considerably shortened the time you had to wait to have a go.

Here is a YouTube link to video of **All About *The Bounce* (2014)**, an Oily preparation video on how best to get on and off the trampolines for *The Bounce*.

https://youtu.be/hsLsgRsulNg

8
From PMLD to Autism Spectrum

Conference of the Birds 2004 Oily Cart. The Water Bird played by DJ Hassan and a participant with a bowl of seeds.

Photo: Gemma Riggs.

DOI: 10.4324/9781003091288-9

I have no embarrassment in saying I was quite moved to tears by the enthusiasm, joy and contentment which is achieved by this most impressive of theatre productions.

Mark Brown – *SUNDAY HERALD*

I have left it till now to mention the most radical effect of the *Boing!* show. In 2002, in the lunch break between two performances of *Boing!* in a Wandsworth Special School, one of the teachers approached me and asked if some of the senior students could have a go on our trampoline in their break. I asked who these students were and was told that they were on the autism spectrum, that they all loved trampolines and would be carefully supervised. Why should we object? In came four or five very mobile students, one of whom climbed onto the trampoline unaided and bounced towards the ceiling with great confidence. I had never seen the like. We were used to working with Profound and Multiple Learning Disability students who had to be manoeuvred onto the trampoline with great care, often involving the use of an electric hoist. What we saw in that lunch break was a huge contrast to the magic carpet rides that we had become used to providing in the Special Schools.

With help from teachers, we pieced together how Special Schools had changed in the years following 1996, while we had been concentrating on work for the PMLD pupils. More and more young people with special educational needs had been integrated into mainstream school but there remained two groups who were in the main still being educated in Special Schools. They were the young people with Profound and Multiple Disabilities and those considered to be on the severe end of the Autism Spectrum.

We began to research and to consult to see if we needed to create different material for these two different audiences. I should sound a note of caution here. Terms like PMLD and ASC have their uses in determining the curriculum, allocating educational resources and indeed in providing a shorthand for schools, families and theatre companies to negotiate with one another. We sort of know what one another mean when we say, *This show is suitable for people on the spectrum.* Or *This might be better for the PMLD classes.* But these terms are reductive, sometimes even pejorative, and they tell us more about what people cannot do than what they can do. There are also many instances of dual diagnosis and of people who do not fit into any of the categories.

Whenever possible I think it best to approach an individual or an audience with an open mind. Yes, make a note of the phrase or acronym that has been applied to someone at some time or another, but do not rush to conclusions. Take your time, use the evidence and be wary about labeling.

Having had my say about labeling, I shall try to define the differences between people who are on the Autism Spectrum and those defined as PMLD. I present these generalisations with apologies. I offer them merely as some tips from a practitioner that may be useful in the making of a Sensory Theatre piece.

- An ASC audience is likely to have more mobility and be more flexible physically than the PMLD equivalent. A PMLD audience often comes in wheelchairs and requires hoisting. This begs the question; do you leave the participants in their chairs or not? What extra space will need to be allowed for wheelchairs?
- An ASC audience is more likely to benefit from a conventional story structure that introduces characters and shows how issues and conflicts develop and resolve.
- An ASC audience is more likely to benefit from preparatory work in person, on-line, on video or in print. Although PMLD participants can benefit from multi-sensory preparation, and carers of both kinds of audience need briefing on the variations of shows on offer.
- An ASC audience will particularly benefit from an **airlock** or **chillout** space separate to the main performance space where they can relax and get their bearings after their journey to the hall or theatre.
- An ASC audience is more likely to benefit from follow-up work after a performance. The performance could form part of (say) a term's work on a theme.
- A participant on the spectrum might find it more of an issue to visit an unfamiliar venue or meet new people than a PMLD audience.
- A participant on the spectrum may be resistant to demands they feel are being made on them. A performer playing to an autistic participant needs to take care not to impose his or her ideas but rather to create a situation that performer and participant can explore together. Performers should not be authority figures but relaxed friends.
- A PMLD audience is more likely to have particular requirements of a venue in terms of changing facilities, toileting and physical access than is an ASC audience.

I began to think that it might be possible to create a production that could be performed in two versions, one for an ASC, the other for a PMLD audience. The difference between the two versions would lie in the amount of pre-performance work done for the ASC version and in the adaptations made by the performers as they encountered the participants. To allow the performers the greatest flexibility in adapting to the requirements of the audience, much of the work would have to be done one-to-one for a substantial part of the show. The more any performer can work close up to the participant, the more likely they are to get to know that participant and to develop some common language with them. If we took into account that each participant would also have an adult companion with them, this could readily be added to the total of one-to-one contact time in a show. Surely that would be sufficient. Taking these considerations into account, we decided to proceed.

First, we needed to find a story which we could make work for both audiences. I had come across a 12th century Persian poem, *The Conference of the Birds*, in which there is a haunting central image: a group of birds searching for their Ruler, discover a deserted palace – but where is their Ruler?

The walls of our palace were a pair of huge inflatable wings that could change colour by means of internal LED lighting. The six members of the audience reclined within the enfolding wings on suspended recliners, called Leaf Chairs. They are not cheap nor particularly easy to tour but they reappeared in several Oily Cart productions because they had so much to offer.

Each chair was suspended by a chain from a frame, making it capable of a very wide variety of movement. It could rotate sideways through 360 degrees, bounce up and down and swing in and out. The movement could range from very subtle and gentle to the most exhilarating and be activated both by the young people in the seats, by the performers or by their adult companions. The idea behind the leaf chairs was that they could provide a range of kinaesthetic sensations that would be enjoyable for people on the spectrum and indeed for many of those described as PMLD. However, from the beginning, we were aware that some PMLD participants, because they used custom-designed supportive wheelchairs, would need to enjoy the performance from their usual, day to day, seating.

There was a wide, very accessible entrance between the wing tips at one end of the set and at the other end, there was a large oval, egg-shaped, video back-projection screen. Just in front of the screen was a working fountain in the shape of an egg that came to life when we needed water. In case any water was spilled, the whole area within the wings was covered by a waterproof floor cloth.

We placed the six leaf chairs within the wings, in two rows of three facing one another. Beside each leaf chair was a comfy chair where the companion, normally a family member or teacher, would sit.

The performers wore stylised bird costumes, a feather in the hat suggesting the bird rather than anything more literal, and each character's way of moving was also bird-like but in a minimal way.

The story could either be appreciated as a sequence of self-contained events, each one dedicated to one or two of the senses, or it could be seen as a debate about what would bring the Ruler of the Birds back to the deserted palace.

Each scene was introduced with a similar sequence. The first bird argued that it was the wind that would most please their Ruler. From outside the performance space, there came the sound of large palm leaf fans shaking. Then on the video screen, there appeared the silhouette of a fan fanning. That led to all the performers entering in a choreographed procession using large fans to actually fan the participants. Finally, each participant or companion was offered a smaller fan to experience the sensation for themselves. This sort of gradual build, first sound then image, then the actual event, allowed the participants plenty of vital processing time. This pattern was soon picked up on by the companions and many participants who could discuss where the sound and the video cues might be leading.

This clear gradual structure introducing each new sensory exploration worked equally well for both PMLD and ASC participants in *Conference of the Birds*.

The second bird believed that it was seeds, the food of so many birds, that were the most marvelous thing of all. The seeds were brought to the participants in large, hollowed-out gourds. There were lights in the bottom of the gourds, covered by a layer of seeds. When the gourds were shaken or stirred not only was there a satisfying sound, but also the shifting patterns made by the seeds over the lights drew the focus of the participants. They could easily push the lights to switch them on and off.

The third bird preferred feathers whereas the last bird championed water to bring the Ruler back. Other gourds were filled with warm and lightly scented water from the egg fountain and taken to the leaf chairs where it was sponged and squeezed over the hands of the participants.

The Ruler of the Birds, an abstract being made up of sound and light, was finally induced to return by the appearance of the participants projected onto the oval screen while each one had their Name Song sung to them. The melody of each Name Song had been introduced earlier in the show to make it familiar on the overture principle and each lyric was just one word, the name of the person to whom it was sung. This brought the show to a celebratory conclusion: that the participants themselves were the most enchanting thing of all and had caused the Ruler of the Birds to return.

> Pupils responded continuously to the performance more than we have ever seen them respond to anything else. The children loved seeing themselves on the big screen. One ASC boy who usually runs around

and becomes violent was just mesmerised for 45 minutes then went back to class and just wanted to hug and "love" the staff – a complete transformation.

Feedback from the staff at HILLTOP SCHOOL

Here is a YouTube link to video of **Blue (2006),** an edited version from two performances for young people with Profound and Multiple Learning Disabilities or an Autistic Spectrum Condition.

https://youtu.be/SyshdtT_4BY

9
Sensory Theatre for the Very Early Years

Baby Tube 2013 Oily Cart. Huff 'N Puff played by Ellie Griffiths plays a tubophon for a baby to hear and to feel. Design: Claire de Loon.

Photo: Patrick Baldwin.

DOI: 10.4324/9781003091288-10

Baby Balloon lasts 50 minutes, every single one a delight. This is touch-me-feel-me theatre of the highest order, in which the fourth wall is blown to smithereens.

Lyn Gardner – THE GUARDIAN

All the time we were developing the kinaesthetic, interactive and close-up work for young people with PMLD and people on the spectrum with Oily Cart, we were also still creating theatre for two to five year olds and their families. We were beginning to call these 'all-comers' shows, shows that were open to anyone, with or without any disability providing they were more or less in the right age range. However, we were concerned that a two year old and a five year old were very different beings in terms of their understanding of the world and their use of language.

These all-comers shows always had more people in their audiences (between 30 and 50), far more than in the work we made specifically for people with complex disabilities and for this reason they were less multi-sensory and interactive and tended to use more verbal language, narrative and characters. They played in public venues, studio theatres and arts centres, most often involving a pre-Christmas residency followed by a short tour of week-long runs around England and Wales.

From very early days, we were aware that there were many children in our all-comers audiences who were younger than two. While we expected to find babes-in-arms and toddlers in our audiences – they had usually come along with their elder siblings – it could be disconcerting to find children who were too young to talk watching these shows with complex narrative, characters and verbal language. We began to wonder if a multi-sensory, close-up, highly interactive form of theatre could be effective for another non-verbal, or rather pre-verbal, audience.

Then came a catalyst. In 2002, for the first time I saw a production for babies and toddlers made by a French company. I was not impressed. All the sound and music in this show was taped and the tape ran continuously throughout the performance. There was no opportunity to pause or respond to the audience. To me, the performance was frozen. It is not very gracious to say so, but I was encouraged by this example. I had to be able to do a baby and toddler show that was an improvement on this.

At the time, I was working with the Oily team, on a show called *Jumpin' Beans*. We had planned on a version for two to four year olds and one for four to sixes. We promptly added an extra version for a much younger age group starting at six months to two year olds. This version of the show was called *Up in the Clouds* and was played to seven babies with seven carers. The role of the carers who would certainly be present was crucially important. It was essential to gain their support and participation. The performers had to make it clear that they were invited to take an active role in the fun.

The theme that linked all three versions was jumping. The participants spent time in the Wibbly Wobbly Waiting Room before the performance. This was a specially designed soft play area complete with a very wobbly tunnel to explore made of tractor tyre inner tubes, together with plenty of bouncy balls and some mini trampolines. The teachers' pack featured Creative Movement Worksheets by an early year's dance specialist, Hazel Davies. Hazel devised three age-appropriate sessions to be done to the music for the show.

Then in 2006, Oily Cart received a commission from Filip Bral, director of the Pantalone Art House in Brussels to make a new show for the under-twos to open their new venue. Who could resist?

I decided I wanted to do a show all about inflatables and balloons, as our collaborations with Rachel James who had designed and made earlier inflatable sets had been very successful.

This met with some opposition. Several people assured us that the balloons would burst, and all the children would cry. I took a hardcore line that children know from an early age that balloons burst, and it was just part of the deal you accepted if you wanted all that colour and the bounciness. In fact, very few babies were bothered at all on the rare occasions when balloons burst.

As part of our preparations, Claire and I attended an astonishing balloon-modeling festival, the Millennium Jam, which takes place each year in an out-of-season holiday camp at Mol in Belgium. It really should be referred to as a "balloon and beer" festival as the organisers not only lay on a vast array of balloons of every shape and size, and enough gas canisters to inflate a fleet of zeppelins, they also provide enough beer to keep the balloon competitions going late into the night.

The events are primarily aimed at balloon modelers (though I think everyone should go) and there are competitions and prizes in a surprising number of categories including Scenes from the Bible (using only balloons) and Most Beautiful Wedding dress (ditto).

Claire and I were greatly impressed by the potential of balloons and also taken by a bubbles act that had somehow been invited to attend. The bubble artists created some beautiful effects and wistfully complained how changing social mores had forced them to cut some of the former highlights of their children's act – like shoving carving knives through balloons that they had filled with cigarette smoke.

Rachel James designed and made a giant balloon that would be the centre-piece of our set. We recruited two dancers, Adura Onashile and Keiko Aka-matsu. The show was almost completely free of verbal language.

We were fortunate to find that the great Dutch jazz cellist, Ernst Reijseger, was willing to get the train down from Amsterdam to play in Brussels along-side Max Reinhardt. This is the Ernst Reijseger of whom Werner Herzog said, *He is a magnificent cellist, and he can do anything, play anything on his cello. He could play the civil war, the American Civil War on his cello.* As it turned out he was also magnificent at playing for children under two and their families. Ernst was joined by Max on decks, harmonica and a lot of balloons.

The production also involved a complex (early) LED-based lighting system hidden within the walls of the inflatable which made it possible to change the colours of the inflatable through a very wide range. This system had been put together by our lighting designer, Stuart Willcocks, and our video artist and long-time technical whizz, Nick Weldin.

In Brussels we played in quite a small space with a low ceiling to an audience of between 20 and 30 who at the start found themselves looking at the giant balloon. As the music began, the inflatable began to pulsate with colour in time to the music. A dancer, Keiko, appeared. By rubbing the surface of the inflatable, she made largeish helium-filled balloons pop out of the porthole in the end of the big balloon, followed eventually by Adura, the other dancer.

The two dancers played with the balloons, pulling them down low by their ribbons then releasing them so they would shoot up to the ceiling.

Thus far the audience had been passive, with the children sitting with mum or dad, watching the performance as if through a fourth wall. We were hop-ing to gain their confidence and ready them to join in. At last, a bunch of smaller helium-filled balloons were passed through the invisible wall until every child in the room had a balloon to play with. Now the children were in charge of the game and playing in the same space as the performers, trans-fixed by each dive and twist of the balloons. They played peek a boo with silk hankies hanging from the balloons and shook musical balloons with little bells inside. They were delighted to see their own faces and those of Mum and Dad projected live onto a large white balloon used as a screen.

Next another surprise issued from the porthole in the inflatable – not balloons but something even more attractive to very young children – bubbles. This was the only invitation the toddlers needed, and they followed the bubble trail into the inflatable, followed in the turn by the rest of the audience. Once everyone was inside, the lighting of the inflatable faded to a warm, inviting yellow. In this cosy space, we sat and ate tangerines filling the interior with their rich aroma as we did so.

A glowing red balloon lantern appeared in the porthole and the audience was invited to follow the dancers out into a very different nighttime world. The moon illuminating this world was, of course, the large white balloon. In this tranquil setting the children and their accompanying adults were invited to play with the sensory props to which they had been introduced in the course of the performance. Now they had a good chance to play with them in their own way.

We were all delighted at the reception of *Baby Balloon* in Brussels. We had taken some chances, like basing the production on such an abstract theme as balloons, but the children had been engrossed at every performance and the adults had many complimentary things to say about the quality of the music and the use of video in particular.

We continued with short tours of *Baby Balloon* in the UK for another three years with a changing cast of dancers, Anthea Lewis and Sally-Anne Donaldson, and musicians, including Max Reinhardt (solo), Finn Peters, Jason Yarde and Tunde Jegede.

Working with very early years in a very multi-sensory and close-up way, we had found a wonderful new audience for Sensory Theatre.

> A ticket to an Oily Cart show is like an "open sesame" to an irresistible playground for the imagination and the senses. And though Baby Balloon is intended for toddlers, the sheer invention that's at work, or rather at play, is every bit as inspiring for adults.
>
> Mary Brennan – THE HERALD

Here are two YouTube links to video of **Baby Balloon Part 1 & Part 2 (2006)** Performance at Pantalone Art House, Brussels with Ernst Reijseger on cello.

https://youtu.be/z21RaH2o9-E and https://youtu.be/Z4tI-MF2hVc

Part Two
How Sensory Theatre Works

Jumpin' Beans 2002 Oily Cart. Naomi Cortes, Patrick Lynch, Ruth Calkin and Jo James. Design: Claire de Loon.

Photo: Patrick Baldwin.

DOI: 10.4324/9781003091288-11

10
Sensory Theatre Audiences

In the first part of this book, I have described how I became aware of the different audiences for which Sensory Theatre was developed, starting off with the under-fives and finishing up with young people on the autism spectrum.

In Part Two, I will analyse Sensory Theatre by looking in detail at its component parts:

> How the audiences can be defined
> How the productions are multi-sensory
> How they are interactive
> How the shows use music
> How they use design

And the skills of the performer, writers, directors, choreographers, puppeteers, video artists – and so on.

In the interests of clarity, I should like to define some of the terms I use in discussing Sensory Theatre. In conventional theatre, there are the performers who perform and the spectators who watch and audiences who listen.

But in the Sensory Theatre, while there are still **the performers** who put on the show, I think it helps if we think of the audience as divided into one of three categories:

(1) **the participants**, the people who are hard-to-reach and for whom the show has been specifically crafted. For example, the participants in one show might have sensory impairments and communication with them in the theatre must take this into account. Similarly, if the people in one of our audiences are on the autism spectrum, then there will be another set of factors to be taken into account and different adjustments

DOI: 10.4324/9781003091288-12

Mr. and Mrs. Moon 2012 Oily Cart. Sandy played by Natasha Magigi in the giant sand pit where she and the participants all make sand castles and draw pictures together. Design: Claire de Loon.

Photo: Hannah Sharp.

that need to be made. I am deliberately avoiding the use of the word *spectator* because that implies that sight will be involved, and it might well not be. I will also steer away from the word *audience* which suggests hearing, which is another sense that is not very relevant for many in our audiences. However, all present need to *participate* in a piece of Sensory Theatre.

(2) **the companions** (adult family members or teachers, for example) who come along with the participants to help them access the show.

(3) **the observers** (family members, students etc.) who generally sit and watch from a distance and are not usually part of the interactivity.

First Type of Audience – the Participants

In the first category are the people for whom any production is created. The first thing I do when making a new show is think about the participants, the subjects and processes that might interest them and the languages they use to make sense of the world around them. With the other creatives in the team, I consult participants and their family members, and we try as far as possible to put ourselves in the shoes of those for whom we are making the piece. They are not only the starting point of a new production, but they are also the alpha and omega of the whole process. If we were thinking of making a hydropool show, say, then it would not be long before Max and I ended up in the water.

Recently I was talking one to one of the most senior Teaching Assistants in a school where we have worked a lot. She had had a problem with one of her young people involving a pimply rubber doormat. She had asked the student to take off his shoes and socks and stand on the rubber mat. She had thought it might be an interesting sensation. He had given it a go but was obviously not happy with the result. At this point the Teaching Assistant thought she should give the experience a try herself and, as she put it, *So I did, and it was bloody awful.* The moral is: Never trust your own guesswork over firsthand sensory experience.

Secondary Type of Audience – the Companions

Most of the Sensory Theatre with which I have been involved has included the pairing of the participant with a companion, usually an adult companion. This should be someone who knows the participant well, perhaps a family member, a teacher, teaching assistant or similar. They usually stay close to the participant throughout the performance and act as an adviser, an explainer and a translator helping the participant and the performer understand one another. They suggest things that might be possible and things that should be avoided.

While the participants are the primary audience, the companions must be acknowledged as part of the audience, and they need to be encouraged to play an active role in the show. It is important that both participants and companions are drawn into the energy, the joy and the fun of the production. If the companions are comfortable and happy, their pleasure will communicate itself to the participants and help them to relax and enjoy the show.

However, it has to be said that, because of staffing issues, the companion does not always know the participant all that well and sometimes their suggestions need to be taken with a pinch of salt. Sometimes they do not know the participant at all, and sometimes they can underestimate them. The evolving relationship between participant and companion can need as much flexible handling as that between participant and performer.

Third Type of Audience – the Observers

The Observers are usually a group made up of family members and friends of the participants, people who are training to do this sort of work, representatives of funding bodies and so on. Whereas there will always be a more or less equal number of Participants and Companions, there probably should be a similar limit on the number of Observers. Their role is to observe and be unobtrusive. And so, it helps if they are a smallish group and not a crowd. The main objective is the involvement of the participants. Observers sometimes do not have the greatest view and probably will miss out on the close-up sensory input. The pleasure for them is to see and hear the primary audience having a great time.

Sometimes in performances for family groups, one family member might start off as a companion but then swap places with one of their family who had started off in the observer group. Quite often I have seen this swap initiated by a participant, who wants both Mum and Dad to join in the fun. In my opinion letting the participants run the show now and then is a very good idea.

Relaxed Performances

Many young people on the spectrum or with other complex disabilities love going to the big musical shows in the West End and on tour. But every now and again, there are complaints from some conventional theatregoers when people on the autism spectrum, for example, sometimes move around in the auditorium or even – Lord help us – make noises.

Apparently, some people go to the theatre to sit in reverential silence and this strange behaviour is reinforced by the design of theatres common in Europe and North America where the participant/spectator is meant to remain in a particular seat throughout the performance and look at the stage at the other end of the room. The theatre space is not designed for the audience to move around in or even to turn around in. Clearly this is not to the taste of many people on the autism spectrum who have exploratory and iconoclastic attitudes towards the theatre and quite a few other social phenomena.

> Why can't we walk around?
> I want to sit over there.
> What's wrong with talking to the people on the stage?
> Why don't they talk to me?

Then there is the issue for many on the autism spectrum and other complex disabilities of sensory hypersensitivity; people who can be brought to the point of melt-down by loud or sudden noises, bright or flashing lights.

To some extent this problem has been addressed by the staging of "relaxed performances" where, in the conventional theatre, they turn down the volume at particularly noisy moments or dim the lighting at especially bright moments, or, indeed, turn up the lighting when the stage picture darkens. In addition, the audience are told that they are allowed to move in the auditorium and a special "chill-out zone" is provided to which people can move and relax if things are becoming too intense on stage.

Social Stories are often provided in print and online to prepare the young people for the experience of the show. Social Stories are illustrated guides to a show, introducing ideas about a theatre visit and the characters, themes, complementary activities involved to participants who may find encounters with new people and unfamiliar places less worrying or disquieting with some clear preparation.

I whole-heartedly approve of the freedom to move around the auditorium and in and out of the chill-out zone where you can prepare for the show experience and relax if necessary when the performance is on. So, yes, let us have lots of relaxed performances. But could we also have a lot more of what our hard-to-reach audiences really need: a theatre that can genuinely adapt to the specific requirements of a particular group of people; something more ambitious than a tweaked sound cue here and lighting cue there.

People defined as PMLD or who are on the autism spectrum are like the rest of us, ever changing, from hour to hour and from day to day. They are not all of them all of the time reduced to anxiety by darkness. They are not all of them all of the time noise averse or touch sensitive. We should not prejudge anyone based on clumsy labeling but respond to people as we find them.

Enhanced Performances

Because of Oily Cart's reputation as a provider of theatre for young people with complex disabilities, the shows for under-fives regularly attracted bookings from SEND schools as well. This started to become an issue when I saw the possible danger of mixing groups of boisterous young children on the autism spectrum with a family audience which often included babies and ɔddlers who sometimes looked vulnerable when the larger young people ɔegan moving around. I decided to persuade the venues to offer a version of the under-fives show that was adapted to the particular requirements of the young people on the autism spectrum. We called these versions Enhanced Performances and over a three-week run, there would be two or three on offer in the week for schools and at the weekend for families.

The numbers for the Enhanced Performances were reduced from 50 children and adults down to 30. This allowed more space for wheelchairs and made it easier for wanderers to move around. Lower numbers made the experience less stressful for participants and enabled more one-to-one interaction with the performers. The verbal elements in the shows were trimmed down and the sensory interactions were ramped up. A Social Story was produced to help with preparation.

There is a great deal more about Social Stories as a vital means of preparing participants, especially for those on the spectrum, in Chapter 30 of this book.

The first show to receive this treatment was *Land of Lights* (2015) at the arts-depot venue in North London for a Christmas run. Along with the venue, I was unsure whether this tactic would work for the audience or at the box office. Selling shows for a targeted group in a new format takes some preparation and a degree of staff training. Venues have to buy in to the idea of even smaller ticket sales. This is a big ask. Not many venues are willing to lose capacity and income from ticket sales. However, our anxieties proved unfounded and the Enhanced Performances were most successful in giving the targeted audiences a better quality experience. The strategy was repeated with *In a Pickle* (2016) and *Hush a Bye* (2017) at artsdepot and other venues on tour.

11
Sensory Theatre Is Multisensory

Bubbles 1997 Oily Cart. Design: Claire de Loon.
Photo: Paul Harris.

How many senses are there? Nearly everyone would agree there are at least five: seeing, hearing, touching, tasting, smelling, and then I would argue for the kinaesthetic sense which is the sense the body has of its own position and movement in space. There is also the sense of temperature that I believe can be very useful in performance work.

DOI: 10.4324/9781003091288-13

Detailed descriptions of the kinaesthetic sense are to be found in Chapter 17 of this book, and the sense of temperature is discussed in Chapter 18.

Most conventional forms of theatre rely on seeing and hearing for the performers to communicate with their audiences but because our Sensory Theatre often involves participants whose vision and hearing is impaired, we cannot rely on these sensory channels to communicate and engage everyone. Instead, we need to offer additional, complementary experiences and so keep alternative channels open.

However, this approach needs handling with care. When we began to make our first show for people with PMLD, *Tickled Pink*, in 1997, I think I made the mistake of involving too many senses at a time. There were moments when there were vivid colours, sparkling mirrors, deeply vibrating bass clarinet sounds, billowing clouds of incense and rocking in hammocks – all at the same time. Each sensory stimulus would have been fine on its own and some were individually quite beautiful but put them all together and you get what I learned to call the **Disco in Hell** effect.

I should have kept in mind the saying, **Less is More** and not piled up sound on spectacle, perfume on texture, vibration on whirling dance, all on top of one another. We certainly do not need for all the senses to be stimulated in every sequence in a show. A more effective plan would be to concentrate on one or two senses plus seeing and hearing for one scene in a show, then put together another combination of sensory stimuli for a second scene, and yet another for a third – and so on.

Background and Foreground

One way for clarifying presentation, especially when it comes to visuals, is to have a plain background with objects in front of it so that they stand out more clearly. This clarity of focus says to the participant, *This is the important bit. This is the bit to concentrate on.*

In the 2015 Oily Cart production, *Light Show*, the set and the costumes were white and when something was introduced that we wanted the participants to focus on, it was in a bright colour.

This process of using contrast to help with focusing and processing works with all the senses, not just the visual sense. If you would like someone to focus on a particular sound, it helps if there is silence before the sound and silence after it. You cannot have music without the silences to frame it. If you would like someone to appreciate a particular kinaesthetic movement, for example rocking in a rocking chair, it makes a real difference if you ensure that the chair is absolutely still for a couple of seconds before you allow the chair to rock. And also make sure that there is a further moment of stillness afterwards. An activity will always be more clearly defined by stillness and silence before and after it.

High Performer to Participant Ratios

It may seem obvious to say this, but it is important that you make the space in which a piece of Sensory Theatre is performed as welcoming as possible. Whether you want to completely make over a school hall into an enchanted wonderland or if your aim is to transform a corner of a classroom or a living room into an oasis of multisensory tranquility, a key factor is to consider how comfortable your audience will feel in this space.

Many people in a Sensory Theatre audience can be disturbed by spaces that are too noisy, too bright or dark, too hot or too cold. They can be unsettled by too strong a smell or simply by being in an unfamiliar place. That is one of the reasons why it is so important to introduce the performance space itself as well as the characters and the scenery with photos and/or video to participants in any pre-performance preparatory material like a Social Story.

But the situation is complicated by the fact that there are many people on the spectrum or with other complex disabilities who find simply being in a crowd disconcerting. The more people a participant has around them the more difficult they may find it to focus on the essentials. There is also the possibility of sensory overload and meltdown.

Of course, much theatre works by attracting an audience large enough to buy sufficient tickets so that the show can be made and the actors paid. But with Sensory Theatre, the larger the audience the more dilute will be its effect.

In commercial theatre, reliant on box office and bums on seats, there is a need to concentrate on the senses that will convey information over fairly long distances, like the senses of seeing and hearing. But if a Sensory Theatre production only concentrates on what can be seen and what can be heard, it is missing out on a lot. It jettisons at least two thirds of what is available to the sensorium of a neurotypical person. In terms of *immersion*, it's shallow. It is not multi-sensory; it is a bit sensory.

But the most compelling reason for the smaller size of audience in Sensory Theatre is not that it makes it possible to employ a greater range of the senses nor that it is much more welcoming to participants who are made uneasy by a crowd. The strongest argument for the small size is that this permits genuine one-to-one work between performers and participants.

If you try to work with more commercially viable ratios (for example one performer per 25 participants) then the less immersive and the more generalised the experience will become. There is no realistic way that the performer can deliver a personal response to each participant in an audience of 50 or more. You will not be able to establish eye contact or make a personal response to a specific participant's reaction.

Forgive me if I say it again – in Sensory Theatre, the success of the performance is in inverse proportion to the number in the audience.

Here is a YouTube link to video of *Something in the Air* **trailer (2009)**

Oily Cart and Ockham's Razor present *Something in the Air* at the Contact Theatre Manchester, as part of the Manchester International Festival. There are six participants with their carers. Each pair in the chairs has their own chair driver. In this performance, the aerialists, the musicians and the crew are joined by the performers who were previously resident in local schools.

https://youtu.be/3_QtmvWZaEw

12
The Senses One by One – the Sense of Seeing

Tube 2013 Oily Cart. Look 'N See played by Griff Fender. Design: Claire de Loon.
Photo: Ben Cooper.

DOI: 10.4324/9781003091288-14

Seeing is one of the dominant senses in performance, along with hearing. Of course it is not unusual for people with PMLD to have little or no sight and that is one of the major reasons why I first began to explore multi-sensory media.

The number of ways in which we can deploy objects or characters to engage the sense of seeing is vast and includes:

Performers

Performers come top of the list with their expressions, their gestures, dancing and singing. A performer is a most versatile *resource*. You can put on a show with just one performer – and nothing else. Of course performers also communicate via a substantial number of other sensory channels, for example signature perfume and the sense of touch.

Costumes

Costumes enhance the performers; work with their colour and their movement – the swaying of a headdress, the swishing of a cape – can convey an enormous amount of sensory information and of course they also work with the senses of touch, of hearing and of temperature – to which I will return a little later.

Objects

Objects (also known as props) can be as engaging and informative to some participants as a performer. An object may make a connection when nothing else will do.

In some SEND Schools, **Objects of Reference** are tangible things that are systematically and consistently used with a pupil to represent people, places and activities. They are often used alongside the spoken word. For example, a pupil going to the hydropool is given a towel to hold. There is an identical towel hanging by the doorway to the pool. Through repeated use of the object of reference, the pupil comes to associate that being handed the towel *means* "We're going to the pool."

I have frequently used a particular Object of Reference as the basis of a performer's characterisation. With many of our participants to simply say "My name is Brush" is pretty meaningless, but if from the very beginning that character has a brush and uses that brush to brush the back of a partici-pant's hand then, after some repetition, the participant will get to recognise that character and have a notion of what that character likes to do. The appearance of the character, the Object of Reference, the costume, plus the gestures and movement patterns make a stranger into someone very identi-fiable, a friend.

Puppets

Somewhere between an Object of Reference and a performer's character comes the puppet. A well-designed puppet is the essence of a character with all extraneous detail stripped away. It can be unambiguous and readily understood.

Puppets give us the opportunity to play with scale. A character can be por-trayed by an actor, then the same character, played by a puppet can be seen flying through the clouds, swimming at the bottom of the ocean or as a giant – the possibilities are endless.

Of course there are many different types of puppets. The ones which I have found particularly useful for Sensory Theatre are shadow puppets because they can be used to give remarkably clear black and white as well as coloured images.

The most basic shadow puppet screen must be a white sheet hung by clothes pegs from a washing line stretched across the room. The simplest kind of shadow puppet can be made from stiffish cardboard attached to sticks with drawing pins.

If you have a large enough sheet, then you can very easily make **human shadows**. In human shadows, the shadow puppets are the performers them-selves who stand behind your sheet screen, but in front of the light that casts their shadow onto the screen.

The light source for the shadow show can be as simple as a desk lamp between the puppeteer and the screen, angled at about 45 degrees to the screen. It helps a good deal if your light is fitted with a domestic dimmer switch. Then you can have your puppet ready for action on the screen as the lights fade up, and at the end of the scene, you can end the action by fading the light down.

Another very useful light source is to use an old-style **overhead projector** (OHP) cheaply available second-hand online. The big advantage of an OHP is that you operate the puppets as they lie horizontally on the bed, meaning that they will stay still when you want them to and cannot fall from the screen at inconvenient moments.

Another virtue of the OHP is that if you place two of them side-by-side focused on the same screen, it's possible by fading down one as you fade up the other to cross fade from scene to scene. I have often used an object of reference such as a feather or a bowl of water on an OHP to announce and reinforce a sensory experience.

(See Chapter 27 – Puppets and Pixels, for more about other forms of puppetry.)

Lighting

In the Oily Cart show *Land of Lights* (2015) for three to five year olds and their families, we played with a landscape from which all the lights had vanished until the audience found a way to bring them back.

As the audience entered the performance space, they found themselves surrounded by scores of tiny buildings with windows, doors, roofs, and chimneys – all in darkness. The children could peer inside with the torches we handed out but all was dark and still. Where had everyone gone? A tiny puppet girl explained that even the stars had gone missing and all her neighbours had gone out to find them.

What ensued was a sensory delight involving the children in much messy play. They were invited to look for the stars in bowls of bubble and plates of jelly. They searched in flowerpots full of seeds. Once the stars had been found the tiny girl flew with them up into the heavens where suddenly the sky lit up and the lights in the houses flickered into life amid sounds of celebration.

It's often the simplest things that work the best. Take the glitter ball in all its manifestations for instance – from the hand-held bauble to the ballroom giant. Another example is that provided by the gourds filled with dry seeds in *Conference of the Birds* (2004). As the young audiences rummaged amongst the tactile seeds, they continuously covered and uncovered battery-operated lights at the bottom of the bowls, in the process making their own lightshow. Also excellent are jugglers' balls with LEDs inside that glow and can change colour.

Thanks to the wonderful pioneering work of Flo Longhorn (author of *A Sensory Curriculum for Very Special People* (1988)) it's no longer a secret that the Poundland shops of the UK are filled with flashing, tinkling, bleeping treasures to be explored just as much as the high-end tech of stage lighting.

In the past decade, LED stage lights have become much more employed in close-up Sensory Theatre, for at least two reasons: namely one LED light can produce a myriad of colours and patterns and importantly, it can to do this without becoming uncomfortably hot.

For *Light Show* (2015) Jack Knowles, an innovative lighting designer who worked on several Oily Cart productions, came up with a wonderful design that made brilliant use of the fact that the participants were lying on loungers and looking up at the underside of large white parasols. Jack's idea was to put LED lights in boxes on the floor, focused upwards to project their light and colour into the parasols. If Jack had been lighting in the conventional way from above, the participants could not have avoided getting the light in their eyes – and unlike with conventional lighting, there was no risk of the young people getting their fingers burned on the lights (LEDs) in the boxes right beside them.

Video

But perhaps the greatest technical advances in Sensory Theatre over the past 10 to 15 years have been in the area of video.

When I began working with video in the early 1970s, it was using Sony ½ inch monochrome tape. There was a separate reel-to-reel recorder, connected by a thick cable to a camera. I am sure I can remember editing the tape with a razor blade and sticky tape – but perhaps I was not meant to do that.

Now we can video in a hundred times more detail and in far lower light levels with a mobile phone. And nowadays, video projectors are light and robust and you don't have to position them half a mile back from the screen to project a reasonably sized picture. For the show *Stranden* that I wrote and directed in Sweden in 2019, the back projector actually touched the back of the screen. What's more, video images can be edited on your laptop or smart phone. Nowadays video is begging to be used, no razor blade or sticky tape in sight.

Large-scale video projection can show a participant right at the heart of a multi-sensory and interactive experience and for many it helps them to understand what's going on, bringing confidence and understanding to the process.

It also enables the participants to relive a pleasurable experience after the performers have long since moved on to the next venue. In the noughties when we visited a school with a video-based show, like *Conference of the Birds* (2004), we would record a video tape of the show to leave behind so that participants could watch themselves over and over again, often showing more pleasure at the repeats than the original, demonstrating what worked for them and what did not. Nowadays such reminding and reliving can be encouraged by material placed on line, for example on YouTube or Vimeo.

Classroom Installations

But I always come back to the value of a tangible display in the corner of a classroom or a school hall. In the preparation resources for a show, we often suggested that the participants, in advance of any performance, collect objects relating to the themes of the show and use them to make a small display. For example, for the school-based performances of *Something in the Air* (2009), we asked participants and their companions to make friends with the Nest People who lived in nests high above the stage by offering them gifts. The Nest People's favourite colour was red and you could choose to bring them anything – so long as it was red. The red objects were put together in a large green nest for the Nest People to enjoy and remained behind long after the production had ended as a reminder to the participants of their adventures.

Participants were invited to bring other objects to shows such as the Blues Bags for *Blue* and tubes for, you guessed it, *Tube*.

Signing

Makaton is a unique language programme that uses symbols, signs and speech to enable people to communicate. Using Makaton, in particular, is another way in which the visual sense can be used to complement the other senses to clarify a production, although not all schools (or families) use this particular language.

Timelines

In **Chapter 30 – Shows that start before they begin**, I describe a whole range of resources that can help to enhance the experience of the participants. Timelines are a form of simplified visual programme that may be useful to young people on the autism spectrum. The show is represented in a short series of simplified images or Makaton symbols. The participant or carer can follow the progress of the event as it unfolds from beginning "Hello" to final "Goodbye." It can be reassuring to know what is coming next and that eventually the show will end. There is an example of a Timeline in Chapter 25.

13

The Senses One by One – the Sense of Hearing

Tube 2013 Oily Cart. Tubee Doo played by George Panda. Design: Claire de Loon.
Photo: Ben Cooper.

DOI: 10.4324/9781003091288-15

The sense of hearing, along with seeing, is one of the two senses that are the mainstays of the conventional stage, but its importance is even more apparent in Sensory Theatre where the power of the human voice to engage and to inform is quite obvious even when the participants do not themselves use spoken language.

The other great wonder that is brought to us by our sense of hearing is music, although other senses are also involved in the hearing process. I suspect there are few people who are not affected by music. Even people whose hearing is profoundly impaired can be seen to engage and become happier, more melancholy, more excited or calmer, in harmony with the music. Many who seem unaffected by anything else will respond to music.

Even people whose auditory system is so damaged that it cannot transmit data to the brain, can "hear" without hearing. In my form of Sensory Theatre, I always include music, most often played live, even to those who are defined as deaf. I find that bass sounds, the lower notes, are often more effective for those defined as d/Deaf. I have a definite preference for instruments like the double bass, the euphonium, the tuba, the bass clarinet and the big bass drum. They produce **sounds that are felt as much as heard**.

In the trampoline show, *The Bounce* (2014/15), we placed a sub bass speaker under each trampoline which added considerable heft to the sound of the kanun (an Arabic plucked string instrument), played by the virtuosic Maya Youssef. And for the *Underworld* multisensory sequences that took place underneath the trampolines, Max and Maya created kanun tracks with radically lower pitches that, through the sub-bass speakers, produced the kind of bass signals that could vibrate the bodies of the students on the trampoline directly above.

In *Kubla Khan* (2017) the music was provided by the brilliant sitar player, Sheema Mukherjee and utilised the sub-bass speakers again, this time in conjunction with an octave pedal to maximise the impact of the music as a vibration the whole body could feel.

There is a much older, unplugged version of this called the Resonance Board. You lie on a piece of plywood, raised 4cm or so off the floor by blocks of wood around the outer edges. (Plans for resonance boards are readily available online.) Then a performer (or a family member or a teacher) drums on the board around you. The drummer can conjure up a wide variety of reactions.

The Oily Cart show *Drum* (2010) came in three versions, one for babies and toddlers, one for young people on the autism spectrum and one for those with profound and multiple learning disabilities. *Drum* took the basic idea of the Resonance Board but replaced the board with a 150cm diameter drum.

Children and teenagers lay on the drum as the drummer drummed around them. Babies and toddlers sat on the drum. They bounced cheerfully up and down to the beats.

Altogether there were three giant drums in the show, although only one of them was playable. The second drum was both a shadow puppet screen when placed on its side with a light behind it and as a light box when placed on its bottom with a light underneath it. The third drum was used both as a large rocker (the participants, one at a time, were placed inside its rim as it rested on its side, then rolled to and fro) and as a ball pool container when placed face down and filled with the plastic balls.

The drums were made by the wonderfully inventive instrument maker, Jamie Linwood. At first Jamie had difficulty in finding a drum skin to fit the drummable drum. It certainly was not a size made by the usual drum skin manufacturers. But Jamie has a vast range of contacts who pointed him to the inhabitants of a village in Thailand who specialised in outsize drum skins and in rearing rather fat water buffalos.

Jamie should really have a whole chapter of this book to himself. He has designed and made instruments for six of our hydropool shows as well as converting the old ice cream tricycle laden with percussion that George Panda played in *Ring A Ding Ding* (2011). Jamie's skills mean that he can make instruments sound unique, stay in tune and survive the rigours of touring – even when regularly immersed in pool water.

Max Reinhardt

Of course, when we are talking about music and sound in Sensory Theatre, Max Reinhardt has been central from the very beginning, writing all the music produced by the Oily Cart partnership and until recently he was involved in the auditioning and the casting of all Oily productions.

Max is a man who wears many hats. He works as a music producer and a world music DJ, hears a vast range of music in clubs and at gigs and has a detailed knowledge of many different musical genres. This know-how meant that it was possible to have music in our shows that reflected the richly multi-cultural society in which we live. Max knows the music and the musicians who can help him put it on stage. So when people ask me how do you make a Sensory Theatre show, I always reply, *Well if you are not musical yourself, then you need to find someone who is.* Strong music is essential in this kind of theatre, and it is likely to be the one single factor that has the greatest emotional effect.

Live Music

If it is at all possible, I believe the music in a Sensory Theatre show should be played live. With a live musician in a show, especially a musician with some sort of background in improvisation, the music can be as flexible as all the other performances and adapt to the reactions of the audiences. Of course, it is possible to work to a pre-recorded track but there is a fundamental difference in the quality of music coming out of a speaker-cone and that arriving directly from a musical instrument. An instrument played close up is unrivalled. The listener can feel the warmth and wetness of the breath and smell the woodiness of the woodwind or the brassiness of the brass.

Deep Voices

But my favourite instrument for use in Sensory Theatre is the human voice, especially in the bass and baritone ranges. We have had two especially effective bass voice singers in the Oily Cart, Mark Foster and Sjaak van der Bent. Both joined the company for *Hunky Dory* in 1998 and have been featured in many other Oily productions. Their voices produce wondrous vibrations that can be felt just as much as heard. Place your hand on the side of their throats as they sing (I am sure they will not mind – post Covid – if you ask in advance) for a truly multisensory experience. In hydropool shows, the participants could put the soles of their feet up against Mark and Sjaak's chest to feel the music.

Other Sources of Sound

There are many sounds in our shows that can be beautiful and significant though I would not necessarily describe them as music. For instance, surprisingly often in our shows, the participants are invited to listen to **water** being poured from one vessel to another. This act can be charged with many different emotions. Pour the water slowly and from a height, raising the container away from the surface as you pour and there is feeling of calm and order. But if you quickly dash the water into the bowl, then there is a feeling of alarm, a little jump of apprehension. Make lots of little splashes in a regular rhythm and it is a cue for a jolly little dance.

Of course, the sound of water was one of the main features of any hydropool show: drumming on the water with calabashes, falling from an overhead fountain or bubbling up from the pool below.

From the early days, I have used a lot of **fanning** in shows. It is another one of the ways in which we can **touch without touching**. It is multi-sensory in that the breeze from the fan is felt on the skin of the participant, while the swishing rhythm of the fan is **heard**. If you use a sandalwood fan, perhaps dabbed with a couple of drops of sandalwood essential oil, then yet another sense is added to the mix.

Here I am writing about the sounds of hand-held paper, bamboo or silken fans, the swish as they are waved, the snap as they are cracked open with a flick of the wrist. I am not talking here about electric fans although they too have a multitude of uses. I recall in a scratch performance we made with Chicago Children's Theatre, we had use of a 150 cm diameter film studio fan with which we conjured up an amazing range of sensory sensations: tactile, temperature and sonic.

Sometimes, with a hand fan, it can be almost as if you are conducting the audience. Long slow movements of the fan and the regular rhythm of the wafting bring a sense of security and tranquility. A rapid change to irregular, stronger movements agitates and disturbs.

The Jazz Structure

Music/sound is often used to conduct the shows in a more general way. I often alternate between organised, arranged sections that are not particularly dependent on the reactions of the audience, moving on to much freer sections that are all about the responses of the participants. The cues that take the performers from an arranged section into a freer section and back generally come from the specialist musician.

Stranden in Sweden

A more recent show, *Stranden* (2019) that Max and I made in Sweden as part of the Scen:se project, involved a number of ocean drums. An ocean drum, if you have not encountered one before, is a rather shallow drum that comes in various diameters, with a drum skin on both its top and bottom sides. A handful of ball bearings are contained in the space inside the drum and as it is tipped gently from side to side, it makes a sound with an uncanny resemblance to the sea rolling back and forth on a shingle beach.

Stranden, Swedish for "beach," was based on the poem *Dover Beach* by Matthew Arnold. The poem concerns the thoughts brought about by the sound of the sea on a pebbly beach. There were two versions of the show, one for a PMLD audience and the other for people on the autism spectrum. The setting of the show had the atmosphere of a seaside café.

In *Stranden*, to cue the transition from an arranged section, the musician rang a desk bell on the café counter and everything paused. In the ensuing pause, there was the opportunity for the participants to process what had happened and to realise that one episode had ended and another one was about to begin. Now it was up to the musician (at these points very much the conductor) to judge the moment to move everything on. The musician used an ocean drum to make the sound of the sea that was the cue for the next section to begin. This sequence was carefully repeated in between each new section.

It is important that the musician is the one to make these decisions because she is the one who is not assigned a participant to work with, in the moments of one-to-one interaction that pepper the freer sections. She must be a little apart and able to take a more objective overview: are all the participants still engaged or is it time to pick up the ocean drum and move things along into the next section?

14

The Senses One by One – the Sense of Touch

Tube 2013 Oily Cart. Huff 'N Puff played by Ellie Griffiths. Design: Claire de Loon. Photo: Ben Cooper.

DOI: 10.4324/9781003091288-16

The skin, which is the organ by which we perceive touch, makes up nearly 20% of our body and is our largest and probably most sensitive organ. The sense of touch brings hundreds of delights but a few problems too. Touch is about stroking and tickling and embracing and squeezing and patting and all those potential delights. But it is also a sense of what is acceptable to the social and cultural groups to which we all belong and what is acceptable to ourselves as individuals. All of these standards can vary from individual to individual and from society to society. Unless you are working with a group you know particularly well, it's always best to ask if what you are planning to do is acceptable and find an alternative if necessary.

Generally speaking in the UK, it is acceptable to touch someone's hands and forearms, especially if that someone is a child. But if someone says, *Don't touch.* Then just do not. That is one of the main reasons why when working work with people on the autism spectrum or who are defined as having Profound Multiple Learning Disabilities, we always need to have an adult companion present. They are not simply an interpreter and consultant, they are also an adviser on the prevailing social norms and above all on what the participant wishes.

The companions are most often wonderfully helpful. Many is the time I have asked questions like: *Would he mind if I touched his hands?* only to be told: *Oh, take his socks off too. He really likes having his feet touched.*

But on other occasions, you will be told that a participant is tactile defensive and that he or she tends to have a negative reaction to touch. While this is often associated with the autism spectrum, it can affect anyone with sensory processing issues.

Behaviour that suggests Tactile Defensiveness might be seen in someone who:

> Becomes anxious in putting on clothes.
> Tries to avoid being touched.
> Has difficulty with regular activities that involve touch like tooth brushing or washing.
> Does not like to get messy and does not like new textures or objects.
> Quickly becomes anxious.

If you were having to decide whether to bring anyone who reacts to touch in this way to see a Sensory Theatre production which often involves touching, I can see that you might be reluctant. But I would argue that this is just the sort of person who should come along – providing we keep certain factors in mind.

Preparation

As with many other things in Sensory Theatre, preparation is vital. The person who is arranging for the participants to see the show should have been given, in print or online, the details of the show, where it takes place, what the performers will do and what the participants will be asked to do and particularly what they will be asked to touch. (This would be in the Social Story for the participants in the case of a typical Oily Cart show, together with accompanying Introduction for Carers.) If the booker thinks any of this might be too much for one or more of the participants, it would a good idea to discuss the issue with a member of the Oily Cart team. These introductions also include lists of the materials used in a show, which is significant information for allergy sufferers and their carers.

There is always hope that a tactile defensive participant might be less resistant to touch in the actual circumstances of a Sensory Theatre piece where the performers will respond flexibly to the reactions of each individual. They will allow someone who is finding it all a bit too much to have a time-out and the performers will always offer an alternative sensory approach to someone who is rejecting touch. For example, **fanning and misting** are two ways of addressing the sense of touch without actually touching.

For many people, the performance of a piece of Sensory Theatre is still unfamiliar. Even with proper preparation, the Social Story or the like, it will be a revelation. And the reactions of the participants are often surprising as well. I have been creating new Sensory Theatre pieces every year since 1988 and time and time again I have heard parents and teachers respond with astonishment to the reactions of their young people to a show.

> We saw reactions from pupils which were amazing! For example, a tactile defensive pupil reaching out for a balloon and volunteering his hands for a massage! And pupils refraining from self-injurious behaviour whilst on the magic carpet ride – smiling and interacting.
> *Boing!* (2002) East Shore School, Portsmouth

The Privileged Position of the Sensory Theatre Performer

I believe there is a special kind of status allowed to performers in Sensory Theatre by the participants. Because they are in a performance, the performers are not subject to the same rules as we are in day-to-day life. It may seem that I am overestimating the emotional intelligence of some labeled as Profound and Multiple Disabilities that they can distinguish between an adult playing around, being silly and one who is being quite serious. But I believe that most participants can tell the difference between an adult performer "play-acting" something naughty and actual bad behaviour. It means that the participants can laugh at someone making a bit of a mess, say, while in no way feeling this behaviour is what they should copy.

Messy Play

The young people that I work with are often being told to keep themselves clean and tidy and to not make a mess. As a general rule, I believe that performers should always set a good example – but there is one exception and that can be summed up in two words: **Messy Play** or if you prefer a more dignified term, **Sensory Play**. Messy Play is a key part of Sensory Theatre and although it often involves all the senses, it very much involves the sense of touch. Not everyone enjoys it, but it certainly appeals to the great majority in Oily Cart audiences including PMLD, ASC and the very young.

So what is so good about Messy Play – apart from the fact that everybody has so much fun, and it involves every part of your body and makes you forget your isolation and welcomes you into a group of friends?

Messy Play is commonly about putting your hands into bowls full of different materials and textures such as dry beans followed by warm, scented water (*Conference of the Birds*) or jelly followed by soap suds (*Land of Lights*).

Yes. Some of these things might represent a choking hazard with some participants but that is yet another reason why in Sensory Theatre, each participant is alongside an adult companion who is playing right along with them.

My top tip for keeping Messy Play under control within a Sensory Theatre piece is to incorporate both the **setting-up** and the **tidying up** into the action. Very often the setting-up can be a sensory delight in itself. Any scene where the participants' hands or feet or whatever are about to get wet, can be preceded by a moment in which sleeves are rolled up and warm dry towels are placed on laps (a lovely sensory experience in itself). What is more, the scene should be followed up by another patting, squeezing and drying, warm towel moment. For example, you could have a short musical routine that the cast are singing and dancing with mops or brushes. Do not pretend the tidying up is not happening. You will only get egg on your face. Better by far to glory in it.

Messy Play Favourites

Here are of some of my favourite Messy Play activities in ascending order of messiness, all the way through to playing with water and soap where you need to make sure you have a waterproof floor cloth down, a mop and bucket handy and some form of waterproof cape for each participant.

Bowls of Delight

Each participant will need a bowl. The bowl can be any design: shiny metal, wood, a calabash or a colourful plastic (chosen to fit in with the theme of the show). Fill a quarter full with dried beans, butter beans or chickpeas etc.

Approach the participant from in front. Give the bowl to the companion to hold. Take a handful of beans from the bowl, hold them up and trickle them back down into the bowl. Now hand over to the companion and encourage them to have a go. Of course let the participant try anything they want to do. When it is time to finish, spirit rather than snatch props away.

Shaving Foam

You need a couple of towels on stand-by for this one. Each participant will need another washing-up bowl or similar. Approach from the front and give the bowl to the companion. Present a can of unperfumed shaving foam. Give the can a little shake (but be sure it is a little shake) and then very deliberately spray a fist-size blob into the bowl, carefully listening to the hissing sound. If they are up for it, you could put a blob on your own nose, or the companion's nose or even, after a very cautious approach, on the participant's nose. Next step – a blob on the palm of the participant's hand, and then lift the other hand over and gently bring the two hands together. That may make a rude noise. Celebrate that. Then hand over the lead to the companion. The shaving foam will soon fade away (if you have remembered not to shake the can too hard). On a cue from the musician, remove the bowl and put both the participant's hands in a folded towel (preferably warm) and firmly squeeze and pat them dry.

Cornflour Gloop

1. To make the cornflour mixture, all you need is cornflour, water and a bowl, plus water and a cloth or two to clean up. You will need about 120 ml of water to 235 ml cornflour.
2. Add the water to the cornflour slowly and mix with your hands as you pour. Continue adding water until the mixture slowly flows on its own. You can add a drop of food colouring if you like.

You will have created a lovely slimy gloop that feels **solid** when you squeeze it and **liquid** if you loosen your grip, when it will flow through your fingers.

Jugs, Pipes and Bowl

Towels may well be necessary for this. Approaching from in front, give each companion a bowl. Holding it up high, bring on the jug of water. Start pouring the water into the bowl then raise the jug up as high as you can, pouring as you do so. Spirit the jug away.

Return with a plastic tube 15 cm long and 2cm wide. Simply **blow air through the pipe**. Give a second pipe to the companion so that they can join in. The two of you can sing through the pipes too. Blow through the pipes on to the back of the participants' hands, onto their forearms and wherever else is welcome – another example of **touch without touching**.

As ever if the participant is reacting to a stimulus, try some variations, to see if these get more or less of a response. When you feel that the participant is ready for something more, **blow the pipe directly into the water**, making bubbles and bubbling sounds. Try singing as you blow and blowing water and bubbles underneath the participant's hands as they rest in the water. Blowing between the fingers usually works well too.

On a cue from the musician, gradually begin to phase out the pipes and the bowls.

Bubbles

I would be surprised if someone has not written a whole book about bubbles and bubble making. I believe toddlers are hard-wired to be delighted by bubbles and for many of us the delight lasts a lifetime.

For this kind of bubble play, you are going to need the sort of bowl for each participant that I've described above, a towel or cape to go over their laps and another towel for wiping hands and faces. The other essentials are:

The Recipe for the Bubble Mixture

900ml of distilled water (or de-ionized water), from autoshops or pharmacies
100ml of GOOD (but not concentrated) washing-up liquid
25ml of Glycerin, from chemists

It is important **not** to make bubbles when mixing the solution and to store it in an opaque container. Leave solution for at least 24 hours after mixing. The older the solution the better it gets. You can use tap water but if you are in a very hard water area, the result will not be as good as with the distilled water.

Blow your bubbles using your favourite bubble wand or blower.

The Famous Bubble Pie

How to create a great big mound of condensed bubbles that can be blown through the air like Ibiza Foam.

To Make the Bubble Pie Blowers

Use any plastic tubing approx. 40mm diameter (try plumbers' merchants or diy stores). At one end, attach loosely woven material such as gauze or muslin using rubber bands. The tubes used in the shows generally have three layers. You can experiment with your own fabric to get the best results. Gauze bandage is good but do not take it from the first aid box please.

Dip the cloth end of the Bubble Maker into a small bowl with the bubble mixture. Lightly place the cloth end into the palm of your free hand and begin to blow. You will feel the warmth of your breath blowing into the palm of your hand. Slowly raise the Bubble Maker away from your hand as you keep blowing. You will be amazed by the great column of tiny bubbles growing ever taller between the Bubble Maker and your hand. How tall can you make it?

Now you can take the Bubble Maker away from the hand and blow or waft lumps of bubbles away – like Ibiza foam – and with all the other companions joining in it can become quite a party.

Another good thing about foam is that it does clear quite a lot of itself away. But this is one of those areas of messy play where you will need a waterproof floor cloth on your playing area to save the parquet floor, plus a mop and bucket. Beware of slipping!

Of course you will want the participants and their companions to have a wonderful time but you will also want to keep the booker/school-keeper/caretaker/premises officer happy. The aim should always be to leave the hall or stage as you found it so make sure that you have enough time and energy after the show to do that.

Curiously enough most of the methods in this book are equally effective for both people on the autism spectrum and for people placed in that PMLD category. If there are differences in the reactions in these groups, they can often be resolved by the nuances that individual performers bring to their relationships with their individual participants. But, when it comes to the sense of touch, there do seem to be clear variations. Many people on the spectrum appear to have strong opinions about the ways in which they are touched.

Temple Grandin and Deep Pressure

I first became aware of this when I began to read the books of Temple Grandin. Dr. Grandin is a professor of animal science at Colorado State University and is herself on the autism spectrum. In several books she has written of her states of anxiety when she was a child and going into adolescence. To deal with this, she built herself what she called The Squeeze Machine. She had observed that in the USA when cattle or horses needed to be kept under control for treatment, they were often placed between two boards driven together by compressed air to firmly grip the animal. What intrigued Dr. Grandin about this process was that this pressure, rather than alarming the animals as one might have expected, seemed to have a deeply calming effect.

Wondering if this might work for her, she built a Squeeze Machine for herself and found that it alleviated her anxieties. Into her sixties, she regularly spent time in the machine. This idea about deep pressure having a calming effect on people on the spectrum has led to the development of a range of devices that give a person a greater sense of their own physical presence, of their existence. Weighted clothing and blankets and versions of the Squeeze Machine that resemble an old-fashioned mangle are now commercially available and used in many schools and centres working with people on the autism spectrum.

In *The Bounce*, I used weighted blankets and weighty beanbags with people on the autism spectrum on the trampoline. The movement of the trampoline bed accentuated the pressure of the weight.

The towels and dressing gowns that I have employed in the hydropool shows and many other productions, are inspired by the calming effect that basic wrapping or swaddling often induces.

But just as deep pressure relieves anxiety and feels comforting, its opposite, **light pressure**, can be seen to disturb many on the autism spectrum. Casual, accidental touch is felt to be unpleasant and at the other extreme to a firm comforting, committed hug. Claire de Loon often refers to the experience that she had in rehearsal for a hydropool show with the performer Sjaak van der Bent. She was very reluctant to get into the water. Sjaak took her hand firmly and started to sing in his beautiful deep voice. He enticed her into the water in no time at all. His confidence left no room for hesitation.

> We brought our son, S. to the afternoon show and he loved it. Later he said he felt calm inside and had happy tears. To see him calm for that long and totally absorbed was moving and delightful for us. Also the show was brilliantly conceived, aesthetic and showed a deep understanding of ASD.
>
> *Something in the Air* (2009), parent feedback at
> Contact Theatre, Manchester.

15
The Senses One by One – the Sense of Smell

Box of Socks 1988 Oily Cart. Maureen Hibbert as Alien amuses the school dinner ladies. Design: Claire de Loon.

Photo: Gina Glover.

> The pupils were made to feel very special and the positive nature of the event made for a memorable and highly personal experience. The atmosphere was mesmerising but at the same time calming and contagious for joining in. So much theatre is not accessible to children with significant learning needs. I will never forget the joy on the children's faces.
> *Gorgeous* (2011) feedback, Delamere School, Trafford.

Smell is certainly one of the more difficult senses to incorporate in a piece of Sensory Theatre. One person's evocative fragrance is another's horrid pong.

DOI: 10.4324/9781003091288-17

Even the word "smelling" carries dubious, unpleasant connotations that you do not get with seeing, hearing or tasting.

One issue with smells is that they are problematic to deliver. Even working with a small audience of six or eight, it would be difficult to find one smell that we all would agree was pleasant. Or even to find one smell that all would agree was unpleasant.

What's more, it's tricky to quickly introduce a new smell into a space and it's even more of a challenge to get rid of a smell when it's time to move on to the next thing.

Then there's the fact that if you are working with a number of different smells, to find (say) the one that people prefer, after two or three scents have been sampled, your nose seems to tire and it becomes much more difficult to tell one smell from another.

However, if you make a production that is based on a trail or promenade performance in which the audience is moved from one area to another and each area has its one distinctive smell, then scent can reinforce the different identities of the spaces. It helps if you are working indoors where you are able to confine a smell to one space simply by keeping the doors shut till it's time to enter and then closing the doors behind you when you move on.

Of course, this is not to suggest that this is the only way to use the sense of smell in a sensory theatre presentation. For example in *In a Pickle* (2012) each performer presented a sweet-smelling bunch of herbs to the participants at the beginning of the show – a wonderful act of welcome a wonderful act of welcome. Battery-powered ultra-sonic essential oil diffusers work without heat or flame and are very good at making a waiting area or large performance space more inviting. They are especially useful for afternoon performances in school halls where lunchtime smells linger.

I have experimented over the years with essential oils in various other delivery systems but I have become more cautious with their use because so many of them are contra-indicated for certain complaints and allergies. For a time, we believed lavender essential oil was widely acceptable but more recently we have found people who react badly to it.

For several years, we worked with the scent research and development team at Seven Scent who are part of the PZ Cussons conglomerate as part of Oily Cart's involvement with Manchester International Festival. This allowed us some access to the laboratories where they blend their perfumes and a glimpse of a storeroom in which there appeared to be an example of every scent in the world. I was particularly delighted that they had a life-sized testing house with its own bedroom, living room, bathroom and kitchen where new products were tested.

In 2009, PZ Cussons and Seven Scent sponsored and helped with the MIF production by Amadou and Maryam. The renowned Malian duo created a performance in a blackout using only their music and an array of scents to conjure up an evening in Bamako.

But I was most interested in the research that Seven Scent were doing with the Seashell Trust in Cheadle Hulme. The Seashell Trust is a charity supporting children and young adults with complex learning disabilities and additional communication needs from across the UK. The organisation evolved from the Royal Schools for the Deaf and they have a long-standing interest in how the sense of smell may be used to augment communication particularly for the B/blind and the deafblind.

Seven Scent helped us to use perfume to identify characters in a production and to create clearly distinct ambiances in the different scenes in our production, *Gorgeous*, made for the 2011 Manchester International Festival.

Gorgeous came in two versions: one for young people on the autism spectrum and the other for young people classified as PMLD. It was very much about self-image and the presentation of self. We were determined that each character would have his or her own distinctive smell and Seven Scent helped us to develop these identifying aromas. They were supplied in two forms: a small white pen with which each performer could apply a little dab of his or her identifying scent and an eau de toilette spray with which they could refresh the scent on their costume before meeting the participants face to face. They also supplied us with enough pens and sprays to supply all the schools on the tour in with the other resources in the preparation packs. The schools could use the fragrances on the posters of the characters, on their objects of reference and their corridor decorations.

The interactive play element of *Gorgeous* was also very smell-based. In one scene, each participant was given a pestle and mortar into which we scattered a handful of star anise. Then to a highly rhythmic chant the participants, aided by the companions where necessary, pounded and crushed the star anise, unleashing a wonderfully pungent aroma and transforming the atmosphere in the room.

Because my main aim in this book is to give as much information as possible about making a piece of theatre for people with complex and profound disabilities including autistic spectrum conditions, I hope I will not upset anyone if I say that one of the best preparations you can make before starting on a session of Sensory Theatre is to brush your teeth. Certainly, deodorants and perfumes are generally not a good idea, as some members of our audiences who are hypersensitive to smell, can react badly to strong smells. In preparing our performances, we only use smells that we have carefully researched and tried out in rehearsal and previews.

As part of the production *Tube* (2013), we commissioned Nik Ramage to design a smell-o-tube device. Nik has made many beautiful and ingenious items for Oily Cart shows, starting with the giant track for the *Roly Poly Pudding* in 1996. His smell-o-tubes, based on a balloon pump, proved particularly useful in the work with young PMLD people. Young people defined in this way tend to have some difficulty when asked to actively smell something. Neurotypical people, when asked to smell something, commonly point their nose in the direction of the object and take a sharp intake of breath up both nostrils. But that can require a degree of co-ordination that some can find difficult and that is where the smell-o-tube comes in. There was a small pad just inside the black tube of the pump to take a drop or two of scent. When you gently pumped the end of the smell-o-tube, it would blow air over the pad with the scent.

The advantage of Nik's device was that using two tubes, we could offer the ASC participants two distinct perfumes to choose their favourite smell. The performers first modeled how to use the smell-o-tubes by using them themselves. Then they were offered to the participants and carers to try. The tubes could be pumped very gently or they could produce a mild tornado.

I have said this before but as part of any preparatory material that you put out in advance to your audiences, it really helps if you include a list of all the materials that you will use in your production, particularly anything that could conceivably be upsetting to a participant or a companion. Then at least you have given them or their companions the opportunity to request that some smell, loud noise, material or activity could be turned down, withdrawn or just kept away from a particular individual. It's another opportunity to fine-tune your production to the requirements of each participant. This is an extract from the **Introduction for Carers** for *Tube*:

Fragrances

The characters each have a distinctive fragrance created with essential oils. Look 'N See smells of lavender, Huff 'N Puff smells of roses and Tubee Doo smells of mandarin oranges. These perfumes are also used in the smell-o-tubes, in the water on the umbrellas and on the towels.

In the final analysis, when it comes to the sense of smell, I often come back to a simple pot filled with a living herb plant bought from the garden, nursery or supermarket. I love basil or thyme but any culinary herb is worth a try and if someone takes a nibble, well, they are culinary so there should be no harm done. Roll a few herb leaves between your fingers and you can waft the aroma towards the participant with a fan. For *There Was an Old Woman* (2014), I used sprigs of Christmas trees on the floor to create the aroma of a pine forest and in *Mole in the Hole* (2010), the audience sat on fragrant bales of hay in the moles' underground tunnel.

16
The Senses One by One – the Sense of Taste

Baking Time 2003. An Oily Cart/Carousel Players co-production. Bap (Juliet Dunn) and Bun (Ruth Calkin) making a mess. Design: Claire de Loon.

Photo: Patrick Baldwin.

Like smell, taste is problematic. It's awkward because the same food or drink will often arouse very different responses in different individuals. In addition, people categorised as PMLD will often have dietary and medical issues that must be taken into account. A substantial number of them will be fed by tube either through the nose or through the stomach wall. In those cases, nothing by mouth will be allowed.

Over the last decade, as the demographics of Special Schools have changed, with more and more young people being incorporated into the mainstream

DOI: 10.4324/9781003091288-18

wherever possible, the Special Schools have been increasingly medicalised. Sometimes you will encounter nurses feeding via a tube during performances because a participant is sticking to a regular feeding schedule. Sometimes a nurse will join a participant for a while to drain his or her lungs through equipment attached to the wheelchair. As far as the performers are concerned all is just as it should be. None of the participants or the companions will raise an eyebrow and why should a performer? Just give the nurse or teacher the space to get on with the procedure while you, as performer, focus on your own performance or on another participant for a while.

Choosing the food or drink that you would use in a sensory theatre piece is a subject that needs to be approached with great care. You don't want to involve anything that might offend anyone's dietary rules based on medical need or religious or cultural values. By the time all these factors have been taken into account the choices have been sharply reduced.

In *Kubla Khan* (2017), the Emperor treated the guests at his palace to a feast consisting of honeydew melon either cut into slices or mashed up and this was acceptable to all of the audiences involved. Actually, I believe we still need something that is more directly inclusive for people using tube feeding. I believe that taking a small amount of something easily mashed (like a banana) and with a fine brush placing a tiny amount on the lips of a tube-fed participant might be a way forward.

Another method worth trying is fizzy water. Just unscrewing a bottle of fizzy water close to a participant's mouth and nose can be a lovely surprise for some people but always adhere to the adage for interactive sensory work: if the participant appears to be enjoying a stimulus, continue. Obviously, if they show any sign of discomfort or if the companion is concerned about the process – then stop.

17

The Senses One by One – the Kinaesthetic Sense

The Bounce 2014 Oily Cart. Jump played by Tom Jones. His object of reference is a trampoline. Design: Claire de Loon.

Photo: Neal Houghton.

DOI: 10.4324/9781003091288-19

Why do babies like bouncing on a knee or toddlers like swinging on swings? It's not about what they are seeing or hearing or smelling or tasting or touching, it's all about the way they are moving. This is the kinaesthetic sense at work.

It is the sense that tells the brain of our volition and position in space. It's an indispensably useful sense enabling us to move around in the world, but it also brings us a great deal of pleasure. When we watch children in a playground, running, skipping, dancing we are seeing them glorying in the sensations of the kinaesthetic sense, the delights of movement.

We seek out these pleasures in games and sports, in riding scooters, bike and trikes, at funfairs and theme parks, on the dodgems, the helterskelter and the big dipper.

Of course exercise is good for us physically but in my opinion it's more than that; these sensations of being alive in our bodies are important to us mentally and spiritually.

The kinaesthetic sense has an essential part to play in establishing communication with people who are the most hard-to-reach. For example, how can we create a link with someone who is Deafblind, with very little hearing or sight, when it is difficult to show them anything or give them anything to listen to? Taste can be very much affected by personal preferences. That leaves us with touch, an excellent way of establishing contact. And of course, the kinaesthetic sense. With this sense we may communicate a wide range of messages and moods.

For example, let us see how a performer might work with someone who is Deafblind on a trampoline. The surface of the trampoline will amplify the movements of the performer and the participant. If both start from a state of rest and the performer makes some slow, regular, calming bounces, the participant will experience very similar movements themselves and the steady reassuring pattern will convey a sense of calm to the participant. When the performer feels that this mood is established, they can pause a while before introducing a faster and more energetic rate of bounce that will make the trampoline experience feel much lively and vigorous. Other variations that can be introduced including moving the source of the bouncing (provided by the performer's hands or feet) around the participant and back again. It is most important that the performer watches for the participant's responses and reacts to them in turn. So basically, if the participants shows a reaction to a change of pace and the performer responds to that, by doing more or less of it, this may lead into a playful dialogue of bounce.

These sorts of interaction may be felt more intensely by people who are more restricted in their movement in everyday life (because, for example, they are wheelchair-users.)

This is why I find it extraordinary that in many of the examples of Sensory Theatre that I have seen, relatively little work with the kinaesthetic sense is involved. To be blunt, so many Sensory Theatre audiences seem to sit in the same place from start to finish while an assortment of sensory delights are brought to them. It may be convenient but it's certainly missing a trick. I believe this especially because a major factor in the development of the Oily Cart was the drive to find the best way to include the kinaesthetic sense in our theatre.

The process began when Max Reinhardt and I were researching for *Box of Socks* (1988), our first production for people in a school for young people with Special Educational Needs. As the young people waited in the school hall for the buses and taxis to take them home, a teacher and some of the bigger students were putting other students, one at a time, onto a Navy hammock laid on the floor. Then a teacher on one side of the hammock and a senior student on the other would raise the hammock up in the air and swing its passenger, sometimes gently, sometimes exuberantly, up and down and from side to side, creating chortles of delight and cries and Makaton signings of *more, more!*

A week or two later in the hall of another Special School, one of the teachers, who was also a weekend rock-climber, had attached a climber's rope to a big steel beam in the ceiling. On one end of that rope was a harness made of webbing and Velcro. A queue of students of all ages were waiting for their turn in the harness. Once someone was strapped into the harness, the rock climber teacher would take the end of the rope and haul them higher and higher, checking all the time that the flyer was comfortable.

Then the participant would be raised and lowered and twirled round and round and round to create chuckles and shrieks of delight. You could see from the reactions of these young people that they thought it was just brilliant!

So why are we not we seeing more of it? And why after 30 years does kinaesthetic work remain neglected in shows if not in schools? Actually I can see why many people would be put off by equipment like ropes, pulleys and carabiners not to mention the health and safety issues. But there are many quite straightforward, and safe ways to involve the kinaesthetic sense in Sensory Theatre.

For example, there is the Oily Cart's original inspiration, the Navy hammock. And we can take a lot of the backache out of hammock work if we use the sort of frames on sale everywhere to support hammocks. Garden swing seats and rocking chairs also provide great opportunities for an audience to have a kinaesthetic experience. What is more, this kind of moving seating provides an alternative to the beanbag on which some can be made comfortable but certainly not everyone.

Many participants are more comfortable supported on wedges or other shaped foam blocks. However, they might get even more out of the experience if the blocks were placed on a wheeled platform rather than the floor. Using such platforms, with safety belts as necessary, the participant can enjoy twists and turns, and be pushed through the performance space with the facility to zoom in and out on the action, and be freed from the fixed point of view.

Another basic but effective means to move participants around in the performance space is to sit them on a piece of smooth material like the underside (leather side) of a sheep skin rug and pull them around by gripping the side. This will also work with other material, like ripstock.

I have also used wheeled office chairs to seat an audience. Once again seat belts were needed to keep participants sitting safely. It also helped to have pieces of padding, foam rubber in assorted shaped and sizes on hand to tuck participants snugly in place.

There is no particular reason why wheelchair users should not remain in their chairs throughout a performance, especially if they are in seats that are designed to meet a participant's specific requirements. In a wheelchair you may still drive yourself or be steered in and out of the action.

So far I have only been writing about exploring the kinaesthetic in work for people with Profound and Multiple Learning Disabilities, particularly those with restricted movement. One teacher described wheelchair users to me as *getting lots of backwards and forward but very little side to side or up and down.* So, our first trampoline show, *Boing!* (2002), as described in Part One, Chapter 7, was very much about extending the range of movement available to PMLD people via the kinaesthetic sense.

But during the tour of *Boing!*, a production made specifically for PMLD people, we encountered a very different audience. A senior autistic class visited us on the set during a lunch break and, together with their teachers convinced me that they too would benefit from trampoline work – but in rather different ways. When these young people on the spectrum had their turn on the trampoline they bounced with great enthusiasm – a couple of them getting pretty close to the ceiling.

We clearly needed a different kind of show for this kind of audience and once again we turned to retired Special School Head, Eddie Anderson whose expertise in Physical Education for SEND schools had been invaluable in the development of our previous pool and trampoline shows.

In *Boing!*, we had used the trampoline to create the impression that we were on a flying carpet in some orientalist fantasy sailing over an oasis. It was serene, it was calming and it gave the PMLD participants plenty of opportunities for movement.

But now we came to realise that we had to do something with these other people we kept encountering in SEND schools, the people on the spectrum, many of whom preferred leaping to serenely gliding.

The successor to *Boing!* was *Moving Pictures* (2003) once more centred on a trampoline and introducing live video feedback, with some performances specifically aimed at young people on the spectrum. This version worked well enough, but it was obvious that these audiences on the spectrum needed a good deal more vertical space and that ceilings of Special School halls tend to be on the low side. By 2009, we had decided to put trampoline work to one side, while we explored other ways to defy gravity and put more movement into participants' lives.

Then we met Ockham's Razor at Manchester International Festival where so many good things have happened. The company was then made up of Alex Harvey, Tina Koch and Charlotte Mooney with a mission to create, in their own words, *physical theatre on original pieces of aerial equipment.*

At the festival we saw their very ingenious, funny and exciting show, *Every Action*, and talking to them afterwards I explained our long-term plan to make theatre that would free the audiences we work with from the effects of gravity and let them soar through the air like aerialists. Anyone could see Ockham's tremendous intelligence and expertise. Could they advise us?

They went off into a huddle. Ockham's do this. There is no single auteur. They are a collective. They came back and said: *Yeah. We'll do that.* I asked: *You mean you'll give us advice? No – we'll do the show.*

And that was the start of an amazing co-production, *Something in the Air.*

My aim was to take one of our relatively small audiences: six participants together with six adult companions safely, comfortably and thrillingly up in the air where they could rise and fall, swing, bounce and spin in their chairs. I am not technical at all and did not have the faintest idea how to make this happen. But the Ockham's were wonderful. They would worry away at the problems over weeks extending from early January through to June 2009.

We had to work out the seating and our designer, Jens Cole, was invaluable here. We knew that each participant had to be close to their companion to provide moral support and to provide a link with the cast on the ground.

We had to work what belts would be needed to keep our participants of all sorts of sizes safe in their seats when they might be up to three meters high in the air.

This was a show with many enchanting, kinaesthetic elements. Charlotte on her trapeze gliding past you close enough to touch and singing Max Reinhardt's evocative music right into your ear. Then Tina on her bungie bouncing to the floor and back up to the rigging and the participants bouncing right along with her. They might not quite be covering the distances that Tina and Charlotte were going, and they were not quite reaching the speeds that the Ockham's were reaching, but if you were in one of those chairs, it felt as if you were not just the audience but the daring and magnificent stars of the show.

And this was still a show where the individual participant could exercise plenty of choice. You did not have to zoom up the full 3 meters. If that felt too much you could ask to be lower, or even come right down to the ground. The view was also pretty good from there.

As a participant you chose the kind of show that suited you. It could be visceral, filled with swoops and spins, or it could be much more relaxed and graceful or it could have as many points in between as there were participants.

In 2014 with the production of *The Bounce*, we returned to the trampoline with the innovation of having two trampolines working in tandem, so that we could work with twice as many participants per session.

The redesign of the set also took into account our attempt to open up trampoline performance to people on the spectrum. They could walk up two curving staircases to climb on and off the trampoline. But the biggest issue in providing for people on the spectrum was the need to provide headroom above the trampoline for the big leaps that many in this group enjoy. We managed this pretty well, though on occasion it was a close-run thing. Newer Special Schools in the UK, which tend to have roll call of a hundred or so, do not really have much use for big halls with high ceilings. Tour bookers needed to check carefully that there really is sufficient headroom in the schools that have not been visited before and build up a database of measurements and photographs.

For *The Bounce*, we also looked for better ways for helping PMLD people on and off the trampoline. Of course many of them were able to walk on and off via the staircases helped by their adult companions. It is also possible in shows where the companions are family members, for the mum or the dad to carry PMLD people onto the trampoline. But for the most part, and certainly for older and heavier participants, we used hydraulic hoists now ubiquitous in the schools but which we usually had to import into public venues.

I had never been a fan of the hoists though there is no doubt they have saved many a teacher and many a parent plenty of back trouble. But the person in the sling never looked very comfortable to me.

Then I remembered one of my favourite mantras: *Have you tried it yourself?*

I do not know why I had not. I suppose I was thinking that getting someone up onto a trampoline was not really part of the show. That was someone else's business. But why? Surely everything connected with the show, before, during and after the performance was our business. So during the rehearsals Max and I were slung in a sling up onto the trampoline over and over again.

And you know what? In some ways it was comparable as a kinaesthetic experience to the sensations that we had conjured up with Ockham's Razor in *Something in the Air*. So now, when we had choreographed it, set it to music, made it as graceful as it could be, then it became part of the performance. Hoisting, the part I had always rather looked at with half-closed eyes, was all right.

I suppose for many of the participants it had never really been that bad. The equipment was ergonomically designed. The operators had (usually) been well trained and were certainly well-intentioned. Now we could make this essential activity into a dance with waltz-style swoops and twirls, where it fitted very well into a show that was a celebration of the kinaesthetic sense.

It was a strong reminder that if there was something that simply *had* to be in a piece, (like you certainly could not have a trampoline-based performance without getting the audience on and off the trampoline) then you had to perform that essential element as perfectly as possible. *The Bounce* worked very well as a show and particularly well for audiences who were on the autism spectrum.

Franklin's disability often means that he is always being asked to conform or work hard to fit into a social norm that is not suited to him and so he struggles but as soon as we walked into the space, Franklin's differences were embraced and even celebrated. I felt like we were in a bubble of Franklin's world and it was just magical. It was a stark contrast to the harsh world outside. I found the whole experience very emotional to watch and the Oily Cart Company have reminded me how wonderful my son is and we should be encouraging people to accept his differences rather than make him "fit in."

The Bounce, Parent, JW3 Centre

18

The Senses One by One – the Sense of Hot and Cold

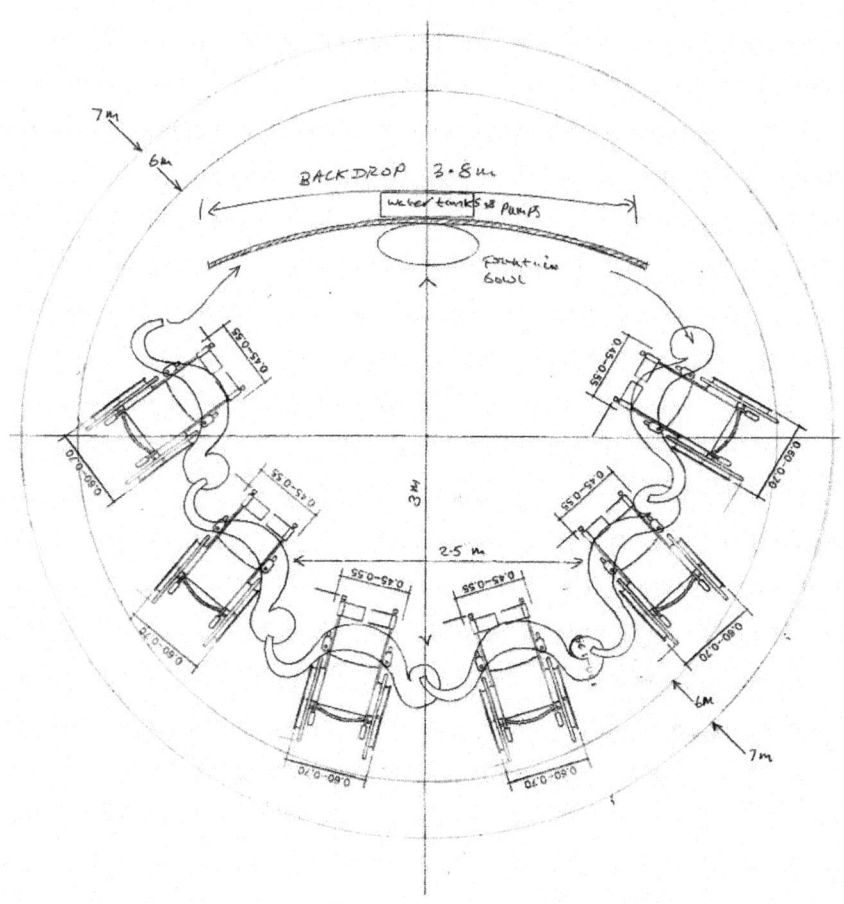

Kubla Khan 2017 Oily Cart. Plan for water channels with six wheelchairs.
Design: Jens Demant Cole.

DOI: 10.4324/9781003091288-20

The sense of temperature is not regularly listed as one of the senses and yet in a sensory theatre context it has a part to play. I have frequently used fanning with both hand-held fans, overhead Indian-style *punkahs*, film set wind-effect fans (so popular in music videos), all very effective ways of changing temperature to suggest a change of location or simply to refresh the participants after a particularly strenuous activity. For me *a change of temperature will take me to a different place.*

I have also used heaters, for example hair dryers, to similarly change the ambiance.

But the most-straight-forward hand-held fan is an essential part of a Sensory Theatre's multi-sensory toolkit. It enables to performer to *touch without touching* and is therefore extremely useful when one is interacting with anyone (there are substantial numbers) who is touch-averse or tactile-defensive.

But temperature work really comes into its own in any work set in a hydropool.

Hydropools are mostly smaller than swimming pools but they are considerably warmer. This sort of temperature is necessary for the people in the PMLD category who are frequently unable to keep themselves warm enough in the water by their own exertions. It is often necessary to pour containers of pool water over their chests and shoulders to keep them feeling comfortable.

But at any time changing the temperature can have significant effect on the participants. It's very obvious in a hydropool production when the participants come out of the water, they will rapidly start to cool down. If you wrap them up in a dressing gown and towels they will start to feel cosy and warm. It's a very welcome sensation. In a land-based show, even if it's only the hands that have become wet, I believe it's important to firmly wrap the hands in a *warm* towel and pat and gently squeeze them.

In any of my hydropool productions I have always tried to play with temperature changes both at the poolside and in the water. In the welcoming session to the hydropool production, *Big Splash* (1999) we used a number of boxes for the young people to interact with before or after the changing. (People were either waiting to change or having to wait before going in the water.) In these boxes were miniature scenes basically connected with the themes of weather and temperature.

To interact with the boxes you first had to find the way to open them. This did not demand fine motor skills, only that the participant rest his or her hand on a biggish lever. That done, the door would swing open and then there was a truly magical moment – or maybe this is one of those things that really and truly does it for me – the lights came on, a waft of warm scented air blew from the box, the tiny clothes on the rotary washing line began to revolve as the tiny clothes pegged to the line fluttered in the breeze.

As with other sensory events it is probably impossible to say that the event is only affecting one sense. It was not just the sense of temperature that was at work here. There was the effect of the lights coming on the sense of vision, of the breeze blowing on the sense of hearing and on the sense of touch. And of the lightly scented breeze on the sense of smell. But I would protest that the defining sense in the event is the warm breeze blowing from the box. The other senses are the supporting cast.

In *Splish Splash* (2018), by contrast, it was a cool breeze that dominated. In this piece the participants were searching though treasure chests scattered around the pool. One of these chests did indeed contain the finest plastic baubles that Pound Shop can offer. Once again the participants had to work out how the lock was operated and when they were successful the lights made the jewels sparkle and shine. But the crowning moment came as a powerful pump blew cool air out of the box and towards the treasure seekers. In the heated water of the pool it was very unexpected, very welcome.

In *Kubla Khan* (2017), based on the poem by Samuel Taylor Coleridge, the audience sat in a semicircle of chairs with a wonderful wooden channel at touching distance in front of them. It is important to note that this was not a hydropool show.

The idea was that this channel was to be identified as Alph, the sacred river of the poem, and the audience were to be taken on a voyage along the length of the river with all its beauties, and dangers, it warnings and its revelations.

> The shadow of the dome of pleasure
> Floated midway on the waves;
> Where was heard the mingled measure
> From the fountain and the caves
> It was a miracle of rare device
> A sunny pleasure-dome with caves of ice!

Max Reinhardt's powerful music played mostly on the sitar by Sheema Mukherjee provided a wonderful frame to show off Coleridge's brilliant lyric, and the wooden channel provided a visceral equivalent for the verbal twists eddies and currents.

There were three versions of the production: one for young people on the spectrum, another for people with profound and multiple learning disabilities, and a third for the deafblind. This was an extraordinarily wide range of people, but then this was a performance that employed an extraordinarily wide range of media from the literary complexity of Coleridge's lyric to the visceral events in the channel, with many tactile and temperature changes that could engage someone who made no use of verbal language.

For these participants the performance was a multi-sensory experience that took them on a voyage through the poem, the changes in the temperature marking the different stages on the journey.

At times the channel would flood with cool water and the participants would put their hands (and even their feet and their faces) into the flowing scream. Then came the opportunity to experiment with the sand in the water, building up sandbanks trickling damp sands from on high into the water.

When we arrived at "those caves of ice" ice cubes were placed in the channel on the back of participants' hands and ultrasonic foggers blew mists across the waters.

It is noticeable that if you are blowing warm air or cool air the effect will be enhanced by scenting the air with an appropriate warm or cool essential oil: for example mint for the cool air, and ginger for the warm. Again it is hard to disentangle the effect conveyed by one sense from all the others clamoring for the attention of the sensorium.

19
The Sensory Audit

Light Show 2015 Oily Cart. Silhouette of Plane (Ellie Griffiths). The outline of the umbrella announces the arrival of the rain, in a very funny scene with plenty of water in the air. The six rocking chairs are for the participants. Design: Claire de Loon.

Photo: Gareth Howells.

DOI: 10.4324/9781003091288-21

I believe that for many developmentally typical people some senses get more than their fair share of attention. The senses of seeing and hearing, probably because they dominate the environment largely constructed by-and-for the developmentally typical, have a tendency to push other senses into the background. Senses like smell, touch, taste, the kinaesthetic sense have their moments, of course. Taste comes forward when it's mealtime, touch when you are stroking a baby's head, smell when you are holding a rose, kinaesthesia if you are visiting a theme park.

My suggestion, when it comes to making a piece of Sensory Theatre, is that, when you are devising, you always check to see how many of the senses it includes. It almost certainly will contain things to be seen and things to be heard. But if you really want to make Sensory Theatre, it needs something in there that will delight one or two of the other senses – something to touch or to smell perhaps. As for me, I am always on the lookout for more kinaesthetic elements.

Please do not get me wrong; I am not saying that you can never have a scene that is just to be seen or another one that is simply to be heard. Actually, I think something purely visual, or only auditory could be brilliant. Imagine a scene in a complete black-out where the only things that happen are sounds. Or the only things that happen are textures, or smells. I believe you would need to think carefully about the anxieties that might arise in the audience for that sort of Sensory Theatre, but it would be interesting.

It is also interesting to wear noise-cancelling headphones as part of the development of a piece of sensory theatre. It will certainly give you some idea into how the scene might be experienced by a D/deaf person, and then ask yourself the question "Is our scene made more powerful or is it weakened with the sound at this level?"

In a similar way wearing boxing gloves or heavily weighted clothing when developing new material gives insight into the perception of someone whose view of the world may be changed by a different set of mobility or fine motor skills.

I strongly recommend that any rehearsal room where Sensory Theatre is being made should have access to a wheelchair and a hoist with slings.

A final word of caution – when you have run your sensory audit over your material and found that maybe you have only addressed one or two senses in a particular scene, that might be quite enough for that scene. You certainly do not want every sequence to be crammed with material for all the senses, **disco in hell-style**. On the contrary, it is always a good idea to leave plenty of time and space for the participants to process what is going on. I just want to make an appeal on behalf of the neglected senses. As part of your practice, see if there is a scene somewhere that would welcome the addition of a perfume or a taste or a tactile sensation or better yet, a little more silence or stillness.

20
Sensory Theatre Is Close-up and Interactive

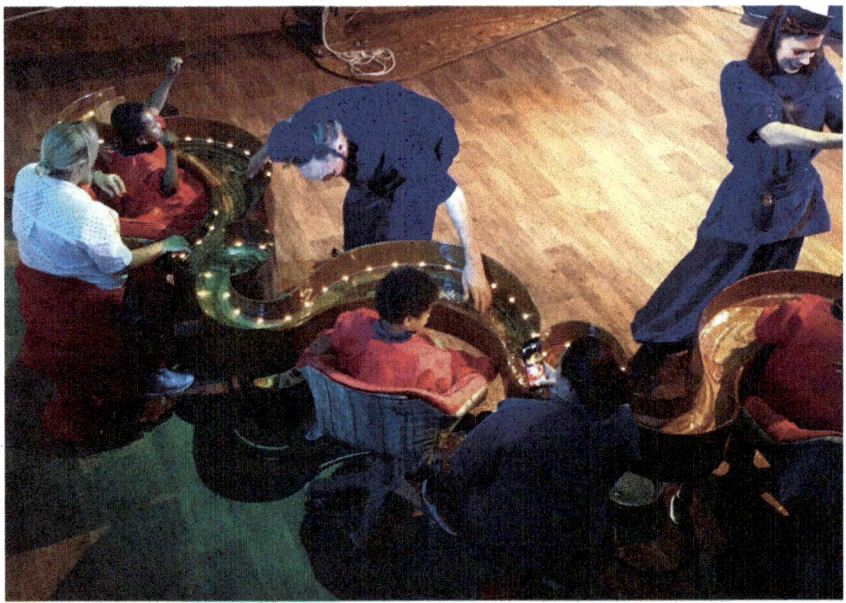

Kubla Khan 2017 Oily Cart. Participants and performers, Griff Fender and Stephanie Rutherford, enjoy the water close-up in a classroom. The sinuous contours of the water channels contain water, ice and lights. Design: Jens Demant Cole and Holly Murray.

Photo: Jens Demant Cole.

I believe that in Sensory Theatre, an interactive and close-up style of performance is of equal importance to a multi-sensory approach.

The first and most obvious reason I would offer is that nearly all of the sensory pathways function much more effectively if you are close to the person with whom you want to communicate. Someone who does not see well is probably going to see something better if it is close up and filling their field

DOI: 10.4324/9781003091288-22

of vision. Someone who does not hear well is going to hear better if they are close to the source of the sound. The more distant sounds will fade and so the close-up sounds will be the ones in focus. So that is why, for at least part of my shows, there will be a close-up and preferably a one-on-one performer-participant relationship. Put simply, if you're trying to connect with a hard-to-reach person, most of the time, it will work better if the two of you are close together.

If the performer is close by, then this will generally sharpen focus for the participant. In a large theatre, with a large audience surrounding you, it can be difficult for the participant to know which sound, sight, smell or other sense they should be concentrating on. There are so many choices clamoring for your attention.

If you are a performer in a Sensory Theatre piece, your is aim is to establish a highly interactive relationship with the people in your audience, a relationship in which you can perceive and creatively respond to each and every reaction from the participants. It is relatively easy to achieve this when you only have to focus on one or two participants. If you can thoroughly involve the adult companions (more of this later) then you may be able to sustain this kind of performance with two participants, sharing your performance between the two of them. But when you begin to work with larger numbers of participants, it becomes progressively more difficult to customise your performance and you find yourself resorting to tricks like "spotting," that is, directing your focus to a participant near the front, then to someone at the back, then to someone in the middle of the audience – and so on. Good performers can give the impression that they are addressing the participant personally with techniques like this, but the larger the ratio of participants to performer grows, the less likely is it that the performer is actually reacting to an individual participant's responses.

Theatre has often been described as a shared experience and I know that any production in which I have played a part has had a shared experience as a particular goal. But when a piece of Sensory Theatre is made for such a hard-to-reach audience as people on the autism spectrum or other complex conditions, then overcoming the sensory barriers dividing performer and participant individual should take precedence.

Intensive Interaction

Now although I have discussed interaction in general, there is a way of working specifically called "Intensive Interaction." This was developed during the

80s and 90s by a number of exponents working separately including Dave Hewett and Melanie Nind, Dr. Geraint Ephraim and Phoebe Caldwell. It is Phoebe Caldwell who has had the greatest influence on me and the Oily Cart team.

Phoebe's approach is definitely not theatrical, but it is very effective. I have taken part in one of Phoebe's courses, read her wonderful books and watched a number of her videos.

Her advice on how to approach people on the autism spectrum who are prone to meltdown and other behaviour that could be injurious both to themselves and others, has been hugely helpful. It was Phoebe Caldwell, along with Temple Grandin who introduced me to the idea that it was sensory overload caused by the fragmented way in which the senses were conveyed to the autistic brain that brought about the panic attacks, meltdowns and similar distress.

Phoebe introduced me to the idea of seeking to create an autism friendly environment that could let an individual on the spectrum know what they are doing and what is going on around them. She inspired the pauses, the moments of stillness, the repetitions that provide processing time in my productions, including performances for those defined as affected by Profound and Multiple Learning Disabilities.

Perhaps even more valuably, Phoebe has shown me how we should take the time to gain the confidence of people on the spectrum so that it was possible to sit close up to them, tune into the language of their breathing, their gestures and the sounds they make in addition to any verbal language.

She teaches the value of not rushing to confront someone prone to distress but asks that at first, we should wait at a distance, echoing but in a more gentle way, the gestures and sounds that they make. She asks for us to always look for the signs of consent and never advance if there are signs of resistance, but gradually make our way to join them. She argues that we should sit beside the person on the spectrum if they will allow it because this is a relatively unthreatening position from which to relate to one another. Then we should adjust our breathing to match theirs but slowing the pace and the urgency that we have been hearing and seeing from them.

Particularly in her videos, Phoebe provides numerous examples of how by echoing and modifying their sounds and shadowing their gestures, she can draw very complex and guarded individuals out from their inner worlds and self-stimulation towards a new engagement with other people and the world out there.

For me this is one of the most compelling reasons for Sensory Theatre to be played as close up as possible. If the language of your interaction with a participant can be made up of shared patterns of breath or when you and the participant can develop a shared language by modifying a short sequence of sounds or gestures, then the closer together the two of you can be, the better.

The Downside of This Close-up Interactive Approach

An issue with maintaining high performer to participant ratios is that the number of people in the audience must be limited. When I am making a show for hard-to-reach audiences, the size of the cast at my disposal generally is five: three performers, one specialist musician and a stage manager. Given the economics of the UK touring business, I think this is an acceptable number. I know many companies working for young audiences that tour with fewer than that.

But, given that I have a company of five, I think the ideal number in the audience is five performers to six participants, each one of whom will come with a companion. The stage manager and the musician have got more than enough to do, so that leaves the three performers to focus on the close-up and interactive moments. If each of these performers is assigned to two of the participants, then they can alternate between those two, with the companions coming in to help as necessary.

But these numbers are not set in stone. At the time of writing, it seems to me that PMLD class sizes in the UK are more like seven or eight per class than six and it would be useful to investigate if, with a group of five performers, we could perform a show with sufficient close-up elements for eight participants.

Although I believe that close-up interaction is an essential element in engaging the most hard-to-reach participants, this does not mean that every moment of the show should be performed close up. That could get oppressive. I believe that you can have too much of a good thing and that any Sensory Theatre performance benefits from changes of pace, style and energy.

The Role of the Companion

The role of companion is certainly essential to any Sensory Theatre performance. The companions know their participant (or at the least should have been briefed about them before the performance) so that they can interpret and advise the performer. The performer can introduce an activity to a participant, but then hand it over to the companion to continue, while beginning the introduction to the second participant/companion pair.

Actually, this process rarely happens in such a clear-cut way. The second companion often begins the activity as soon as they get a notion of what is needed from watching the participant/companion pair next door. This approach is often necessary if not preferred.

Long Shot and Close-up

The terms "long shot" and "close-up" are often used when talking about film-making. I believe these terms are also useful in discussing a Sensory Theatre piece. The close-ups in Sensory Theatre are the one-to-one and the one-to-two performer-to-participant scenes. The long shots cover everything else. For example the opening scene in *Blue* (2006) when all the performers, all the participants and all the companions meet one another and the basic situation is explained:

> Here we all are waiting at a railway station for the train. We're all going away on a train and each of us has brought just one bag with us. It's called a Blues Bag and in that bag is our favourite thing, the best thing in the whole world.
>
> *Blue* (2006)

The participants were the first to show us all what they had in the Blues Bags that they had brought along to the performance. The young people had all been asked to bring to what they thought was the best thing of all. This *best thing of all* was often a photo of mummy or daddy, or a pet, or a favourite toy or video box set. So first of all, we would have a chat about these things as they were pulled out of the Blues Bags. After that the performers in turn showed us what they had in their bags, singing and showing us what their favourite thing could do. The first character to show us the contents of her bag was Belle and her favourite thing was the Wind which she evoked with a large hand fan. Other fans were distributed amongst the participants, their companions and the other performers who fanned to the rhythm as Belle sang a haunting blues, *Feel the wind in your hair* . . . The song then led into the first of the close-up moments.

In this and any close-up moment, the focus was firmly on the performer-participant relationship aided and abetted by the companion.

If the performer noticed that their participant was responding well to a slow, regular fanning rhythm then they would give them more of that. Another performer might notice that they were getting a better reception for a lively fan rhythm and gave a little more energy to that to see if more would be welcomed. And so on. No two performers would be performing in the same way and no two participants would be having identical reactions.

If a participant wanted to get up from their seat and move around while they were being fanned, then that was absolutely OK. The show, especially in the close-up moments, belonged to the participants. The performers were not there to enforce a plan to which the participants must adhere. They were there to create a situation in which the participants would be totally engaged, and they could be the ones in control. We wanted them to feel that what *they* wanted to happen – would happen. The performers were their willing assistants, not their masters.

The musician brought the fanning sequence to a close. It was his turn to reveal to everyone that he had the Groove in his Blues Bag. The close-up fanning was replaced by a long shot leading into the close-up shaker sequence.

The show was a series of alternating close-ups and long shots ending in a riotous all-together celebration when the train finally arrived to take the characters away.

Being a Playfellow and Where to Draw the Line

It is only when safety was an issue that the performers would direct the action and suggest to the companions that they should intervene. If, for example, someone was wandering around exploring the area back-stage between the video projector and the screen on which it was projecting (in more orthodox theatre productions this area would be inaccessible), the stage manager would almost certainly direct the wanderer away from this area where he or she was casting their own shadow onto the screen. But our performers do not want to suddenly transform from funny, delightful characters who want the audience to play more and more wonderful games into authority figures saying *Uh-oh – you can't go there*. If it meant some participant's shadow suddenly walked onto a shadow screen, well, was that so terrible?

However, if some participant was doing something that looked like they might hurt themselves or somebody else, like heading for the electrical connections, then it was time for someone to intervene and that someone was generally the stage manager. Of course, prevention is better than cure, so the potentially dangerous items like the electrical equipment are best hidden away under a table.

It is a big mistake for the stage manager or anyone else to get involved in a chase with the unofficial backstage visitors because from a participant's point of view, this is a Really Good Game. It is better for the stage manager to stay with the potentially dangerous equipment and let the performer who has been assigned to the wanderer from the beginning come up with some business that is more beguiling than the chase and tempt the participant into a different game.

This is not always easy but the aim of the performers and the stage manager (if you are lucky enough to have one) is to remain relaxed and engaging play-fellows and not become security guards enforcing the rules and regulations.

In fact, I think **the political role of the performers** and the way they inter-act with the audience is one of the key factors in the success or failure of a Sensory Theatre project.

People who are hard-to-reach often seem to live in a world filled with au-thority figures. There are figures like a parent, a teaching assistant, a nurse, a dinner lady or a teacher, all around them, and all with the best will in the world, telling them what they can do and what they cannot.

Now it may be that at first glance the performers in a Sensory Theatre pro-duction appear to be authority figures, but that impression should not be al-lowed to persist. The performers should never be seen by the participants as people who are there to give them instructions or to be role models. Rather they should be seen as someone to have fun with, someone who will help you do what you want to do, not tell you what you cannot do.

It seems to me that, given a nudge, very many of the people with whom I have worked in Special Schools and Centres over the years are more than willing to take on this game-playing role when things need not be taken too seriously, and we can all have a bit of a laugh. The pressure to behave cor-rectly, the pressure that is always there in everyday life, is relieved.

Of course, this is relatively easy for the performers of Sensory Theatre. It is only rarely that we do have to be taken seriously. Performers do not have to be responsible for the people they are working with day after day, week after week as is the case with, for example, teachers or teaching assistants. In their professional lives there will be times where a teacher or a TA needs to assert their authority and be taken seriously. But the performers can be playful and fun almost all the time – except when it comes to issues of health and safety.

Here is a YouTube link to video of **_Ring A Ding Ding_ (2012),** a short trailer for the show for 3 to 5 year olds at The New Victory Theater in New York.

"A tabletop set turns 'round and round' as Alice and her friends search left and right, high and low for her runaway pet in this colorful and creative piece of participatory theater."

https://youtu.be/j2IYqMkKzKE

21
Wonderlands – Design in Sensory Theatre

Big Balloon 2008 Oily Cart. The aeronaut (Griff Fender) in his hot air balloon oversees the action at the Unicorn Theatre. Design: Claire de Loon.

Photo: Edgar de Oliveira.

For the great majority of the shows that I have made, the set design (to use a good old-fashioned term) has been created by Claire de Loon and because her design has been driven by the requirements of the audience, it has been at the very heart of every show. It was not just the sets, it was also the costumes, the puppets, the posters and the resources, all designed by the wonderful Claire and the talented team that she gathered around her.

It is no exaggeration to say that without Claire, there would be no Oily Cart. We met at Glasgow Citizens' Theatre in 1971. Having worked together

DOI: 10.4324/9781003091288-23

for so many years, we share a knowledge of and commitment to Sensory Theatre.

Basic Design Principles for Sensory Theatre

Claire's primary aim in creating a performance is to make something that she believes is beautiful, and to make it as beautifully as she can. She believes that if she brings her very best to the work then her experience tells her that others will find it beautiful too. Young people respond to beauty as well as their adult companions and it is a sign of caring and respect from the company to all the participants.

She considers the show to be an experience that starts long before the performance and continues after the event. Preparatory and follow-up resources should echo the visual signature of each show and include objects of reference and other sensory markers wherever possible.

The journey into the performance from home or the classroom is an important part of the show and signage such as corridor decorations and ushers' costumes need to be designed accordingly. It is important to make the journey as reassuring and inviting as possible through clear messaging and interest. Incorporating pictures of the characters, triggered sound effects, textured curtains, intriguing underfoot (or under wheelchair) surfaces, perfumes and, if possible, live music, can all add to the experience.

Easy transitions into the performance help participants and companions alike. Wherever possible, there should be an airlock or waiting area outside the performance space to facilitate the way into the world of the show and to act as a refuge or chill-out space during the performance.

The entrance to the performance space itself should be wide open so that more reluctant audience members can watch from outside. Exits need to be clearly visible. A trail/game can be a very effective way to draw in very young audiences.

Seating for audience, companions and performers should always be carefully considered because of the many different seating requirements of a typical Sensory Theatre audience.

There should always be enough space for participants who like to wander to circulate safely.

Lighting should be used to make the space inviting particularly when the participants arrive at the start of the show.

We use costumes/dress-ups for the participants and involve them in making pre-prepared *passports* or *gifts for performers* to make everyone feel part of the setting from the outset.

Claire uses contrast to make the visuals easier to interpret. For example, the red costumes of the Nest People stood out in the green world in *Something in the Air* (2009) or the dark velvety dry area contrasted with the sparkling white poolside in *Dreams and Secrets* (2000).

We use Objects of Reference to identify characters and settings. Wherever possible Claire incorporates tactile connections with the set, characters and props. The designs for *Ring A Ding Ding* (2011), *In a Pickle* (2012), *Land of Lights* (2015) by Claire, *Kubla Khan* (2017) by Jens Demant Cole and *Stranden* (2019) by Petra Hjortsberg were particularly successful because in all of these shows, the participants were **literally hands-on**, actually touching the stage/set for much of the performance.

Ideally participants should be left with reminders of the experience. In *Big Splash* (1999), schools were given a cassette tape with music, a worksheet and sensory objects that echoed the ones used in the show. The final gift was a string vest turned into a bag that could hold the sponge, brush, spray mister etc. for a mini water-based sensory session. When visiting schools years later, it was clear that these kits were still in use and Oily Cart continued to get requests for replacement audiocassettes. (Now Oily Cart put the music and video for these sensory sessions online.)

The Journey and the Airlock

All of my Sensory Theatre projects involve a journey to the performance space even if it's only the journey from the classroom to the hall. However, it may be a lot more complicated. In 2009, for the Manchester Special Schools students participating in a performance of *Something in the Air*, it was not just a journey down a school corridor but halfway across the city. To my mind this journey and the arrival at the end of it was an essential part of the experience. It built up anticipation and it allowed the participants a gradual transition from the everyday to the wonders of the theatre. Why not make the journey across town in the school bus part of the show? Why not have the participants dress up before they climb on board and listen to the soundtrack, live or recorded as they ride? What if the buses are decked out with green seat covers and pots of living herbs?

On arrival at the venue, the audience made its way into the Airlock (waiting area) usually positioned in a room near to the entrance to the performance space. The transitions from one space to another were important milestones on the journey of the show.

Some people in our hard-to-reach audiences may have problems with thresholds. For some people even transitioning from their home into the street or entering the school door can be a problem. Sometimes this can be alleviated by a clear exposition of what is involved in the preparatory material/Social Story that participant/adult companion pairs will have been sent in advance of the performance. All of this preparatory material should also be available in the Airlock in print and on iPad.

Airlocks should be comfortable with kinaesthetically interesting seating and examples of some of the props that will appear in the performance. An Airlock should be a place to get your breath back. Obviously, it should be as near to the loos as possible. It's a place to have something to drink and eat before you go into the show, and it is also a place to retreat to during the show if things get too much or if medical attention is needed. It should be stressed that participants may return to the performance space when they are ready.

In most productions, a character from the show will come to the Airlock to say hello before the performance starts. They will set the friendly tone and invite the participants to follow them into the performance space.

Seating

Another design feature with which Claire and the rest of the design team have wrestled over the years is the issue of seating. Ever since I saw the delight that hammocking brought to the audiences in *Box of Socks*, our first production for Special Schools in 1988, I have been searching for seating that allows the participants a range of movement that brings the kinaesthetic sense into every show.

In 2004, in *Conference of the Birds*, Claire introduced us to the brilliant Leaf Chairs that she had seen in action in schools and other venues. This type of chair is suspended from a frame. In it, you can sit up or lie down. You can bounce as well as swing from side to side and to and fro. The adult companions can very easily turn the participants to focus on the relevant action. We experimented with ready-made seating like the garden swing seats and rocking chairs in *Blue* (2006), rocking recliners in *Light Show* (2015) and hairdressing chairs in *Mirror, Mirror* (2016).

Although at one time I used beanbags in Sensory Theatre shows and I still find them useful in the Airlock before going on into the show, for the main performance area where the participants and the companions might well be staying for 30 to 40 minutes, I now prefer forms of seating that offer more kinaesthetic possibilities. The wonderful "nest chairs" that Jens Demant Cole designed for *Something in the Air* (2009) were the ultimate example. These chairs not only raised the participants and their companions up in the air with the aerialists, once there they could swing, bounce and swing alongside them.

Under Your Hat 2001 Oily Cart. An epic installation designed by Claire de Loon at the Southbank Centre. This interactive promenade show for under-fives took dressing up to another level.

Photo: Amanda Webb.

The Devil in the Detail

A key part of Claire de Loon's approach was the extraordinary attention paid to detail and I believe that focus on detail is an essential feature of all Sensory Theatre. Within our audiences, particularly those who are considered to be on the autism spectrum, there are many agendas that vary greatly from the neurotypical. Their priorities are not mine or yours, but their own.

Now forgive me as I generalise. Sitting in a room with one or two other people, a neurotypical person tends to prioritise people's faces and voices.

That's where they put their focus. That's the way their minds are made. But someone on the autism spectrum might just as easily focus on the texture of the carpet, the flicker of the neon tube or the colour of the ceiling. Because it is difficult to predict how a participant on the autism spectrum might prioritise their perceptions, I try to ensure that each one of the experiences available in a show are equally valid. It makes it a **360° theatre** in which each dimension has significance.

So, we think carefully about the floor covering and not just the non-slippiness of it, but the texture, the colour and even the smell of it. But what about up above? We need to consider that too. Look, listen, smell, feel, move, rest – wherever you choose to focus, there is a discovery to be made.

Designing for Water Shows

An even more specialised area of design that Claire has pioneered is Sensory Theatre in hydropools, from *Bubbles* (1997), through *Big Splash* (1999), *Dreams and Secrets* (2000), *Waving* (2001) to *Pool Piece* (2008) all for Oily Cart, and *Tonic Water*, for Giant Productions, Glasgow (2000).

As you probably expect, there are particular design issues associated with making touring shows for hydropools. I have never encountered two hydropools that are the same size, so Claire has had to design modules to fit in and around a great range of shapes and sizes from semi-Olympic to barely a splash pool. Unfortunately, it is not possible to use a regular swimming pool because the water is too cold for many of the PMLD people who find it difficult to maintain their own body heat.

Although there are many beautifully decorated pools in Special Schools, there are also too many with dodgy dolphin murals and heaps of garish pool equipment. They require some ingenuity to turn them into enchanting spaces. Yes, many of the pools have sound and light systems but these seem to be designed for discos. So the designer of a touring hydropool show has his or her work cut out.

There are three main areas to be considered in a pool: the walls around the pool, the space above the pool and the water itself.

In *Dreams and Secrets* (2000) the pool itself was transformed by bunches of pearly white balloons filled with helium that floated above the heads of the participants and performers in the water. The floating weights that prevented the balloons flying away were little plastic bottles filled with sparkling, coloured beads that looked particularly good underwater. The balloons were an economical way of occupying quite large areas if necessary, and in particular they were excellent at filling in the empty space up above the water where it was difficult for anything else to be positioned. The number of bunches could be varied according to the size of the pool.

In *Pool Piece* (2008), the space above the water was filled with 20cm mirror balls. They were suspended from the ceiling by fishing line attached to magnets. It required a member of the crew to wade through the water to put them up and take them down with a special extending pole.

The awkward and sometimes large spaces that have to be filled in pool shows make extreme demands on lighting, and any lighting in the vicinity of water and young people makes special health and safety demands on the designer and the lighting designer. For our first hydro shows, we bought a professional diver's torch that was, we thought, amazingly expensive. For subsequent shows, we had a brainwave and bought some 12-volt pond lights from a garden centre that were amazingly cheap. Their low voltage meant that they were designed to be safe to use in the pool. With these lights we could create magical effects below and above the water. In a low-ceilinged pool, the lights under water pointing upwards produce wonderful kaleidoscopic patterns on the ceiling.

A regular design feature of water shows has been a cascade of water. Water is pumped from the pool up above the heads of the participants. It rains down to form a very cold curtain of spray. This looks spectacular in the lights and the sound is magical. Some young people love the shock of the cold water. Others prefer to experience it from under an umbrella.

For hydropool shows, there is a requirement for a changing room area that is as welcoming as possible. In the model for hydro work that I prefer, we welcome two participants and two adult companions for each session. A lovely way to greet all four is to present each of them with a warm and dry dressing gown as they arrive in the changing area. In the case of people classified as PMLD, changing into a swimsuit can sometimes take a fairly long time and requires the attention of both companions, and preferably a third carer. I do not imagine that it is too pleasant for the participant who is left waiting and it is great if one of the performers can sing to them or fan them so that they feel included.

It is important if the performers do not feel neglected either. In a typical hydro show, I would probably have four performers, two of whom go in the water in the morning leaving the other pair for the afternoon shift. The whole team, including the musician, need his or her own dressing gowns and plenty of barrier cream, shampoo and body lotion.

The costumes for the performers working in water also have special considerations. Much attention needs to be paid to the head and shoulders of the characters, these being the most visible parts in the water. All costumes take a beating in the chlorinated water. This means that replacements are often needed on tour. At the end of each performance, the cast spend at least an hour washing and drying all the sponges, towels, costumes and robes before they can be used again.

Any materials used need to be checked in chlorinated water before use, to see if they turn brown or fade. You have to shop around for suitable materials. Ships' chandlers can supply suitable rope, marine paint and buoys, plumbers' merchants can supply tubing and garden centres have pumps and low voltage lighting.

Plastazote is a synthetic foam that comes in sheets, in tubes or in blocks that can be carved. It has the added benefit of floating in water. The colours are limited but all in all, it is a hydropool show essential.

Inflatables

Claire and I tend to go through phases. In the early 2000s, we produced a series of memorable shows involving inflatables designed and made by Rachel James of Location Inflation. Rachel had pioneered the use of computer-aided design to create the patterns for the panels that go together to make an inflatable. As a result, her work is intricate and organic. Inflatables are lightweight and take up little space in the van but when inflated, they can fill a stage or a school hall.

Rachel's inflatables appeared in *Jumping Beans* (2002), *Conference of the Birds* (2004), FreeTime at Somerset House (2004/5) and *Big Balloon* and *Baby Balloon* (2006).

The advent of LED lighting that emits little heat meant that we were able to light the inflatables from within and introduce a very wide range of colours. If there is a snag with inflatables, it is the noise produced by the electric fans that blow them up and keep them up. Our solution was to use lengths of 500 mm diameter flexible spiral duct to keep the fan(s) well away from the inflatable and in a separate room. The fans also needed protective boxes for extra soundproofing and safety.

One of Oily Cart's great strengths was the closeness of its creative team. From the inception of every production, the design and the music were incorporated into the work on a par with the writing and direction. Claire,

Max and I developed our knowledge and ideas together and built up a shared approach that endured and flourished for over 40 years!

Here is a YouTube link to video of **The Art of the Cart: Oily Cart Design Exhibition (2015).**

https://youtu.be/bfDvy9Hrees

22
Staging a Show – *Stranden*

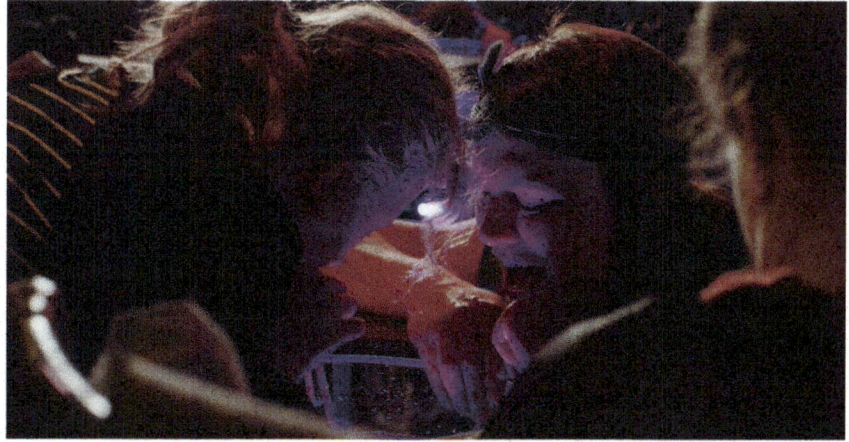

Stranden 2019 by Folkteatern Gävleborg/Scen:se, Sweden. Eva von Hofsten with participant. They are engrossed in the changing LED light show taking place in front of them. The light shines through a bowl of water built into a tabletop. The colour can be changed remotely. Even a gobo pattern can be introduced.

Photo: Michael Tebinka/Folkteatern Gävleborg/Scen:se.

I wrote and directed *Stranden* for Folkteatern Gävleborg and Riksteatern (the Swedish National Theatre). It was part of the Scen:se Project that toured extensively in Sweden in 2019 and thanks to our Swedish collaborators, especially on the technical side, it incorporated significant improvements in lighting and video that I liked very much.

The logistics of the production period were complicated. The three UK artists involved, Debbie Bandara (choreographer and assistant director), Max Reinhardt (composer and my long-time music director) and myself were rarely together in the rehearsal room as we commuted to and fro between

DOI: 10.4324/9781003091288-24

the UK and Sweden. Still, everything came together in the end due in large part to the efforts of the technical and stage management team and the energetic co-ordination of our producer from Folkteatern Gävleborg, Anna Thelin.

For this production, I worked with the designer Petra Hjortsberg. It was based on the 19th century English poem, "Dover Beach" by Matthew Arnold and was intended for participants with PMLD or who were on the autism spectrum. So why do I like this production so much? It is partly because it enabled us to tell the story in at least two contrasting ways. In the poem, the sounds of the tide withdrawing from the beach (the sound of the Ocean Drums) suggest to the narrator the way in which the Christian faith that had given meaning to the world had faded and died. We sang almost all the words of the poem in the performance. I don't know how meaningful those lyrics were to all of our participants, but I do believe that we were true to the arc of the story and the emotional journey on which the poet had wanted to take us.

On the other hand, the piece could very well be experienced as a visceral series of events, experienced in the moment, where the meaning lay in the music, the visual images, the tactile sensations, the movements of the bodies, the props and the chairs. I am proud of the way we could say without words that the world in which we had started had become increasingly threatening until it burst asunder.

And I am especially proud of the feedback from teachers that Eva von Hofsten reports in her piece on the Scen:se Project in Chapter 40.

> "After almost every show the adults that accompanied the young people, told the actors that, 'this is the first time that we have been invited to a performance that is actually created for our students.' Some also added that before, they had often been invited to performances for young toddlers, sometimes together with the toddlers. The performers reported that the venues were relieved that they finally could offer something for young people with complex needs."

I believe that we engaged with those audiences for *Stranden* and that we connected with them. Not always but often enough to make it worthwhile. You could see it in the way the participants focussed. You could hear it in the intensity with which they listened. It was confirmed by the feedback of the adult companions, the teachers and family members.

The setting was a seaside café. The audience (six participants and six adult companions) sat in a semicircle in specially constructed seats facing a back-projection screen made to look like curtains flapping in sea breezes (electric fans). The video projections were of sea, sky and the participants' faces.

The six seats for the participants, made in the workshops of the Folkteatern Gävleborg, were a wonderful solution to several seating issues. They were comfortable and there was the possibility of adding cushions and padding when necessary. They could be steered readily, braked securely, their height could be adjusted with a foot pedal, and they very much suggested the furniture of a 19th century café terrace.

Best of all, each of them fitted neatly into a semi-circle of tables (rather like desks) when they were brought into the performance space from the welcoming area (airlock), where each of the participants had been made comfortable in his or her chair.

In the centre of each of these tables was a hole (approximately 300 mm across) and fitted into this was a clear plastic container (approximately 250 mm deep). Right under the bottom of this container was an LED light that could be remotely operated through a wide range of colours by the stage manager. This excellent system was devised by Robert Berglund (the lighting designer) and David Zackrisson (the stage manager and video editor).

The idea behind this fabulous contrivance is that many of the people in our audiences whether defined as being on the autism spectrum or PMLD will see, hear and smell things more readily if they have the objects producing these sensations right there on the tabletop in front of them. To enable scene changes, there was a lid to close over the tabletop marking a clear end to a scene, before a new object was introduced.

For people who make little use of verbal language or of symbolic language either, this was a wonderfully direct, visceral way to connect Sensory Theatre audiences to the world around them. The object glowing in the hole in the table with the ambient lighting kept low, was a very clear point on which the participant, adult companion and performer could focus, while the raising of the lid and closing of the lid clearly punctuated the action to give time for processing.

The scenes on the tabletops were as follows:

1. The lids were raised and clear plastic water jugs were brought on. Warm, scented water was poured into the bowl. Participants were encouraged to put their hands into the water.

After this we introduced small colanders to pour water and sponges to squeeze water over their hands and to dab between the fingers. Changes in the under-bowl lighting complemented this developing business with the bowls.

This scene ended as the jugs and other props were removed and the lids were closed.

2. Warm towels were brought to each table. The participants' hands were placed on the towels and the towels folded over them. The hands were patted and gently massaged.

3. The lids were opened, and small Ocean Drums introduced.

   The Ocean Drums contained lots of ball bearings. When the drum was tilted from side to side the rolling balls made a sound remarkably like the sea as it rolled onto a pebbly beach.

   The Ocean Drums were positioned on the tables where the light from under the table shone up revealing the changing patterns made by the ball bearings as they rolled about creating the sounds of waves on the beach.

4. A large piece of blue silk was wafted over the heads of the audience so they could hear, see and feel a storm brewing.

5. A transparent umbrella was given to each participant/companion pair who sheltered under them as water was sprayed onto them, draining off into the bowls in the tables.

6. The umbrellas were blown away in a dance to the far corners of the room. The performers encouraged the companions to shake the seats of the participants. The degree of movement depended on the reactions of the participants. Some of our audiences enjoyed being whirled around the room in their chairs like a funfair ride, while others preferred something gentler.

7. On a cue from the musician, the action paused. All went quiet. The performers struggled to speak or to move. (In the poem on which this is based, the characters are rendered helpless because the world in which they live has lost its meaning.) But the participants, when asked, could move and make sound so bringing the circle that had been broken back together as the chairs rejoined each other and their tables. That which had been destroyed was restored.

Stranden was a show which depended on some relatively complex effects, the adjustable and moving chairs, the light bowls set into the tabletops, the scenery – waves, water and clouds – were on video back projected at very short range onto translucent curtains that could be made to waft and undulate by a handful of electric fans.

When all the components of any production have been devised and created then it is up to the performers to ensure that everything is delivered to the participants and their companions. It is the performers who, by carefully monitoring the reactions of the audience, will make any changes necessary to ensure that the show is truly getting across.

23
Venues – Open and Closed

Pool Piece 2008 Oily Cart. Bubbles played by Nicole Worrica. Design: Claire de Loon.
Photo: Patrick Baldwin.

DOI: 10.4324/9781003091288-25

When come it comes to choosing venues for Sensory Theatre work, the choice often comes down to closed venues like schools, or public ones like theatres or art centres. There are advantages and disadvantages to be considered in either case.

The advantage of a **closed venue** like a school as a performance space is that it is familiar to the young participants. It's on their own ground and the facilities they need for changing, for toileting and any medical procedures will be readily to hand.

These considerations are especially important for audiences labeled PMLD where there can often be last minute changes. For example, a group of six participants have been on their way to the performance in the hall. Suddenly one of them is taken ill and has to be substituted. In the school this problem is easily solved but if you are on the way to or actually at a public venue, it is usually impossible.

The **open venues**, by which I mean theatres, art centres, public meeting places of any kind, have the disadvantage that even the most modern of them do not have facilities as suitable as those to be found in the schools. But increasingly in the UK I find that the staff in the venues are well aware of the issues and go out of their way to provide what is needed. However, in the present era, so radically affected by the Covid 19 pandemic, I think it is likely that theatre and other arts venues may find it more difficult to find funding to improve facilities to deal with issues like toileting and access.

I also believe we should consider that some people on the spectrum can be stressed by interruptions to their school routine and taking part in trips and activities with which they are unfamiliar and might well be more comfortable at a school or other closed performance. With proper preparation, however, these same young people will find that travel to the venue, meeting new people and the theatre experience wonderfully widens their horizons.

(There is a good deal more about preparing the audiences for the experience of the performance in Chapter 30 of this book.)

Of course, travel is expensive, requires high staffing levels and does not always go to plan. It is not uncommon for transport problems to disrupt a performance schedule in a venue to the extent that the audience arrives when the show was expected to finish!

However, companies like Bamboozle and indeed the Oily Cart have spent decades persuading theatres and similar venues that if they are receiving public funding they should be providing, if only from time to time, work which can be accessed by all the people who make up our society. Why should theatre be reserved for people who conform to the norms, when theatre is uniquely capable of creating the languages to engage everyone.

Venues like the Unicorn, arts depot and Stratford Circus in London, the MacRobert in Stirling, the Gulbenkian in Canterbury, and indeed, Lincoln Centre in New York have taken on the need to lower audience numbers and raise production values as the necessary cost of Sensory Theatre that will break through to audiences who are the hardest to reach. These pioneering venues show their commitment to all members of their community.

Venue performances have the tremendous advantage that they can be enjoyed by family groups. Such events are quite rare in schools, but it is beautiful in a venue when parents and siblings enjoy a piece of theatre together.

One of the great advantages of the public venue performances to the participants is that they take the students out of the schools and the older people out of day centres and into wider society. So the participants get to see more of the world and the world sees more of them.

Of course, there are many other possible venues to be considered – hydropools, nature trails, parks, for example. If they satisfy the requirements of the participants, they may well be worth a try. For example, there is the *living room* model of Helium Arts (described in more detail in Chapter 34) where their performances of *Pop-Up Picnic* take place for a child with complex conditions in the middle of the family home, with only the child and other family members present.

And as we found during the Covid pandemic, where companies like Oily Cart were performing in people's front gardens and in the car parks of schools, any place where they could be seen and heard but otherwise kept at social distance, even that sort of performance could lead to real engagement.

24

Music That Is Felt as Much as Heard

Something in the Air 2009 Oily Cart/Ockham's Razor. Twelve egg chairs are raised into the air while musician Arun Ghosh plays the clarinet. Contact Theatre, Manchester International Festival. Design: Claire de Loon and Jens Demant Cole.

Photo: Duncan Elliott.

Music is, arguably, the single most effective medium in Sensory Theatre. Max Reinhardt, composer and music director has been my inseparable partner from the prehistoric times when we performed *The Exploding Punch and Judy Show* together – learning the hard way that perhaps we should be doing something else. It's not an accident that the name of the company we co-founded with Claire de Loon, Oily Cart, is a word play on D'Oyly Carte, the name of the great comic operetta company that originally produced the work of Gilbert and Sullivan.

DOI: 10.4324/9781003091288-26

In the irresponsible early years of our little company, the plan was that we do our own potted versions of the D'Oyly Carte's hits. We did manage a two-man *Parrots of Penzance* (1984) but backed away from further homage.

However, music has remained central to all our work since and while the Oily Cart has made productions without words, we have never made a show without music. The reason is simple: as we have moved further from mainstream theatre and into Sensory Theatre, it has always been clear that the majority of our audiences, however you chose to define them, were delighted by the music, whether it moved them by its beauty or had them dancing to its beats.

From 1988 when I began making theatre for people who were, to use the terminology of the time, in Severe Learning Disability Schools, I realised that we were playing quite often to people who were defined D/deaf and yet they seemed in no way excluded from the performance. I learned there were many ways of hearing. Maybe some people would need another medium to help them follow a verbal dialogue, like signing or a hearing aid but for the most part they were being affected by the sound of the music.

Perhaps because of uncertain job security in our part of showbiz, from quite early on Max also began building another career as a DJ. Over the next couple of decades, he graduated from the tennis club next to his house to the august heights of BBC Radio Three's Late Junction by way of innumerable clubs playing what you might call world music. In so doing, he acquired a vast knowledge of music and musicians from around the globe. All of this musical diversity has played a major part in the development of our work together.

Max and I have always had live music in our shows from the earliest days when it was mostly Max and his guitar on through a period when he explored the world of electronic keyboards.

As the company began to grow from the initial duo, we were always on the lookout for actors who could sing and preferably play an instrument too. This strengthened the musical side – I was never more than a barely adequate singer – and the musical level of the company rose, especially after I moved on to being full-time artistic director and writer in 1988.

In the 1990s, performers who really could play an instrument such as Sue Eves (clarinet) and Geoff Bowyer (keyboard, musical saw and marimba) joined the company and were the core of Oily Cart for a good part of the decade. Sue was also a really good puppeteer who was a key part of the company in eight productions over a period of six years.

Geoff had been a true rock legend before he joined the cast. At the end of the 60s he had been part of an outfit, basically a jug band, called the Purple Gang. Curiously during his rock 'n' roll years Geoff's main instrument was the washboard and it is rumoured that he jammed with Jimi Hendrix playing this instrument. As is proper with a true survivor from the 60s Geoff cannot remember if this story is true or indeed anything else about the period. What is true is that Geoff was one of the funniest people ever to appear on-stage with the Oily Cart.

The other funniest person ever to have done that was Griff Fender who still remains a member of the band Darts who had three successive number twos in the UK charts and became Britain's biggest-selling chart act of 1978. In 1983–84, they played in the West End and on Broadway with *Yakety Yak*.

Max's range of contacts brought some wonderful virtuosi into our shows. What's more because Max is so involved in world music in a huge city like London, with such a fabulously diverse population, we have had the opportunity to bring examples of music from around the world into our productions.

Apart from the fact that music can be exciting and moving and conjure up a vast range of other emotions, songs and chants are also an excellent way of putting across information. People who are hard-to-reach and might appreciate extended processing time can benefit if the information is conveyed in the form of music and song. If a performer speaks an instruction once, repeats it to make sure it's been heard and then repeats it again to make sure it's been understood, it is certainly not entertaining or poetic and it might even sound boring.

However, if music is added to the mix so that the instruction is rather more like a chant, or a groove it will sound like fun and can be performed like a dance. An example could be found in *Gorgeous* (2011) in which, at one point, we were asking the participants to put a handful of star anise in a mortar and grind it up with a pestle. I suppose we could have dealt with this by saying: *Right, now put the spice in the bowl and grind it up, like this.* Instead, we chanted as we ground our spice in our mortars.

> So now we put some in the pot,
> This pot that we've got.
> Let's put some in and grind it,
> Grind some in the pot.

So instead of reeling off verbal instructions to persuade the audience to do something, the process was turned into a game, a piece of carnival fun in which there was no right way and no wrong way but always many another way to join in.

I like to include promenades in my kind of Sensory Theatre, getting everyone to move around the space, usually to move the audience into the next scene. There's no better way to show that we are at a new point in the story than by physically moving to one. Getting an audience to move as a group can take time if you just tell them about it, but if instead chant something like:

> Stand up everybody
> No time to lose
> We're going dancing
> With our shoes
> We're dancing, dancing
> Can't be far
> Follow Mrs. Shoe in her car
> Hold your shoe up
> Hold it down
> Take your shoe and turn it
> Round and round
> Come on everybody
> No time to lose
> We're dancing, dancing with our shoes.
>
> Now stop everybody
> Can you tell
> What's that scent
> That we can smell?

From *There Was an Old Woman* (2014)

In this scene each participant has found an odd shoe and is following the Old Woman in her car to bring the shows to her house. When you have the audience in position for the next scene, you simply stop clapping and singing and everyone will stop with you. It helps if there is some kind of marker on the floor to follow. Tape on the floor is fine, but if you have lighting, you could light up a pathway with the stage lights or use battery torches to show the way.

Another possibility is to have the procession being led by a puppet or a cart or a pram, but I would always use music to indicate the stop and start moments.

The Deep Bass Voice

Over the years we have had a remarkable range of instruments in our productions from authentic barrel organ to orchestral marimba via musical saw, but when we focused for a time on work for people with the most complex disabilities including deafness, we started to realise that there was one sound that was essential. This was the sound of the human voice and particularly the human voice in its bass and baritone ranges.

For me the breakthrough came with *Hunky Dory* (1998) when we had two of the most rich and deep voices of all singing in the same show, the voices of Mark Foster and Sjaak van der Bent. Sjaak has a wonderful opera trained voice while the sound that Mark's voice makes is a phenomenon that makes rooms vibrate. It's not a hearing just a hearing experience, it's a multi-sensory experience, with vibrations you can hear and low, low vibrations you can feel.

In the somewhat unlikely event of your coming across Mark in the steaming heat of a hydropool, the thing to do, if you are invited to join him in the water, is to relax and float while he places both your feet on his chest. Then he will sing to you and the powerful vibrations will travel through the soles of your feet, and on up your legs and all along your spine until they reach the very top of your head and disperse around you. Your whole body will be energised.

It's akin to the experience of a didgeridoo massage, where you lie on your front while the didgeridoo is played as it is moved to and fro along your spine.

Oily Cart explored many ways to introduce deep, vibrating sounds starting with the bass clarinet played by Carolyn Hier in *Tickled Pink* (1996). In *Over the Moon* (1997) David Hallen played the tuba. Quite a few young people loved the sound so much that they tried to climb down the bell of the tuba. Steven Heath performed a 10-minute long solo on the didgeridoo in the water in *Pool Piece* (2008). In *Tube* (2013), George Panda and the cast played instruments created by Jamie Linwood, out of drainpipes and the coils used to shield underground cables, to produce some remarkable low-end sounds, while in *Light Show* (2015), Adam Storey delighted everyone with his virtuoso jazz on the bass. More recently in *Splish Splash* (2018), we were thrilled by the fabulously deep-toned floating instruments again designed and built by Jamie Linwood and played in the hydropool by George Panda.

We were particularly impressed by the cast who showed a lot of confidence and ability in dealing with pupils with a wide variety of needs. The best part of the music was the way the cast altered the music and singing in response to each individual pupil.

Paddock School, Wandsworth. *Moving Pictures* (2003)

25
The Problem With Narrative

Timeline for *Drum* 2010. Oily Cart. The show is broken down into seven scenes. Reading from left to right, it starts with Hello and ends with Goodbye.

Some years ago, I was part of a team working with Mencap, the UK charity for people with a learning disability. The plan was to make a DVD showing some of the cultural activities available to people with profound and multiple learning disabilities. This DVD included examples from Project Artworks in Hastings and Oily Cart in London. The title for the compilation chosen by Mencap was *In the Moment* because it was seen by Mencap as a valid description of how people categorised as having Profound and Multiple Learning Disabilities live their lives. They might be said to live them **in the moment**, neither raking over memories of the past, nor rushing to embrace what was yet to come.

Of course this is a generalisation but it might be one that benefits anyone wanting to make a piece of Sensory Theatre because it helps us to think about the work vertically rather than longitudinally. In a piece of conventional theatre, you move purposefully through a chain of events, each link reveals more about the characters involved and the situation that has developed. At the end there is a sense of closure.

But with a substantial number of people in the PMLD category, there are questions about memory. Some may well remember in a neurotypical way, but others may have poor short-term memory so that, for example, they may not remember at the end of a 45-minute performance what happened at the beginning.

DOI: 10.4324/9781003091288-27

In a piece of conventional theatre, the ability to remember what happens over the whole length of a performance is significant. Conventional theatre is often concerned with the development of character or with the unfolding of a story over time, how one event leads to another and then another and so on. But if you are not able to remember what a character was like at the start, how can you measure how they have changed over a period of time? Or if you cannot remember what the situation was like at the beginning, how can you assess how it has changed when you get to the end? The absence of memory also means that ideas of cause and effect don't have much meaning, so that you will not be able to anticipate how one thing leads to another or guess how a chain of events might turn out. If you have a conventional sort of memory and can remember what came before and anticipate what comes next, then you can be surprised or disappointed.

But if some of the people in your audience have these short-term memory issues, then you need to explore different approaches to storytelling than you would find in a traditional piece of theatre.

I believe that Sensory Theatre is about the performers finding ways to communicate with the participants and their companions. The performers sort through a selection of methods and the different languages made available to us by the sense until they find the ones that do the job of communicating with the participants.

In a Sensory Theatre piece, you do not necessarily build to a decisive conclusion at the end. You might arrive at a working relationship between one participant and a performer quite early but between another participant and another performer, it could happen somewhere later on. It can happen at any time and at any place in the scenario.

In any one of my Sensory Theatre productions, it is usually the musician who keeps an eye on the interactive moments between performer and participant during which there is a good deal of free improvisation. While the performer/participant/companion trios are improvising a section of the show together, it is the job of the musician to observe what is going on as objectively as possible and make a judgment as to when to move the show on. The musician must spot when the majority of the trios have established a good relationship and then play a music cue that will bring the ensemble back together and take everyone on to the next stage of the show. It can be a difficult call to make.

The Jazz Structure

I often refer to this structure where a firmly choreographed and rehearsed ensemble moment is followed by something much more improvised with the performers operating independently as a "jazz structure." In jazz music, you will often find a tight, rehearsed introduction, followed by improvised passages, finishing with the ensemble playing another final tight, rehearsed ending. (Yes, I know there are great many jazz tunes that are nothing like that but if you take this generalisation with a pinch of salt, it may prove useful.)

But maybe all this is getting too theoretical and what we should be looking for are some basic rules for building a Sensory Theatre piece. Here are a few such basic principles that I would not abandon without a good reason.

Episode One. The Welcoming Space: The Airlock

I would always stage the show in two adjacent spaces if at all possible, with the first space being a low-key, relaxing and welcoming area where we first meet our audience and introduce resources to prepare them for the show. This will often include material on iPads. I call this space the **Airlock.** It includes appropriate comfortable seating.

This space also serves as a place to move back into and relax if things get too much for a participant during the show or if a place is needed for medical procedures, toileting, changing and so forth, but also contributes to the narrative by allowing the participants to have an interactive experience of the characters and situation (via an iPad for example) and to handle props or costume items that will appear later in the show. Most of all the Airlock gives the participants an opportunity to relax and focus after their journey to the performance space.

Episode Two. Entering the World of the Show

The second space, which should be a short, convenient distant from the Airlock, if not actually adjacent, is where the main part of the performance takes place and should be wonderful. I think in terms of transforming the usual (school/theatre) space into something enchanting. I like to call these spaces **Wonderlands**.

The design theme for the show will determine the actual look of the piece, but it is a good idea to allow the participants to take a good look at the set from a distance and then approach it slowly. All the approaches into the main space should be well lit and the sound levels should be kept low.

If a participant is going to be alarmed, it is likely that this is where it will happen.

Episode Three. Make Yourselves at Home

Once the participants and their companions are in the space, they should be made comfortable in the seating and warmly welcomed.

Episode Four. First Sensory Event

From now on, the structure depends on the specific details of the production but this scene is basically a gentle prologue. A general principle would be to leave any scenes with low lighting or loud noises to later in the action when the audience will be feeling more confident.

Episodes Five to Seven. More Sensory Delights

Roughly three more scenes, each based around a different sensory element. The scenes not only focus on different senses but they have different characteristics. So a gentle introductory scene might be followed by an upbeat comical one. Next a quieter mood would calm everyone down before a very playful scene. And so on.

Leave using low lighting to the later episodes.

Episode Eight. Prepare to Say Goodbye. Name Song?

As we approach the end of the performance, it's good to build up the light levels so that we have a sense that the journey is ending and things are returning to normal. I would probably have a Name Song using the names of each of the participants as the only lyrics set to melodies that have occurred before in the show and so seem familiar on the so-called *overture principle*.

Episode Nine. Goodbye

A Goodbye Song is a good way to send a clear signal that the show has ended. The performers line up by the exit to wish everyone well as they leave the performance space.

26
The Performers in Sensory Theatre

Something in the Air 2009. Sprout played by Tina Koch from Ockham's Razor, hangs upside down from the rig. She is holding the first and smallest red ball ready to drop. Contact Theatre. Design: Claire de Loon and Jens Demant Cole.

Photo: Nick Mackay.

DOI: 10.4324/9781003091288-28

The quality of the performers is another key to the success of a Sensory Theatre piece.

More than the pre-show preparation of the audience, more than the script, the design, the music, the video, the choreography and the puppetry – because the performers are the ones who can **modify in a moment** what was made in the rehearsal room so that it meets the requirements of its audience.

To do this a performer, working one-to-one or one-to-two needs to be:

> **observant** – able to spot whether or not they are successfully involving the participant with whom they are working
> **creative** – able to improvise new material on the spot in order to engage the participant
> **playful** – and do all this is in a relaxed light-hearted way

This is a lot to ask and performers new to Sensory Theatre are often anxious about how to prepare themselves for the work. My best advice is that they should observe what the more experienced members of the cast do and try to emulate them. For this reason, I always try to put casts together in which there are at least two members with previous Sensory Theatre experience.

But of course, it is not so simple, especially when it comes to performances for people on the spectrum. Performers who are newcomers to Sensory Theatre ask questions like: *What do I do if the young person I am supposed to be working one-to-one with ignores me or runs away?*

Audiences of people on the spectrum will definitely be unpredictable. It is one of the real challenges of this form of theatre – but it is also one of the great joys when you see how a performance can free an individual to be more truly themselves. Each performance is *for* them, it is not something they have to fit into, there is no *right* way for the participant to do it, and no wrong way either.

Of course, in an audience of six, there will be six individuals, often bewildered by social convention, and each with their own agenda to pursue. So there can be an underlying anxiety. For people on the spectrum the world, especially as it is perceived by the scrambled senses sending signals to their brains, often creates fearfulness though this can be assuaged by proper preparation.

For example, before the participants come to the show, they should have experienced the Social Story and other preparatory material on video or online.

In addition, during the visit to the production each participant should have a companion, (teacher, carer or family member) who can answer their questions and reassure them if they become stressed. There is also the possibility of taking someone back to the airlock to give him or her the chance to chill in the relaxed atmosphere if that becomes necessary.

With the pre-show preparation, the work of the companions and the careful structuring of the show itself that gives its audiences the time and the extra cues to focus, the participants on the spectrum may well experience the show as more stable and less confusing than everyday reality. As the performance proceeds, they will start to relax and feel welcome in a carefully evoked ambiance that makes more sense than the world out there.

The worries of performers in Sensory Theatre do tend to focus on participants on the spectrum but I believe there is another hard-to-reach audience who may at times seem oblivious of the performers. These are the people said to have Profound and Multiple Learning Disabilities (PMLD). With these participants, there can be so many things between us blocking our mutual understanding. There may be sensory issues: they cannot see, they cannot hear. Or intellectual issues: they cannot remember, they cannot anticipate, or they cannot use verbal language. Or they have medical issues or they need to be fed via nasal or gastric tubes. I have frequently seen performances when the school nurse will be clearing air passages while the show goes on. Many in the PMLD category are under medication to keep them in a stable condition, but these same drugs may produce drowsiness and other side effects.

The situation is not improved by the fact that these people are usually defined and labeled in terms of what they cannot do rather than what they can. A person categorised as having Profound and Multiple Learning **Disabilities** is *disabled* by that definition which tells us that the person labeled is unable to do multiple things. The labeling pathologises the person. Sometimes because they are expected to fail, they are not given challenges, nor put in stimulating situations. And because they are not strong, often feeling weak and ill, they rarely protest and sometimes there is no one to advocate for them. In fact, there is so much to do in terms of feeding, changing, medicating, washing, all practical, all essential, that there is very little time left in the day to do anything more.

On your first contact with a PMLD audience, they may seem withdrawn, slumped in their wheelchairs, or not looking around, sometimes just looking at the floor. Apparently not engaging with the world around.

Yet give this audience an experience that it is relevant to them, like a ride on the bed of a trampoline, a truly kinaesthetic experience, and everything changes. If you are on the trampoline with them, close to them where they can see you better, hear you better, then you may find your way into a dialogue with them. But this is not usually a dialogue of spoken words. You are listening to their breathing, reacting to their facial expressions and their body language. Perhaps this is complemented by some Makaton or other signing and suggestions from the companion at the trampoline side. Then you offer a sound, a gesture or a change of pace or rhythm on the trampoline. You are alert for any response. Sometimes there is nothing. Sometimes the response is so subtle that it is only noticed by the companion.

> *Look at how he's tracking.*
> Or
> *She's very relaxed.* Sometimes you only find out what happened from the school or the family after the performance has ended.
> *Did you see how he gave you eye contact?*
> *Is that unusual?*
> *Oh yes.*

Given patience, given time, that person you met at the beginning, so slumped, so disengaged, has revealed a different side of themselves thanks to the dialogue the two of you developed. Often it is a development that has been witnessed by a teacher or family member who was close to that trampoline, and it is in that way that a successful method of engaging with a participant can be extrapolated from the show and incorporated into their home or school life.

Differences in Approach to Autism Spectrum Groups

Curiously although there are strong parallels in the ways that both the PMLD audience and the autism spectrum groups may be approached, there is one striking difference.

For a complex of sensory and cognitive reasons, many young people categorised as PMLD often have difficulties focusing on the world and the people around them. I find it works best to approach a PMLD participant in a very direct way, approaching them from in front and at their eye level, keeping everything as clear as possible. It is better not to rely on verbal language but supporting yourself with the use of song, sensory props and playfulness.

A More Oblique Approach to People on the Spectrum

On the other hand, a much less direct approach may be more successful for a participant on the autism spectrum. Many of those on the spectrum can it find it challenging to have someone, especially someone with whom they are not familiar, come up to them, look them in the eye and try to engage them in conversation. Demanding a response is rarely successful.

In my experience, it is generally more productive if you approach someone on the spectrum while casually playing with a sensory prop, for example a ball or a slinky, and engage his or her interest by displaying *your* interest in the prop. If the participant shows some interest, then you might offer the prop to them to play with, or simply put it on the floor near them. In other words, you gain the interest of the person on the spectrum, not by directly demanding it of them but by demonstrating just how interesting the object you are playing with can be.

A more common issue occurs when a companion briefs that *their* young participant reacts badly to loud noises, or meeting strangers, or to dimming the lights, or other similar reactions. Sometimes the warnings turn out to be justified, but quite often, the predicted reactions do not materialise.

I believe this happens because the companions in this case are forecasting what would happen in normal circumstances in the school or in the home. But a Sensory Theatre performance is such an unusual event that anyone who has not experienced one will find the outcome hard to predict. Time and time again, I have been told both by teachers and by family members just how wonderfully surprised they have been by the reactions of the participants that they have observed.

Other Sensory Theatre Audiences

Two to Five Year Olds

I am sure that there are another hundred audiences – at least – for Sensory Theatre but there are only two of them, after PMLD and those on the autism spectrum, with whom I have had substantial experience: children under two and children aged from two to five. I discussed some of the actual shows with which I have been involved with these audiences in Part One of this book. But I should like to write here about these audiences from a performer's point of view.

I believe that most difficulties in performing for these age groups stem from an expectation that these very young people will behave as a mini-adult audience; that they will sit in rows, stay in their seats and not want to talk and interact with the performers (and I am not talking here about getting all the participants to yell *behind you*).

But young people in the two to five year age range often get restive if they are asked to sit still and be quiet. On the other hand, they can become over-excited or overwhelmed by the experience of being in the crowd in a large theatre space (I would say anything over 50–80 seats). With this sort of age range, I am not campaigning for the six-strong audiences that I prefer for the PMLD and autism spectrum groups. It would be very interesting to do some development work with the two to five year olds in such small groups but to avoid the problems of overwhelming or overexciting, I believe an audience of 50 or so including adults is just about right. This size of audience brings all the participants close to the stage action where everyone can see and hear. It also means that there can be many more opportunities for the participants to move around and explore the show in a kinaesthetic way and that there are ways in which the senses of smell, touch and taste can also be readily incorporated; processing under arches of real pine branches or crunching through shallow boxes of forest bark when going into a woodland scene, for example.

The performer in this form of Sensory Theatre has to be alert for any suggestion from the audience. Preferably you should act on any suggestion from a participant, or give a good reason why not, even if it is of the *That's a good idea too. But let us just try out her idea first* – variety. It's also often necessary to pay extra attention to the younger shyer children so that the more confident, older children do not monopolise the process.

The Under-Twos Audience

This audience is almost always made up of parent/child pairs. I find that 15 adults with 15 children makes for a workable group. It does not have to be mother and child or father and child, but children of this age need to be absolutely sure of that adult's support.

It follows that the performer must take great care that all the adults feel included, entertained and an essential part of the action.

Children below the age of two are unlikely to make many verbal suggestions but you can rely on them moving everywhere in the performance space and playfully exploring anything that takes their interest. If that interferes with your choreography, then you will just have to change your choreography. The performers are not there to perform a rehearsed and perfected theatre piece. Rather you are in a wonderland filled with a mass of multisensory material to inspire **enhanced play** with the adults and the very young children.

The Strengths of a Sensory Theatre Performer

Although a performer in this area of theatre faces many challenges, if you have been properly prepared, you will be able to handle them.

First you are part of a team that has prepared and rehearsed what they are going to do. This team is presenting a multi-faceted theatre piece in which everything, the story, the music, the design, the lights, the perfumes, the textures, the tastes, the temperatures, the visceral, the kinaesthetic, has been blended to ensure that there will be enough varieties of language and of sensory events to ensure there are plenty of opportunities to engage the hard-to-reach.

Second you will have worked on a character that is clearly delineated and the participants should have had plenty of processing time beforehand using the preparation material, for example the Sensory Social Story. It helps if each character has a distinctive silhouette, texture and a specific odour, on a scented wristband for example. The characters do need names if only for the companions to point them out to the participants, but my aim would always be for the characters to be identifiable even if the participant can neither see nor hear them.

Building a Character Based on an Object

As mentioned earlier in this chapter, when it comes to performing to participants on the spectrum, I believe it is very useful to have some sort of prop with which you can begin to play together. Let us call it a **Sensory Prop**. Examples of such props could be a folding hand fan, a bubble blower or a flashlight.

Take the example of the flashlight. If you were meeting a participant for the first time in the airlock, say, you should be playing with your light in a way that really interests you. Exploring its possibilities. Making shadows. Lighting up dark spaces. Flashing the light in mirrors.

It's important not get too close or give eye contact to the participant at this stage. The idea is that you will be so focused on your object that you will attract his or her interest. It's excellent if he or she makes the first move. But failing that you could roll the light across the floor to them.

In many of my productions the name of this prop would be given to the character you are playing. It also becomes **the Object of Reference** for your character. The first words your character might say are: *Hello, I'm Flashlight. They call me that because I like to play with my flashlight. I play with it like this, and that, and this. I'm Flashlight.*

Later in the performance, you can reintroduce the light to use as a spotlight whenever a new prop is introduced into the show.

Playfulness is an essential component of any character, and you will need to be playful and seek out fresh qualities in anything you use in the performance. How many things can a new prop do? Can it make a sound? Is it interesting to touch? Can it move in a different way? If you are intensely curious about something, then it will draw the interest of the participants too.

But this should not get too serious. It should be playful – and fun.

Fun and funny are key words in Sensory Theatre. Of course, there can be serious themes and moments of beauty and wonder in our work. But practically all audiences respond well to the moments when we can all relax, lower our guard, forget about the proprieties and be silly. As Richard Burbage, a highly experienced teacher of PMLD classes wrote:

> Don't be afraid to act silly. Pupils can love it when things go wrong, and they are aware a different result should have occurred.

He would demonstrate by dropping a pile of papers on the floor with no damage done at all. But Richard would act up his distress at the *accident*, talking to his students as he shuffled the papers and dropping half of them again.

> Look what I've done, Carol. Aren't I a silly so and so?

And the more that he complained and gesticulated (without seeming in the least truly upset), the more his pupils, who knew him, would laugh. I believe that it is significant that his pupils knew him because then they would be able to compare the Richard who was really upset with the Richard who was acting upset.

But why would anyone be amused by Richard play-acting upset? My theory is that in that PMLD classroom, the teacher (in this case, Richard) is the real authority figure albeit one who is gentle and helpful, not at all threatening. He is the one who tells the pupils, and, to some extent, the teaching assistants what needs to be done and decides if things have been done well or not so well.

Normally anyone in that class would take Richard seriously but when he starts play-acting, then he is not being serious, he is playing around, having a laugh – and so we can all relax.

This is all based on my belief that PMLD people for all their supposed disabilities, are often rather good at judging the tone of other people and especially whether they are being playful or not. If you were dependent in so many ways on other people, rather as any participant classified PMLD would be, it would certainly benefit you to be aware of your caretakers' changing moods.

A PMLD person is dependent on many other people, not just their teachers and their teaching assistants. There are their families, mothers, fathers, siblings and quite frequently, foster families. Medical personnel too are often a continuing presence. All are people who are dedicated to helping you, but who are, in the process, telling you what to do. How you should do this, but never do that.

But how must it feel if you find yourself as a participant in a Sensory Theatre performance? The performers are dressed in a different way to the adults in your families or in your schools. They feel different, smell different, move differently and do not seem to tell you to do anything much. It's more that they want to play with you and have fun and show you that the world is full of possibilities.

But it also feels that things move at a different speed in this Sensory Theatre world. You have more time to think about what is going on. And things repeat so that you get another chance to figure things out. Sometimes you'll hear something – running water for example. Your teacher sitting beside you will say, *It's water.* Maybe she'll sign it in Makaton. After that there's a video of water up on a video screen and then you can actually feel the water running over your fingers.

But in fact, all this can go off in lots of different directions because the performers are looking for ways in which to hand over the lead to the participants. This is more likely to happen with the neurotypical under-fives and under-twos, but it does happen often enough with participants who are on the spectrum and, with a little more mediation from the adult companions, with people classified as PMLD.

I believe that the participants in our Sensory Theatre audiences gradually realise that the performers who have set up this wonderland in their school hall or theatre have a very different agenda to the adults with whom they usually interact. Most adults want them to be healthy, nourished, able to communicate, but the Sensory Theatre company is not trying to do anything so practical and useful. They just want to explore the world to discover things that are wonderful, beautiful, funny and benign. It's about sharing gratuitous pleasure with our audiences. It's not like real life, thank goodness. It's like Richard when he's play-acting, and we can all laugh.

I suppose some might question if this approach gives a bad example to young people. But I believe that most young people will recognise this as a holiday, a brief interval when the hall is transformed into a wonderland and people dress up for the carnival. Next day, next week, life with return to normal, all the set and all the costumes, lights, smells and visions will have gone away for a while.

So as a Sensory Theatre performer, you have a very privileged status. You are just expected to make the world seem a better place so that the audiences with whom you are playing turn outward to embrace it. What a brilliant job!

What Makes a Good Sensory Theatre Performer?

I believe you have to be curious about minds that think very differently than your own. Do you want to engage with people who are very young or old or on the spectrum or have other complex conditions?

You need to be perceptive and able to spot the subtle signs that someone is responding to you.

You need to be inventive, able to communicate in an instant in numerous different languages, only one or two of them verbal.

You need to explain things to teachers and/or family in clear concise language. In a way, it is the opposite of dramatising things. It is making things as clear as possible.

You need to like flying by the seat of your pants. Sensory Theatre can be very unnerving theatre. You have to love not knowing what's going to happen next. You have to be able to let go and allow the audience to take the lead.

It's good if you can sing, even better if you also play a musical instrument.

And better yet, if you are some other kind of an artist as well as a performer: like a puppeteer or an aerialist, a writer or a director, a video artist or a dancer or even a trampolinist. I have worked with all of them.

And you have to be funny, playful and carry the spirit of misrule and carnival with you wherever you go.

What Not to Do as a Sensory Theatre Performer

Once you have your silhouette, your texture, your perfumed wristband, your sensory prop and your sense of fun all in place, you are pretty well ready to meet your audience.

There should be built-in pauses, moments of quiet and stillness to allow the audience time to process all that has been happening in a performance. The performer should do his/her utmost to respect these pauses. There is a tendency with performers under pressure (the kind of pressure you often get in a performance) to keep busy, adding and creating, because they are afraid that they are going to lose the audience. Do not give in to the temptation. **Respect the pause.** Preserve these still moments for processing.

But while you preserve the pauses, you also need to avoid the **false notes.** An example of a false note in a hydropool show would be when in the silence that follows after a shower of glowing water has poured from a silver bowl into the pool, a performer casually plonks the bowl back on the poolside tiles with a great clatter. The pause, the concentration has been shattered and we struggle to rebuild it. That's a false note.

And finally, there are two or three more things to be careful about:

Please, always approach a participant from the front or the side so they can see you coming. It will give some participants a bit of a shock if you suddenly pop up from the side or from behind them.

And do not jump up with a loud sound from behind cover. On the whole Sensory Theatre audiences do not enjoy shocks. Give them a chance to get used to you. Emerge slowly and give them plenty of time to see you.

If it is clear that you are alarming someone in the audience, the best thing to do is to back away and behave in a shy and tentative way yourself.

Try not to tower over the people in your audience. If a participant is sitting in a wheelchair, on a chair or on a beanbag and you are standing close to them, you will be towering over them and sounding remote. Try to work with the participants on their level in every sense of that word.

27
Puppets and Pixels

Ring A Ding Ding 2011 Oily Cart. Alice (Alicia McKenzie) with the milk float that goes round and round. Driving the float is a puppet milkman with a puppet Alice next to him. Design: Claire de Loon.

Photo: Jack Knowles.

DOI: 10.4324/9781003091288-29

Not all the characters in my kind of Sensory Theatre are played by people. When Max Reinhardt and I started performing together, many of our early shows featured puppets. Puppets make it possible to have scores of different characters in an infinite range of sizes and guises. Puppets are very useful to represent children in a show rather than have adults playing the roles. Several early shows featured puppet versions of performers, thereby playing with the notion of scale. Puppets are great because they work tirelessly and live in a suitcase.

Another advantage of being able put a sizeable crowd of puppets onstage is that a member of the audience can get right up close to and even hold their own puppet character. This is particularly valuable in Sensory Theatre. In *How Long Is a Piece of String?* (2008), every child had a string baby to hold and in *Knock Knock! Who's There?* (2000), everyone sang a lullaby to their own little potato as they rocked them to sleep.

Puppets found their way into the first Oily Cart piece for Severe Learning Disability Schools, *Box of Socks* (1988). The title of the show was prompted by a donation of many odd socks from the Sock Shop and some of those socks became the Sock Puppets from Space. There were four Space Babies, each with a different colour and texture. They were not particularly successful at engaging the participants. Rather they seemed to come between the participants and the silly performers. One distinct puppet character or a single clear shadow silhouette proved more effective. The Space Babies made me think hard about the use of puppetry in theatre for people with complex disabilities. Looking at the list of shows, it is noticeable that while I remained at Oily Cart, I was still making productions for people with severe learning disabilities at the rate of more than one each year, but few of them used conventional puppet characters.

In theory, puppets should be very useful for communicating with people on the autism spectrum. A puppet will most often have an unchanging expression that is easy to interpret and people on the spectrum are supposed to have difficulty interpreting complex human expressions. *Happy face* and *sad face* might be OK, but *doubtful* or *ironic* faces are said by some to be confusing. The reason often given for the popularity of Thomas the Tank Engine in the autistic spectrum (ASC) community, is that Thomas and his friends each have an unchanging expression. They are popular with that community just because they are easy to understand.

Certainly, when we asked young people on the spectrum to bring their favourite thing with them to *Blue* (2006), an early show for young people on the spectrum, a great many Thomas toys and DVDs were chosen by the participants.

I tried again more recently in *Light Show* (2015) with the puppet character, Baz, who appeared in the autistic spectrum version of the show. Baz was a child-sized puppet operated by Plane (at first played by Ellie Griffiths and later by Katherine Vernez). The puppet was controlled with one hand to the back of his head and the other to the back of his hand. Baz had long cuddly arms that were heavily weighted. His arms could be joined together by Velcro pads so that he could give you a good hug around the neck. We were hoping that this would appeal to some young people on the spectrum who enjoyed deep pressure.

All the characters in this show had various papery qualities. They had names of paper objects, such as Fan, Plane and Hat. They each had a sensory prop to go with their character, so Fan had a paper fan, Plane played a lot with paper planes and so forth. Baz himself was named after the up-market writing paper, Basildon Bond. His hat was a paper cone which some of the participants greatly enjoyed knocking off his head to reveal a hairstyle made up of paper strips.

At times, Baz, the three-dimensional puppet, appeared as a black shadow puppet, back-projected on to a shadow screen via an Overhead Projector.

Baz worked quite well in the preamble to the performance, welcoming the young people as they came into the hall or theatre. Some would like to sit beside him and seemed to enjoy his hugs, but I came to the conclusion that maybe it was his fixed, unvarying character that was actually against him building a relationship with the participants.

The strength of a performer in these circumstances is that he or she could present a different personality to each one of the participants. If Plane found that one participant was responding well to a boisterous Baz, then she could develop that side of the character when playing with that participant. If she found that a shy, quiet Baz was working better for another participant then that was the side she might work on for the retiring child.

Sensory Theatre, at its core, is about the ability of the performer to adapt their performance until they engage with participants who may be very different to one another. For me it is this protean quality of the human performer that, if I have to choose, outweighs the fixed focus of the puppet.

Object Theatre

In my Sensory Theatre work I have found that something closer to Object Theatre is more likely to engage than puppets. Objects of Reference, like a flashlight, a fan, a slinky or a ball could interest, even fascinate, while a more fully fledged character like a puppet, something with a face and a voice and a character, could be less interesting. An object is an excellent place to start to build a Sensory Theatre character who then becomes the very embodiment of their Object of Reference.

There was a moment in *Something in the Air* (2009) that was very much about the way commonplace objects in motion had a great effect on the participants. At the start of Scene Three, Sprout, played by Tina Koch, was spotlighted up in the rig. She was dressed in red and wearing a bungee harness. She hung upside down with one outstretched arm holding a small red ball. (See the image of Tina in Chapter 26.) After a very long freeze, she dropped the ball. When the ball hit the stage below, it bounced for quite a long time. The chair-drivers who controlled the height and movement of the chairs were asked to pick up the ball only when it had finally and absolutely stopped bouncing. Then they were to dance around throwing the ball as music played, all watched from high up in the chairs by the participants with their companions.

When the music stopped, there was a second long pause and then Tina dropped a red ball the size of a football. This one bounced higher and longer and more noisily. Again, the direction to the chair-drivers was to wait until the ball was absolutely still and only then dance around with it until the music stopped and there was a third pause.

Then Tina produced a huge red gym ball and dropped it. This bounced very noisily, and it seemed as if it would never stop. Just when the ball seemed to be still, and a chair-driver approached, it would roll again. And again. And again. Until at last, the chair-drivers were dancing with the ball. By now it seemed that everyone had worked out the pattern. All eyes were turned to where Tina was sitting on the rig.

Finally, there were no more balls, so Tina launched herself into space and bounced as high and as long as any of the balls. The audience was absolutely chortling. At this point, the chair-drivers started to bounce the participants up and down along with Tina. It was so exhilarating!

I loved this because it was a joke that did not rely on words, a joke about how objects move and make sounds and so I would say it could be appreciated by an audience drawn from a wide range of abilities.

Baby Drum 2010 Oily Cart. Shadow puppet design for action song. Design: Claire de Loon.

Shadow Puppets

So although I turned away from conventional puppetry in the work for people with complex disabilities, it certainly remained as a core component in the theatre for Under-Twos and Under-Fives.

In the mid-eighties, another type of puppet was added to the repertoire.

In 1985, Claire de Loon and I visited China in pursuit of traditional Chinese Opera. But it was a low-key performance in a teahouse in a suburb of Shanghai that was to make a big impression on our own work.

The backstage was lit by a single large light bulb. That was the only light used during the entire performance. The musician began to play, the first of the translucent multi-coloured leather puppets faded up into view on the screen. That first character was a general. Another general soon joined him. The story unfolded in a way that we had seen before in various Chinese operas. It started off slowly with just one or two characters, little action, plenty of singing but then built and built to battle scenes or court scenes with scores of characters.

But what I actually brought back with me from that trip to China was that I would be able to include shadow puppetry in my work. Before Shanghai, I had thought a perfect blackout was needed, but then I saw that single naked 150 watt bulb in the teahouse where the walls leaked light from numerous openings.

I have used coloured shadow puppets in numerous productions, both for the Under-Fives and for those with complex needs. In the whole school productions *Pleasuredome* (1989) and *Colour Me, Colour You* (1990), coloured shadow puppets were used in various scenes. In *Pleasuredome*, the theme was games and sport. The puppets represented various games, such as snooker. At the time, snooker was popular on the TV and older students followed it with enthusiasm. In *Colour Me, Colour You*, the shadow puppets could be quickly switched from say, an outline of an animal with no colour to the same animal coloured in.

Later in 2000, we mounted *Dreams and Secrets*, a hydropool show. It was inspired by a trip to an hamam in Turkey. In the introductory Dry Area section, we mounted a dreamy Turkish-style coloured shadow puppet show accompanied by live music on the violin. Some of the participants reacted in a very positive way to the puppets while the majority responded to the other sensory delights such as brush and hand massage and the beautiful music.

Overhead Projectors

My interest in shadow puppetry and its light sources and blackouts led Claire de Loon to suggest that we consider the use of overhead projectors in *A Bit Missing* (1993), a production for Under-Fives that was also notable for basing a performance around a jigsaw. The pieces of this jigsaw were sent to the venues (mostly schools) days before the company arrived. The jigsaw could be made beforehand to introduce the performers and the story to our young audience, except that there was a problem: there was one bit missing. Of course the show ended with the missing piece being produced and handed over to the school to finish the puzzle.

The story was told with the use of two overhead projectors (OHPs) back-projecting onto one screen, but with a good deal of live action taking place in front and to the sides. Moving coloured scenery was projected from one OHP while silhouettes of the characters performed on the other OHP. Together they told a fast moving story of the caretaker on his bicycle chasing the robot through the town into the countryside. There were many misadventures and discoveries along the way.

The OHPs were controlled by dimmers, so that smooth transitions between scenes were possible. Just fade down OHP One as you fade up OHP Two. It became a fluent way of working that we repeated over several productions. Actually, in that first OHP production, A Bit Missing, it was far from straightforward and it was only thanks to the extraordinary patience and the ingenuity of Geoff Bowyer and Johnny Quick, the OHP puppeteers and live performers, along with Carol Walton as live performer and musician, that it came right in end.

The OHP scenes in A Bit Missing told an elaborate story but I have found that they are also invaluable to show bold, iconic images as part of shows for young people with complex disabilities. The projector excels in showing a very simple moving silhouette of such objects as a feather or a fan. The image on screen reinforces the introduction and exploration of three-dimensional objects while a cutout figure or a performer's silhouette projected can be very effective as an illustration of the movements in a song. Raheem can nod his head. Everybody! Nod your head like Raheem.

Use of Video

The logical next step is to introduce characters on live or recorded video into the productions. But that is for the future.

I have, however, frequently used projected video as part of the scenery. In Conference of the Birds (2004) and Blue (2006), short video clips were incorporated into the structure that introduced each new sensory element. In Blue (2006) video of fans, shakers, water and the night sky showed what was coming next, while the climax of this show featuring vintage black and white film of a steam train arriving, coupled with clouds of real smoke, brought cheers from the participants.

In Mr. and Mrs. Moon (2013) for under-fives, the scene moved from a beach to the moon and back. This imaginative journey was accompanied by beautiful video images created by Paul Williams. In The Bounce (2014) the bouncing on the trampolines was accentuated by video of balls dancing in time with the music.

I have used live video very often during the "Name Song" section that comes at the end of many productions for people on the spectrum or with PMLD. A large image of each participant is projected onto a screen as the performers sing their name.

Of course performers playing in character appear in all the preparatory videos that introduce many of the shows for people on the spectrum or classified as PMLD. Who knows what will happen in the future but I have come to feel that live theatre with the stage populated by human actors is an important alternative to the digital media that is more and more dominant in contemporary society – especially in this time of Covid. Surely one of the key features in Sensory Theatre is that it comes to its audience via several senses. It should be multi-sensory and should not restrict itself to the manipulation of pixels on a screen or the vibrations of speaker cones. For the moment at least, the sound coming from a vibrating double bass will always be more richly complex than anything coming out of the biggest bass bin and the three-dimensional stage picture created by the colours, the textures and the smells will offer far more sensory pathways to be taken than the widest flat screen television.

28
Auditions

Mirror Mirror 2016 Oily Cart. Sponge played by Fatima Niemogha. Design: Claire de Loon. Photo: Neal Houghton.

DOI: 10.4324/9781003091288-30

If you want to build a Sensory Theatre company, sooner or later you will need to audition to find a performer who will have the personality and the talent to fit right in with the rest of your team. It is not easy and I suppose that not all the auditions I have run have been successful in picking the perfect performer for the job, but it has worked often enough to let me persuade myself that I know what I am doing.

The Adverts

Nowadays most of the advertising that a performer is needed happens on-line. If I had anything to do with it, I would include details of the show and ask anyone qualified and interested to send me their CV, photo, Spotlight entry and anything else online and, above all, a covering letter saying why they wanted to work on this particular production and with this particular audience.

Usually there was a big response from agents sending the details of all their clients but missing out the covering letter altogether. But for me, the personal covering letter was the most important thing because this would tell me that the performer had really thought about the project and, presumably, come to the conclusion that it was not just another gig and they really had something to offer.

The Auditioners

Mostly I auditioned with Max Reinhardt, Max dealing with the music side while I took care of script and direction but we very much auditioned as a team.

If someone played an instrument, we generally started with that. If they wanted to play from a prepared piece from sheet music that was fine but we would always want to see how well they could improvise.

The ability to play, to interact with participants is essential in any Sensory Theatre performer and a common audition feature for Max and me was where we asked the performer to first tell us, as straightforwardly as possible, about their journey from home to the audition space. It is curious but for some people, clearly describing the journey seemed to be the most difficult part. But in a Sensory Theatre show, performers often need to explain things simply and clearly.

The second part of this exercise was to do the story of the journey from home as a song or a rap or both.

What the performer was asked to do next depended a good deal on what they would have to do in the production. For example, they might be asked to sing the story of the journey in the style of an West End musical, or as if they were a dog, or as though the whole event was a beautiful dream – or a nightmare.

Next up, we checked out their movement skills, asking the performer to improvise contrasting moves across the floor to a rhythm track.

After that, we would commonly place a variety of objects on a table, asking the performer to choose two or three of them and then give each of their choices some ways of moving plus a voice or a sound effect. When we had played a little with those ideas on and around the tabletop, we would then ask the performer to add a haptic quality, something that could be felt, to the other qualities of the object characters. *Could this one brush your arm and hand? Or What if that one dances on your back? Would that be like a back massage?* I would give them directions relating to **close-up choreography** to see how they took direction. Close-up choreography is my term for being aware of every movement when performing in a one-to-one situation where the focus is on the face and the hands. Up close, every gesture and expression is important and should be given careful consideration to make the most impact.

One of our most enjoyable audition exercises was called *The Jam Sandwich*. We would place a sliced loaf, a pot of jam, some margarine, a spoon, a knife and a plate on the table. Then we would ask the performer to use these ingredients to show how to make a jam sandwich to someone who had never done such a thing before. After that was completed, we asked them to characterise some of the individual items and finally to re-enact the sandwich making scene in the style of – say – *The Phantom of the Opera* or a ballet. This exercise and the description of the journey explored the performer's ability to be both factual and fantastic. Could they be clear and imaginative and funny?

One of the things I always looked out for when auditioning was how well the performer would fit in with the rest of the touring team. After all, touring is stressful. The company are often away from home, sometimes for weeks at a time. The working day is long, quite often starting at 7.00 in the morning and going on till 6.00 at night and in an Oily Cart Sensory Theatre show everyone was likely to be involved in the fit-ups and the strikes. Everyone had to pull his or her weight and if one of the team regularly turned up late or went missing when it was time to load the van then it could affect company morale. I certainly thought that it was important to point these things out at the audition and to stress how interdependent we all were on the road.

Afterwards, it was simply a question of asking the performer if they had any questions and had they enjoyed themselves during the audition.

29
Rehearsals and Rehearsal Spaces

Once the cast and crew has been assembled, the new show must be devised and rehearsed. In recent years (pre-2019), an Oily Cart production would usually begin with a basic scenario, a design, some of the music and lyrics plus four to five weeks to rehearse. There would always be plenty of time for the performers to develop character, their method of relating to the audience and several opportunities to bring in experts to develop specialist skills in the company: for example, in hand massage or communicating via Makaton.

In the first two or three weeks of the rehearsals, the morning of each day was usually occupied with music and choreography, while the afternoon was reserved for character work, telling the story and interacting with an audience. By the third week it was usually possible to run a scratch version of the whole production.

But the most important function of Oily rehearsals was for the people making the show to get to know the people (under-fives, PMLD, on the spectrum, or under-twos) who would be the participants. The plan was always to spend some of the rehearsal period working in a relevant setting, usually a school or nursery, meeting the young people and the staff, getting to know them while refining the content of the new show. In several cases where we had built up a good relationship with a school, they would invite us to spend several weeks there. For example, all the rehearsals for *Something in the Air* (2009) took place at Michael Tippett School in Lambeth.

Since 1993, Oily Cart has had the closest relationship of all with Smallwood School in Wandsworth. The Oily Cart office, rehearsal room, wardrobe and construction workshop are all located in their playground. The fact that all the main departments of the theatre company were so close together ensured excellent internal communications, especially important when a new show was being created. A decision made in the rehearsal room in the morning

DOI: 10.4324/9781003091288-31

could be discussed with the design department over lunch and the financial and logistical implications talked through with the admin team at the end of the day. This made for a company that was co-ordinated and light on its feet.

Having a resident theatre company is also a significant asset for a school because the casts and the technicians can offer a range of skills from help with lighting and sound, props and costumes for school events, through to help with dance, puppeteering and video skills.

On several occasions, the Oily Cart has also worked with the whole of Smallwood school to create major events to which all the families and local community were invited. When the school celebrated its centenary, the company joined with the school to create a parade with a marching band and giant puppets three times life-size, followed by a fireworks display. When there was a general election, we asked the teachers and children to invent their own political parties, formulate their programme, shoot their election videos, and conduct their own hustings and voting procedures. The actual Mayor of Wandsworth supervised the voting and acted as our returning officer. The *Sweetie Party* won but the party that wanted to flood the whole school and turn it into an aqua theme-park was a close runner up. In 2012, when London was hosting the Olympic Games, Smallwood School and the Oily Cart went one better and staged the Galactic Games that involved teams from different planetary systems competing in games unknown to mere earthlings but vastly popular in outer space. The children, families and even some of the staff had a great time.

But in the final analysis it is the theatre company that gets the best of these deals, especially if that company is resident in a school like Smallwood which is so much more than a primary school. It has a Children's Centre on the premises that works with the families and the very early years, including ante-natal help and there is also a nursery where the children can start once they are past their third birthday. The school itself contains children from four to eleven, but, most relevantly for the Oily Cart, it also has a Language Unit with up to 40 children, at any one time, who are being assessed regarding speech, language and communication issues. These young people are educated sometimes in small specialist classes and sometimes back in the larger mainstream classes, with children of their own age.

During my time as artistic director of Oily Cart, we were creating theatre mostly for the children in the nursery, foundation stage (two to fives) and young people possibly on the spectrum, like the children in the Language Unit. Smallwood was an idea place to be located, to research, consult with families and carers, try out material for these three groups and invite them to several previews and get their feedback. I often found the feedback from the Smallwood pupils' teachers and parents particularly useful because they knew the company very well. Seeing us around the school for much of the year, they had the confidence to speak to us frankly with no beating about the bush.

30

Shows That Start Before They Begin – Preparation

An Introduction for Carers

THE BOUNCE
An Oily Cart production developed with support from Ockham's Razor

The Bounce 2014. An Introduction for Carers. A guide to all aspects of a trampoline show including important health and safety issues. Written by Amanda Webb. Graphic design: Paloma Hernández Santos.

DOI: 10.4324/9781003091288-32

Preparation time is of paramount importance in Sensory Theatre. Given the complexities of engaging hard-to-reach participants, the more processing time we have at our disposal, the more chance we have of dissolving the barriers between us.

When we made the production *Something in the Air* (2009) with the magnificent Ockham's Razor, we could only get together intermittently to rehearse. The whole rehearsal process lasted for ten months with gaps of several weeks between sessions.

We rehearsed in the main hall of Michael Tippett School (a Special School in Lambeth). I will always be grateful to Jan Stogden (the then Head) for allowing us to come on this very irregular schedule that must have meant serious interruptions to the school's routines. Actually, Jan often said that several of her students really enjoyed it when they saw the riggers, a piratical-looking bunch, putting up the massive structure on which the Ockham's and eventually the whole audience would fly.

On the first day of the first rehearsal, a teaching assistant, let us call her, Maria, came to me with a young man (let us call him Aldo). Aldo liked to roam, and Maria's job was to roam along with him. When she found out more about the show, she said that Aldo would love it. He loved funfairs and theme park rides and the whole aim of *Something in the Air* was to take its participants swinging, bouncing and twirling through the air in the company of the Ockham's performers.

When we had finally rigged up one of the flying seats, I invited Aldo to have a go, but he turned down the offer and sat himself down beside me to watch the riggers instead. This became a pattern that repeated itself over and over. Each time we came in to rehearse, Aldo and his tireless TA would join us. Each time Maria thought he was ready to be winched up, but Aldo didn't agree, though now and again he would suggest: *You do it, Tim. You do it.*

Ten months went by. Ten months of a week's rehearsal here, two weeks there, until the show was ready to open. As we were preparing to dismantle the set, in came Aldo and Maria. *He's ready now*, said Maria. Aldo clambered into one of the seats and we gave him a short preview. He loved it and, of course, it took forever to get him out of the seat afterwards.

It had taken Aldo a long time to complete the processing that he needed to fly through the air in the show. It took many more participants a lot less time, but maybe Aldo knew what he was doing. When we first met, perhaps he could sense that we were insecure, that we were working things out. Ten months later, we were confident, and he had seen for himself that we had practiced everything over and over again. There was nothing left to be anxious about.

Only Aldo has ever received this much preparation but the effect it had on him confirms my thinking that when it comes to preparation for hard-to-reach audiences, the longer the better.

At Oily Cart, we had prepared teachers' packs from our earliest times. For *Up on the Roof* (1986), Claire de Loon and Frances Scott produced an extensive set of worksheets filled with suggested activities for the teachers to use building on the anticipation and inspiration of the performance.

The next step was to make ancillary material to prepare the participants for performance. In the first half of the 1990s about half of my output was for young people from three to five years old and all of it was original writing with not an adaptation of a book or a fairy tale in sight. But by this time, I was the father of two and I knew very well that what very young children really like is to have a story read to them while they look at the pictures and then have it read again and again. How could I introduce original material that would be familiar to its young audience?

The Big Books

The solution was a series of large format storybooks, illustrations by John Morris at first, then by Claire de Loon, telling the story of the show. The Big Books were sent to the Nursery and Reception classes of the school where we were to perform at least two weeks before the actual visit. Then at Story Time, the teacher would read the story and the children would, we hope, shout: *Again! Again!*

I pursued this angle for four shows: *Greenfingers* (1992), *A Peck of Pickled Pepper* (1994), *Perfect Present* (1995) and *The Roly Poly Pudding* (1996). We would have liked to continue to produce the Big Books, but we had to prioritise our time elsewhere. We had to content ourselves with the teachers' packs and different shows invited other initiatives. For *A Bit Missing* (1993), we sent a jigsaw puzzle with one piece missing. For *Pass the Parcel* (1998), the schools received a parcel that would be central to a series of scenes based on party games that moved the show along.

Introductions for Carers

Claire de Loon created an introductory teachers' pack for all the SEND shows. These contained a detailed outline of the show and ideas for making activities and games that related to the themes of the show across the curriculum. Suggestions for wheelchair decorations, recipes, art and science activities were included. Every show would have an advisory teacher who helped us throughout the development of the show and the accompanying resources.

When Oily Cart started to offer shows adapted both for young people with PMLD and those on the autism spectrum, it was important to describe the differences between the two versions. In that way, the schools or parents could decide which version was most likely to appeal to their young people.

The introductions contained ideas for preparing people on the spectrum for the experience of the show. For example, in a production where there were to be two performances each day, it was a good idea, if possible, to bring the autism spectrum people into the performance space over the lunch break where they could try out the seating, take a good look backstage and check out the exits. There would be more opportunities for these inspections in schools where the company was visiting for several days.

Over the years, the Introductions for Carers became more and more informative with cassettes of the music of the shows and posters of the characters. Oily Cart's first full scale hydropool show *Big Splash* (1999) included a cassette tape with music from the show accompanied by a voice-over by Max Reinhardt. In this Max talked a carer through a multi-sensory session using the same materials featured in the show itself. At the end of each session, the participants were given a sponge, a mister or a brush that eventually built up into everything required for a *Big Splash* sensory session.

Social Stories

It was not until several years later when we started to work on a regular basis with young people on the autism spectrum that we began to consider a development of the Big Book concept. I had been talking about Social Stories with teachers from the Livity School in Lambeth. Social Stories are an approach to working with young people on the spectrum that had been pioneered in the USA by Carol Gray. In her books, there are numerous examples of how to tackle everyday social and personal matters that people on the spectrum may not understand intuitively. Subjects might include:

Sharing Toys
When Do I Say, Thank you?
Learning Ways to Stay Calm in Class
When the Fire Alarm Goes Off
Getting Ready in The Morning
Thunderstorms are OK

It dawned on me that theatre itself was a particularly complex example of social behaviour. People/performers pretending to be something they were not, telling stories that were not true. What were these people trying to do? Why were they doing it? If it is true that some people on the spectrum find it difficult to interpret some of the complexities of language and of behaviour, if they sometimes become confused by things like irony and metaphor that they take literally, then a full-blown piece of theatre could be quite baffling.

We were well aware that many of the young people on the spectrum could be subject to great anxiety if their routines were interrupted, if they were visiting unfamiliar places or meeting people for the first time. However, if someone was told and preferably shown (online, on video or in photographs) what they were going to be doing in a performance, then there was much less risk that their anxieties would overcome them and lead to a panic attack or meltdown.

This was the sort of information I wanted to put into our Social Stories. We started with *Blue* (2006) with a printed Social Story booklet and a short DVD that were sent to the schools that booked us in advance of our arrival. The book version and video Social Stories were shown to the pupils on their classroom whiteboards, so everyone was ready for the show when the time came. Later, as the technology became available, we put this material online (mainly on YouTube). There was a marked rise in expectation as the information was spread more widely around all the school staff and pupils, and parents could also have easy access to the information.

Here is a detailed example:

The Social Story From *The Bounce* (2014)

Page 1: The Bounce is a show with actors and music. We also have 2 trampolines.
Page 2: Jump and Spring love the trampoline.
Page 3: You can go on the big trampoline with them.
Page 4: The actors will sing to you. The Voice. Bounce. Bob.
Page 5: Boing plays bouncy music. Boing!
Page 6: You can bounce a lot or a little. You can say *More, please* or *Stop now.*
Page 7. The show lasts 20 minutes. Then we say *Thank you for coming. Goodbye.*

Each page was illustrated with a straightforward photograph of the character/s, the set and so on. This is the essence of the show boiled down to its essentials. It starts. The participants will be warned well ahead of time when a show is going to end. (A sudden ending can be quite unsettling to some young people on the spectrum). It finishes. You have choices. The information is aimed at the participants but can also be useful to the companions.

More recently with the help of Nick Weldin, our longstanding specialist video and digital collaborator, Oily Cart added an **interactive** version of the Social Story to the Sensory Social Story and the book/video versions. The participants could choose the sequences that they would like to see repeated. This interactive video was also on the iPads that were available to each participant as they waited in the Airlock. This iPad material was generally very popular.

In the wake of the Covid 19 pandemic, it is likely that online preparatory work will be more widely used as part of the continuing efforts to shield vulnerable audiences.

Characters in Residence

On the rare occasions when I have been asked what I would do if more money could be made available, the answer has always been that I wanted to be with the participants for much longer than is usually possible, so that they can find out much more about us and we can find out more about them. On two separate occasions, with extended versions of *Blue* (2007) and *Something in the Air* (2009), Manchester International Festival made my dream scenario come to life.

For *Blue*, the Festival had booked a week's worth of our standard touring version of the show. But we also had the chance to embed two characters who might have been in *Blue* (but were not) into two Special Schools in Greater Manchester.

On the first Monday morning of the two-week residencies, the young people arrived in school to find that a shack had been erected in a corner of their playground. Each shack was equipped with a verandah, a little bed, a working water pump, herbs planted out in old oil drums, a washing line complete with washing and an old-style portable record player with a few blues LPs to play on it. As the young people went to their classroom, they may have seen the figure of the embedded character pottering about around the shack.

In Melland School, a Severe Learning Disability school, the embedded character was Pancake Bob (Bob Karper), a gravel-voiced bluesman and at

Grange School, a specialist Autism school, the stranger in residence was Boom Boom T (Nicole Worrica) who was more into hip hop. Both had been given the same basic direction: do not talk to the young people until you have to, and preferably not at all until the second day. Be polite about it but try not to talk. This policy, of course, generated considerable curiosity and the bolder young people began to question the characters and speculate about why the Head would let a stranger camp out in the playground. One boy had a theory that the Head, apparently always looking for ways to raise money for the school, was charging the visitor for this low-grade accommodation.

On the morning of the second day, more and more young people were beginning to talk to the performers. They wanted to know where their visitor had come from. Were they going to stay? And in particular did they really sleep in the little bed in the shack?

In exchange for the information, the young people gave their guests guided tours of the school and invited them in to share the school dinners. After another day or so, Pancake Bob and Boom Boom T were guests in the computing, cookery and art classes while inviting the young people to join them in play and making sessions back at the shack.

At the end of each day the characters met with school staff to discuss how it was all going and the next stage of activities. This ultra-flexible approach made for a very responsive programme of interactions while sticking to the main aim of preparing the pupils for their visit to the performance.

Pancake Bob showed his new friends how he got his nickname, with some highly sensory pancake making, that involving sifting flour, splashing milk and breaking eggs. The video of Pancake Bob making pancakes is a classic of good practice that I never tire of watching. You can find it on the Oily Cart 30th Anniversary DVD.

Gradually the back-story emerged. The guests were only staying temporarily. They would be leaving soon to go to the station where they would meet their friends and take the train back home. Perhaps their friends from the school would like to come along to the station. They should pack some luggage with what each of them considered the most important thing in the world inside. Then, at the station, everybody could tell one another about their Blues Bags, sing some songs and have a party; in other words, participate in the touring show version of *Blue*.

What I found remarkable about this preparatory project was that in a relatively short time, it made a huge difference to the relationship between the performers (especially the performers who had been embedded) and the young people in the schools.

But the real delight came at the end of the two-week residencies when the students made their way across Manchester to see the performance of *Blue*. Most remarkable was the reaction of the students from Grange School, the specialist Autism school. The school staff that accompanied them on the visit were prepared for problems because these young people were not used to visiting new places or meeting people they did not know. They had been anticipating panic attacks and meltdowns – instead they were amazed.

The young people clutching their Blues Bags hurried onto the mini-buses with Boom Boom T and the staff members. When they arrived at the Manchester Conference Centre, they jumped out, raced through the foyer and onto the stage where the rest of the cast of *Blue* were waiting and immediately the students were all over them. *I know who you are, Big Jack, and I know what you have got in that big trunk. You've got water in there.* They knew all about the characters. Of course, they did. Boom Boom T had told them all about her friends waiting at the station and the weird and wonderful things they carried with them in their luggage, like the night sky, the village pump, the fans that could blow up a breeze. Now they wanted to find out even more and experience for themselves the marvels in the Blues Bags.

The two teachers were astounded. They had tears in their eyes. This was not how their students were predicted to behave, excited to meet new people and filled with curiosity.

The response from the students of Melland School was more low-key but they too were delighted, and so was I, believing that we had found a way, in quite a short time to introduce young people, prone to high states of anxiety, to develop friendships with people quite unlike themselves and then be transported into the heart of what could have been an unsettling experience.

Two years later, we took *Something in the Air* to the next Manchester International Festival. This time the festival was generously offering us even more money and we were able to embed two characters in each of three Special Schools plus a much larger cast for the show itself and a much larger budget overall. The show itself, featuring Ockham's Razor, was very widely appreciated but I did not quite feel that the character embeddings were as effective as the ones for *Blue*.

Personally, I would blame the writer/director, but I do have the impression that two characters embedded in each school was not as effective a model as the one character per school. In *Blue*, the single character was adopted by the students who saw that he/she needed befriending.

Pool Piece: Repeat Performances

I have worked through a long list of lengths of performance and composition of casts over the years. In *Pool Piece* (2009), a hydropool show for Special Schools, I was interested to see what difference it would make if we offered two performances of the same show to the same participants within a three-day period, accompanied by extensive briefing and debriefing of the school staff.

This involved a six-week long tour performing in six schools altogether. The pool and poolside settings were installed on the Monday and the staff briefed. Over the next four days, we worked with two groups of eight students, a maximum of sixteen students in total. Each participant was accompanied by a member of the school staff. We performed for the first group on Tuesday and Thursday and for the second group on Wednesday and Friday. Each session consisting of 10 minutes at the poolside and 20 minutes in the water, lasted about 30 minutes.

With this format, every participant had the opportunity to travel through the pool installation twice. The second visit gave them the opportunity to develop more confidence and understanding than would be possible in a one-off session. It enabled the performers to get to know students and staff better – and, of course, vice versa. That made it possible for us to adapt our performances to the requirements of the individuals involved. The schools were briefed that the production was specifically intended for young people with the most complex disabilities. We assumed that many of the students would be largely nonverbal and that hoisting in and out of the pool would be required in many instances.

The *Pool Piece* extended performance project certainly succeeded in its immediate objectives and if the finances could be found, I would certainly consider using this model again. Any extended contact with our audiences has a beneficial effect on our understanding of the participants and their companions and so on the quality of our performances. However, it has to be said this show only toured six venues and only two of those were new to the work, with some intense negotiation being required to fill the sixth slot.

Follow-up to the Performance

The other essential when it comes to extending the footprint of the performance, is to consider what comes after the show. How can we make maximum use of the understanding and the inspiration that a Sensory Theatre performance provides and how can we extend the time that it stays in the memory?

I have already talked about the **Big Books** as preparation for Early Years shows. Of course, they also acted as follow-up resources.

We often gave under-fives **a small souvenir** at the end of a show, such as a packet of seeds. My favourite souvenir was a paper bag for *If All the World Were Paper* (2005). The paper bags were handed out at the start of the show and were used as programmes, fans and for sound effects during the performance. At the end, the children were asked to whisper their favourite bit of the show into the bag. They could take that memory home with them to keep.

The Music of the Show

One of Oily Cart's greatest strengths has been the original music written by Max Reinhardt. As soon as finances allowed, we started to record the music in a studio so that audiences could have a lasting reminder of the show to play whenever they wanted. This applied to both Early Years and SEND shows.

Video Reminders

In *Georgie Goes to Hollywood* (1993), our two day-long programme for a whole Severe Learning Disability School, we made a 20-minute video with contributions from every department in the school and staged a world premiere. We left behind a VHS version of the film and a small yellow figure, a Georgie, for the school to display in its trophy cabinet.

After the performance of *Moving Pictures* (2003), our performance for people having profound multiple learning disabilities, we handed over a compilation video that showed the reactions to the trampoline of each one of the participants to be watched and discussed over and over again, allowing plenty of processing time. After the performances of *Conference of the Birds* (2004) and *Blue* (2006) where we had videoed and projected the live reactions of each participant during their Name Song (where the lyric was simply the participant's name), we presented a copy of the Name Songs video to the classes involved.

The Blues Shacks and Bags

At the end of the *Blue* residencies described previously, we left both schools with their own Blues Shack complete with a set of sensory Blues Bags. In the bags, there were all the resources needed for a range of Sensory Sessions related to the themes of the show such as fans, perfumes, shakers, bowls and bubbles.

Social Stories and Activity Packs

We were always delighted to come across schools where they revisited the Sensory Social stories from earlier shows. Sometimes they would ask for a new cassette tape because theirs had eventually fallen apart after several years of use.

Part Three
The Growth of Sensory Theatre

Phil Fogg (Christopher Stevenson) and an audience member gaze around cloud canyon in the 2018 Big Umbrella Festival production of *UP AND AWAY*, commissioned by Lincoln Center and created by Trusty Sidekick Theater Company. Environment Design by Nic Benacerraf, Lighting Design by Simon Harding, Costume Design by Natalie Loveland.

Photo by Alexis Buatti-Ramos. www.trustysidekick.org

DOI: 10.4324/9781003091288-33

31
Canada – Carousel Players

When I made my first piece of Sensory Theatre, *Box of Socks*, in 1988, I was not aware of any other artists doing similar work, at least not on a regular basis.

As a member of the Theatre for Youth team at the Citizens' Theatre Glasgow in the mid 1970s, I recall being part of a company touring a promenade, pirate treasure hunt performance that worked in Special Schools under the director, Peter Leach.

In the late 1970s, Max Reinhardt and I were working with a wonderful company called Theatre Kit who made a piece for London SEND schools. I was told it was about a trip inside a giant brain that you entered via the ear. I regret to say I never saw it.

As Max, Claire and I began to work as Oily Cart, we became aware of other companies working with artists with disabilities such as Strathcona, Action Space and Heart 'n' Soul but as the 80s turned into the 90s, the only companies concentrating on making theatre for audiences with learning disabilities were Interplay in Leeds, Mind the Gap in Bradford and a little later, Bamboozle in Leicester.

Oily Cart was confined to London for quite a few years, although Phyllis Steele of Giant Productions, often invited us to Scotland and Liz Moran, running the remarkable child-centred MacRobert Arts Centre at the University of Stirling, booked us regularly, as did Clwyd Theatre Cymru in North Wales.

Apart from that, there was little international attention until the Vulavulani Theatre Company of Soweto in South Africa, heard about our *Roly Poly Pudding* (1996) and did their own version of the show in 1998.

DOI: 10.4324/9781003091288-34

Then came a momentous meeting with Kim Selody and Linda Carson who, at that time, were running the Carousel Players in Ontario. This led to our first overseas co-production.

Christmas Baking Time 2009 Oily Cart. Baker Bun (Griff Fender) and Baker Bap (Jumoke Oke) create a snowy wonderland with flour. Design: Claire de Loon.
Photo: Amanda Webb.

Kim Selody, Artistic Director of Carousel Players Writes: The Oily Cart in Canada

I first found Oily Cart and Tim Webb in 2000.

I had recently taken over the artistic leadership of a Theatre for Young Audience company in Canada that specialised in participatory theatre for young children. I was told by the outgoing Artistic Director that the company needed to do this kind of work, as it had been mandated by the founder of the company 20 years earlier, but that it was not very "artistic" and the company's public funding reflected this lack of a strong artistic aesthetic. This prompted me to ask the question, "Was there a company out there who was doing participatory theatre that had a strong artistic aesthetic?" My search took to me to London and Oily Cart Theatre.

We began by creating a Canadian production of an Oily Cart show *A Peck of Pickled Pepper*, retitled *Patti's Cake* for my audiences. We had a Canadian cast directed by Tim, using the design and music from the original production. The impact on audiences was immediate and significant. Where the company had been playing to over 500 primary aged children in a school, (five to eight year olds) we were now playing to 80 children (between two and six year olds) and their parents and caregrs in our own venue. Immediately, we could see how much more impactful the work was on children and adults.

The next step was to begin a collaboration on *Baking Time*, a co-production between our two companies. Half the cast were Canadian, the other half were British. We toured the production for four months in England and four months in Canada. It was remounted in England as *Christmas Baking Time*. Then in 2014, we remounted that variant in Canada as *Holiday Baking Time*. It has played several festivals in Canada, and remains as a holiday favorite in our theatre.

The idea of creating a multi-sensory experience that connected very young children and adults was new to Canadian audiences at the time. Claire de Loon's visual aesthetic, combined with Max Reinhardt's music, under the guidance of playwright and director Tim Webb, created a powerful experience for audiences. Tim's constant search for experiences the audience could see, hear, touch and taste was transformative. The humor and quirkiness of the worlds we were creating drew very young children and adults together for a shared experience. Before this, our work was viewed as "just for children" with adults dropping children off and leaving, or sitting at the back not very engaged. Now we had a small theatre full of adults and children being brought into the same world.

Another significant shift for us was away from the kind of participatory work where all the audience is being asked to do the same thing at the same time, which was rather boring theatrically for adults. Tim pointed out that you never really knew what was going on inside someone else's head, and that it was much more interesting to treat each person as an individual. It was also a great tool to "rebalance" the power dynamic in the room, by empowering the very young children to the same level as the adults.

I have been employing these two strategies and concepts in all my creations since working with Tim. The importance of a strong visual aesthetic, that is more installation than set is also vital to the experience. In my view, Claire de Loon is a genius of theatrical design.

For us, what worked so well was seeing the audiences stimulated by the whole experience, creating a feeling of joy and wonder in the room. They also wanted more. Our company began to receive regular increases in funding and demand was growing for the work, so we started to tour nationally and internationally.

One initial barrier we ran into was audience size. As we had played to large numbers in the past, our network of presenters and schools demanded that this work play to larger numbers. We tried a few times, but the result was a disaster. We had to rethink who we were creating theatre for, and the importance of having a greater impact on our audiences. Turns out Tim and Claire were just ahead of their time. Within 10 years of them coming to Canada, we now had several theatre companies focusing on smaller numbers, with greater impact. We also had a WEE Festival for work for the very young.

The importance of focusing on the senses when creating theatre for the very young cannot be overstated. Tim, Claire and Max were a formidable force. The fundamental difference in reaction from our audiences was that now both the children and the adults were fully engaged in the experience. Now there was a true sense of wonder in the room quite regularly.

Baking Time is still playing today in Vancouver, Canada. When I worked with Tim, if something worked, he would say it was "*classic.*" *Baking Time* has now been playing on and off for 20 years, with the original design, music and text. It is truly a classic of theatre for the very young.

32
USA – Chicago Children's Theater

Red Kite, Blue Moon by Chicago Children's Theatre. Joshua Holden, John Francisco, Carolyn Defrin.

Photo: Michael Brosilow.

DOI: 10.4324/9781003091288-35

Tim Webb Writes

We first met Jacqui Russell, from Chicago Children's Theater, at the Oily Cart Summer School in 2006. We were celebrating our 25th anniversary. The show *Blue* was on tour and a visit to a cramped and badly attended performance was part of the Summer School programme. Fortunately, Jacqui was not put off by the underwhelming show and she did enjoy the rest of the activities enough to invite Max, Claire and me to Chicago to work on a new show together the following year.

We three had a wonderful time working for two weeks on a scratch performance called *The Four Winds* with Jacqui and her very skilled company.

I returned with a full script for *Red Kite, Blue Moon* that Jacqui developed into a polished performance. This was the start of several projects for me in the USA, including tours to perform at the New Victory Theater, Lincoln Center and the Brooklyn Academy of Music in New York. I have been invited to lecture on Sensory Theatre at NYU and other university drama departments in Colorado, Hawaii, Florida, Arizona and Montreal, Canada.

In 2008, Chicago Children's Theater also staged a production of the Oily show *If All the World Were Paper*. The Chicago Stage Review called it "*an original creation of child-like theatrical genius.*" Nice one.

Jacqueline Russell, Artistic Director and Co-Founder of Chicago Children's Theater Writes

After attending the Oily Cart Summer 2006 workshop in England, I fell in love with this group of artists and their unique and original method of making theatrical experiences for people with profound disabilities. Those days with them were life changing for me and I felt a kind of inspiration and awe that I had not felt before. I remember one night after a group dinner we went for a long walk – under a clear sky with a bright moon when I invited Tim to bring an Oily Cart show to Chicago and he said to me (something like this) – *No, you need to do your own show for the children in Chicago. Besides, autism has been more your area of focus and passion, why don't we come to Chicago and make a show with you and your Chicago artists. A show for the children with autism that you already serve. It needs to be a show made for them, not a show made for UK kids.*

The response to this show, *Red Kite, Blue Moon*, was tremendous. An overwhelming mix of joy and gratitude. The reaction of the children to the performance was often total surprise – almost shock for the parents when they observed how the children openly and gladly responded to the work. The feeling in the room was almost a healing, shamanistic-like atmosphere.

The collaboration that took place amongst the artists with myself and Tim was incredible and energising. There was always so much love, commitment and wonder in the rehearsal room and it translated to the stage, too. We also had an amazing roster of experts on our team. Autism specialists and special educators who gave lots of content, design and educational input that really shaped the piece and made it even more autism specific and friendly. We also hired a young man with autism and included him in the show – on and off stage. He would open each performance with a show-appropriate "pirate" joke and would also sing along with the cast. When not on stage, he assisted front of house folks and stage managers with prop resets.

It was not all perfect. I think my goals for set design were quite a bit unrealistic and we quickly learned how easily the set could be destroyed by an overly excited child and, in addition, that some areas were not fully secure/safe for the children to jump on. It's a different sort of design from traditional set design – you have to think of it as building a playground for kids, not a set for actors. You must also be extra careful with props. We had these lightweight, rubber rocks meant to be asteroids but one little guy starting eating them during the show!

There were plenty of surprises like that. But plenty more that were simply wonderful. I will give you an example: We had a seven year old child who attended our show who had never spoken to anyone outside of his immediate family. His family brought him to see *Red Kite, Blue Moon* with great trepidation, but still with hope in their hearts that he would enjoy this new experience. Five minutes into the show, he left his mother's lap and joined the actors on stage to interact and talk to them! When asked later why he did that, he told his mother that *he liked those people* (the actors) and *wanted them to be his friends*. His family openly wept when recounting this story to me. That is just one of many, many stories I can share that illustrate the profound and life changing *successes* of this performance.

We were always moved by the reactions and feedback we received. Sometimes we would have a child come to the show who would not enter the room. They would only stand in the doorway, just peeking in the entire time. Actors always included them and brought every sensory experience to the door to share with the child. We would then see that child back again the next weekend in the performance space, sitting in a chair and fully participating and interacting. We also had children who would NOT do anything to participate or interact with us. We would worry that perhaps they did not enjoy the experience at all. Then we would get a note from their family saying they talked enthusiastically about the show the entire drive home and then set out to re-enact the performance in the safety and familiarity of their own house. The list of reactions like this goes on and on.

After *Red Kite, Blue Moon*, we felt we could not stop! We had created something for this underserved and so often overlooked audience and they were hungry and in need of more theatrical experiences. Since then, we have created six more *Red Kite* productions – most very scaled down and designed to travel. We have toured them to Canada and across the United States. Thanks to this work, I was named a Cultural Envoy to Canada by the U.S. State Department and later won an Autism Speaks Hero Award. We have also won very competitive NEA grants for our Red Kite productions, as well. I also continue to train and collaborate with other theatres and universities around the country.

For the past 10 years, Chicago Children's Theater has also offered a summer arts camp specifically for young people on the spectrum, Camp Red Kite.

The only obstacle to this work is, honestly, funding. We are very fortunate in Chicago to have been able to raise the money to do this work but given the intimate and specialised nature of the work and the audience served, ticket sales will never come anywhere near covering the costs.

In the future I want to reach more underserved communities. To do this, I need to continue to identify and train diverse artists who may have limited resources, but a true gift and a passion for this type of theatre. I am currently working in Kansas on a new Red Kite production with Native American artists from multiple tribes. The piece that is now in development will debut at a local Pow Wow and is entitled *Song for Otter*. This work will aim to reach young people in the most underserved community in America and my hope is to bring attention to these gifted tribal artists who lack opportunities and to serve the indigenous children in their community with developmental disabilities.

33
UK – Bamboozle

Anan on the set of *Storm* by Bamboozle at Shanghai Children's Art Theatre.

Photo credit: Shanghai Children's Art Theatre.

Tim Webb Writes

As Oily Cart grew during the 1990s, we discovered to our delight that there was another company, Bamboozle, based in Leicester who were also making

DOI: 10.4324/9781003091288-36

work for young people with Profound and Multiple Disabilities or who were on the autism spectrum. In recent years, their form of theatre has spread rapidly especially in China. In the piece which follows, Christopher Davies, the CEO and Artistic Director of Bamboozle describes their methodology and in particular their experience of working in China.

Christopher Davies, Artistic Director and CEO of Bamboozle Writes: The Enabled Space

Sitting centre stage, five actors. One plays gentle guitar, others harmonise softly. Relaxed; at ease; waiting. Into the studio come six children who are on the autistic spectrum. They are shown to benches and their parents retire to the back of the studio, as they have been briefed to do. One girl does not sit, she stands and sways, as if about to fall. None of the actors move. Her parents hold their breath. She is trusted and stays upright, unsteady, watching. An atmosphere of ease and anticipation.

We are in the studio at the Shanghai Children's Art Theatre. It is the opening of *Storm*, Bamboozle's production based on Shakespeare's *Tempest* and designed for those on the autistic spectrum.

Along the front of the stage between actors and audience is a shoreline. Flotsam and jetsam. Driftwood and nets. Remnants of plastic bags washed up along the beach. The actors animate lengths of driftwood; rising and falling with the swell; the sound of the waves vocalised gently – in and out, in and out – rhythmic, repetitive, mesmeric. The tide builds then subsides – the driftwood waves come to rest on the beach. The actors gather pieces of plastic and float them on the wind – their breath in time with their harmonised singing.

Measured. Relaxed. No need to rush.

Slowly, gradually thin sheets of plastic are carried on the out breath towards the audience – occasionally there is a fleeting eye contact with a child – an invitation. An invitation not an imperative. Children are hesitant, tentative, not sure of the rules. Gradually some take up the offer and one girl blows plastic back towards an actor who responds. A game ensues, back and forth, to and fro. A boy screws up a bag and throws in onto the shore. An actor takes another bag and does the same. Then waits.

Step by small step the children are drawn in. They realise that they can participate. Or just sit and watch. Both are equally valid; there is neither pressure nor expectation.

This scene embodies three of the key considerations when Bamboozle makes a show.

1. **How can we create an enabled space** where the audience can engage with the action on their own terms? Where the focus is on interaction and engagement not getting a response right or obeying the rules. So, when a girl picks up flotsam from the shore, the actor doesn't give any validation, she simply joins in the exploration. There is no expectation. The joy is in the joint interaction. The girl's worth is recognised, acknowledged and valued which is so important for audience members who are frequently shown that they don't belong.

2. The second consideration is to create points in the narrative that give **opportunities for the audience to interact** with the setting or the action. The scene above comes very early in the show so that right from the start the audience are given the message that this performance is for them – on their terms. And the scene is flexible in length – it runs for as long as it takes for the audience to feel at ease.

3. The third concerns the physical setting. **Set and props must either be indestructible or easily replaceable.** This enables the actors to relax and allow audience participation without having to restrain anyone to protect a vulnerable part of the set or a delicate prop. This is key in creating the enabled space where no one is told they can't touch this or go there. Everyone – actors, audience and accompanying adults – can relax. The driftwood is therefore made of a durable and flexible polymer – which is a light substance so that the lengths of wood are not as dangerous as the real thing would be if thrown. The plastic washed up on the shore is replaceable so it doesn't matter if someone tears it up.

And what of the girl who was unsteady on her feet at the start of the show? Her parents had flown 1000 miles to bring Anan to this performance. There is nothing like this for families like theirs in China. On being invited to leave Anan and sit at the back of the room they told us that she has Rett Syndrome and they would like to remain close to give physical support as she could possibly fall. We agreed that if that became necessary then they could, of course, offer support but initially they would try sitting back. Anan spent the whole of the show on the set amongst the action, sometimes standing apparently unsteadily, but never falling – and always engaged. Her parents had gathered up their courage and let her experience the performance on her terms. After the show, close to tears, they told us that this was the first time in her life that they had seen their daughter being herself. They were grateful for the realisation that she could be more independent than they realised. Theatre can change the lives of learning disabled young people.

Bamboozle's experience, particularly in China but also across five continents is that there is an appetite throughout the world for theatre designed to be accessed by learning disabled audiences. Organisations are hungry to learn about our underlying pedagogy and how it leads to high levels of audience engagement. For example, Bamboozle's seminar "How Can Theatre Impact the Lives of Learning Disabled Children" given in Shanghai in 2019 was attended by 200 people in the theatre and watched by a third of a million live online. The interest is there, we need to capitalise on it. We are working in an ongoing partnership with the Shanghai Children's Art Theatre creating a company of Chinese actors; who now perform Chinese versions of both *Storm* and *Down to Earth*, one of our shows for profoundly disabled children. The more we can all spread the word of the impact that theatre has for these audiences the better it will be for children like Anan and their families.

34
Ireland – Helium Arts

Pop-Up Picnic by Helium Arts, Ireland. Thomas Johnston and Niamh Lawlor.
Photo: Brian Cregan.

Tim Webb Writes

Helium Arts based in Westmeath, but active all over Ireland, has fascinated me for a long time because of its close relationship with the Health
Service. The project was begun by the present Artistic Director, Helene

DOI: 10.4324/9781003091288-37

Hugel. Helene and I have mentored the team on several projects including *Pop-Up Picnic* that toured into the family homes of children under five with complex disabilities. Its director, Joanna Williams, describes this project in detail.

Joanna Williams, Director of *Pop-Up Picnic* Writes

This Helium Arts project supports families in absorbing creative and play skills to be used in everyday life in the home of a young child with a disability, providing parents with new ways of bonding with their child using sound, light, music, movement, smell and touch. The project was developed in collaboration with the Jack and Jill Children's Foundation.

The *Pop-Up Picnic* began with research and development mentored by Tim Webb in January to March 2016. The first home performances took place in April 2016 and toured in County Kildare, County Tipperary and to the Mermaid Arts Centre in Wicklow.

I had admired Oily Cart's work for the very young and for people with complex disabilities for many years. As an artist and visual-theatre maker myself I had focused on making work for Early Years and the idea of making a work specifically for children this age with complex needs was something that excited me. It felt like a very natural extension of my practice. I was keen to learn from Tim Webb in a very practical way. My work had always been largely nonverbal, visual theatre set to music. Tim taught me to think and present for all the senses. As I led the team on our collective journey to create the work it was reassuring to have Tim on hand to check in with regarding our instincts.

Audiences were hugely appreciative of the work. It was an amazing thing for two performers, a musician and a puppeteer to walk into a family home as strangers with all the awkwardness that this can bring and within 10 minutes find themselves dancing around the living room with the whole family or sharing an intimate moment as parents and children experience a massage together as we roll an orange across their shoulders or hands.

Parents commented that it was a chance for families to participate in a fun experience as a whole family, which one expressed as being a *rare* experience when living with illness, and that *Pop-Up Picnic* provided *new ways to entertain their child and new ways for the child's siblings to interact and play together.*

Parents enjoyed learning how to use the different senses for stimulation and saw the performance as a *welcome break* from medical routines. One parent was very surprised by the length of Maeve, her daughter's, attention span, describing her reaction as *heart-lifting*. Other parents were surprised at how easy the multi-sensory techniques were: *simple ideas to try at home*.

> The home visits were a wonderful, magical experience that helped to stimulate Maeve in a multi-sensory way. The team tailored an individual sequence of interactive experiences to Maeve's unique needs and presented it at her own pace. Maeve really loved all of the music and singing, along with the cleverly designed resources. We were delighted to be involved in this superb project that genuinely catered for Maeve's unique needs.
>
> (Maeve's mum)

If I had to name one thing essential to this work I would say *responsiveness*. This was embedded in every aspect of the performance, the process that created it, the way the performance was designed, and the commitment of the performers to this ethos. We created a framework to anchor the performers, from which they could jump off and play and explore. Our performers, a musician and puppeteer, had the skill to embrace this and that was central to the success of the production. Their ability to be really present, noticing the smallest of responses, subtly seeking guidance from parents as to how an experience was being received, adapting and exploring all the time meant that each performance was truly tailored to our audience's needs.

From the start the project's production values were high with the intention of creating a piece of sensory theatre of the highest artistic standards. We took time to research our project supported by many partners, from mentorship by Tim Webb, the guidance of the Jack and Jill Foundation whose nurses worked with the families on brokering the initial relationships and the feedback and learning from working with four very special, diverse families.

All the performers and creative team were highly skilled in their fields, music was composed with great care and skill, the sensory objects and props were beautifully made. This helped bring a sense of occasion and magic to the room. Everything we created had its origins in the familiar, with all scenes rooted in the types of play that all parents engage in with their child. A hand-washing sequence following exploration of the sticky oranges gave an opportunity for water play, playful tapping of eggs produced a roomful of feathers to float and tickle, games of peek-a-boo were enhanced by music and props. Everything in the performance was designed to be played with, from the musical instruments to all the puppets and sensory objects that were meant to be handled, explored without caution. Music could respond to the energy of the room, capturing the fun and building with it or it could remain calming and quiet as the mood required.

Our learning from Tim gave us the ability to create a really strong framework. The things we took from his work included the opening name song, the use of ritual to create a different energy, a way to give focus and make something ordinary feel really magical. There was, in particular, the use of stillness, learning to move and present at a slower pace that allowed our audience to process what was happening.

The families and children who acted as our Creative Consultants commented on how with each visit, their understanding of what their child responded to and enjoyed grew, their child becoming more relaxed and receptive to the performers as the familiarity increased.

Our theme of a picnic came from the realisation that we did not require a complex narrative. At the same time for a family as a whole *picnic* was a reference that could be appreciated by all ages. It allowed us to create a *menu* of experiences. We could open and close the show in a familiar way, creating repetition and familiarity while offering different ingredients on each visit, and best of all on our third visit the family could choose to repeat a picnic which was most resonant to their child.

One of the key elements to the success of this project was the time that we spent developing the piece. We spent a considerable amount of time working with the four families in their homes. This allowed us to learn from the children and the families and gave us a great grounding from which to develop the final performance.

For example, when I look back at my notes, very early on we discuss the challenge of being in people's homes, different spaces, large family audiences with siblings of varied ages, intimate audiences of just one child and a parent. How do we create a performance space without making people feel awkward in their own home? How do we define our space while maintaining an open invitation to play? We discussed rolling out a rug, defining places that the more mobile children might sit using mats or cushions. This became our Picnic Rug, with its own sensory plates or patches that children could sit on and still give the performers the space they need.

We learned that sometimes we might even be ignored and to be ok with this, while remaining flexible to what was happening in the room. On occasions a sensory experience we had prepared might not engage the child at all. If this was the case we simply moved on to the next thing.

If we had only been working with one family some of our ideas might never have made it past this stage, but on arriving at another home we often discovered that this was the very moment that was most enjoyed by the child living there. Later, on reflection, we sometimes thought of another way the experience could be enhanced to give it more appeal, for example by adding a scent to a puppet intended for sensory massage.

We realised that our offerings needed to have time and flexibility built in, allowing the performers to be responsive and adapt to the moment. If an experience is really resonating there needed to be room to spend time and explore where it might go.

The audience feedback has been fabulous. Families are often very moved by the experience and overwhelmed by the fact that the piece clearly demonstrates *an understanding* of their child or children. Usually this is a first experience for them of finding something that can be enjoyed by everyone in a family that has a child with complex disabilities needs at its centre. We have been inundated with requests for more performances. In order to respond to this great need we have also developed a version of the piece with a third performer to play to audiences of six families.

This production has had a tremendous impact on my work and the work of the whole team that have been involved along the way. I have continued to explore how all of my work can have elements that appeal to a broader range of the senses, and continue to create experiences that allow audiences to get involved, to play, to experience in the fullest sense beyond the traditional style of passive audience.

35
Japan – Hospital
Theatre Project

To the Sky of Far Away Arabia 2017 by Hospital Theatre Project, Japan. Here the performer is using a shiny bowl to enhance the close-up light effect. The carer is thrilled by what she can see reflected in there.

Photo: Jun Takai.

Tim Webb Writes

Kaori Nakayama founded the Hospital Theatre Project in 2010, based in Tokyo, intending to take storytelling projects into hospital settings but was disappointed with the first results, which seemed too traditional to her. In 2016, Kaori enlisted Claire de Loon and me to visit Japan as mentors. We

DOI: 10.4324/9781003091288-38

worked with two teams, one in Tokyo, the other in Sendai. Together we created two interactive scratch performances. After this the project had a radical change of style, and created five productions which played in public rather than hospital venues and put aside storytelling for a much more multi-sensory style aimed at the child and his or her family. Kaori's theatre pieces have very high standards in design and music and she employs multi-talented casts. She has a remarkably high rate of production having created and toured five shows since 2016.

Kaori Nakayama, Director of the Hospital Theatre Project Writes

Founded in 2010 Hospital Theatre Project, run by a Tokyo-based charity Theatre Planning Network, is a professional enterprise creating performances for children with disabilities.

Originally, we visited institutions or hospitals with a sort of storytelling. However, I was unsatisfied with the attitudes of the institutions but also of my artists – both of them were bound up by conventional rules, which did not allow the children to participate in the performances, thus greatly reducing their enjoyment.

In order to change perceptions and increase understanding, I knocked on the door of Oily Cart in 2015 and invited Tim Webb and Claire de Loon to Tokyo and Sendai in October 2016 to provide training opportunities for performers. This was supported by the Nippon Foundation. After this, we totally changed our style from conventional storytelling to multi-sensory performance and began presenting in public places.

Up until 2020 we have produced five multi-sensory productions with various themes searching for the sense of wonder and met not only the targeted audience but also the unexpected – children with constant medical needs.

Now more families can take a chance and bring their children to the venues longing to enrich their children's lives and bring them joy. Although our prime objective was to create a rich theatrical experience for the families who are not made welcome by conventional theatre, now we have found another goal – to make a wonderful memory for the whole family.

Many families come back for every production. This tells us clearly that the repeated experiences can change not only children's responses and attitudes but also those of their parents and siblings as well as keeping us very wary about generalisations. Every child has his or her own speed and way of developing play and expression, and a person's growth is boosted by their families' relaxed attitudes – when they are with us, they do not use the negative phrases *No, Be quiet, Sit properly*, and so on.

Our Company of Hospitality adapted an idea from the Orpheus Process in music – where no conductor is engaged, all the company actors, musicians and staff are equally involved in the creative activity. To some extent, Japanese artists are trained to be obedient and passive culturally and socially. However, it is crucial that our audiences confound our expectations and surprise us all the time. We must accept this and become our audiences' accomplices so enabling the further development of their curiosity and sense of wonder.

In 2019, we were very happy to have Tim and Claire in Tokyo again for professional training, co-hosted by our government agency of cultural affairs for the first time.

There are so many audiences we have yet to meet – it is just they do not know of our existence yet. But we will persevere.

36
Australia – Sensorium Theatre

Whoosh! by Sensorium, Australia.

Photo: Daniel Grant

Tim Webb Writes

I first met Francis Italiano and Michelle Hovane in 2010 when they came to observe Oily Cart in rehearsal for *Ring a Ding Ding*, a very interactive show for under-fives. We were reunited in 2018 when we all participated, along-side Trusty Sidekick, in The Big Umbrella Festival, the world's first month-long festival dedicated to arts programs for children on the autism spectrum

DOI: 10.4324/9781003091288-39

and their families at the Lincoln Center in New York. Trusty Sidekick presented *Up and Away*, Sensorium played *Oddysea* and Oily Cart performed *Light Show*. It was very exciting to be part of this prestigious celebration of a relatively new art form.

Francis Italiano, Co-Artistic Director With Michelle Hovane Writes

Sensorium Theatre, based in Perth, Western Australia, is Australia's only theatre company making shows specifically designed for young audiences with disabilities. The company grew out of a seeding project in 2010 exploring ways to create immersive sensory theatre for an audience that had been largely neglected in Australia before then. Eventual company founder and co-artistic director, Francis Italiano, worked with a small team to develop the genesis of our first show *The Jub Jub Tree*. Joined by co-artistic director, Michelle Hovane, Sensorium created a schools-based touring show of *The Jub Jub Tree* in 2011 and has since performed three different multi-sensory theatre shows to thousands of neuro-divergent young people aged five to eighteen, around Australia, as well as touring to Singapore and New York.

Our small audiences of up to 15 young people are typically neuro-divergent and can include children with learning disabilities and sensory processing issues, as well as those on the autism spectrum. Some of them may have difficulty moving and communicating independently. For many of them, a Sensorium show might be their first experience of theatre. Our shows use touch, taste, smell, mostly live music and sometimes puppets, and strong visual elements to bring stories to life in immersive environments where the children are "on stage" with the performers. This proximity allows us to tailor the performance based on individual audience member's responses and communication preferences. The invitation to play within the context of the story is key for us. From the beginning, we've trialled different ways for audiences to be active participants in the theatre experience rather than simply passive recipients of a show.

We'd noted that the children we met in special education needs settings sometimes seemed to have imagination and play squeezed out by medical/ therapeutic drivers in their lives. Sensory stimulation seemed to be considered in therapeutic terms rather than as a way to connect to stories, spark imaginations or elicit creative responses. In *The Jub Jub Tree*, we wanted to investigate how much we could use sensory elements as access points to the story. Could we use the senses to get the audience caught up in and carried along by a story? We created a super tactile forest setting for children to directly engage with, made puppets that they were welcomed to touch, and props that could be smelt. Children could feel the life-size Goat puppet's fur and ring his bell, tickle or be tickled by the Rooster, and when it rained in the story, they actually got wet.

Our artists – and the audiences' circle of care – were delighted by how engaged the children were by the world we'd created. Usually more cautious children were reaching out to pat the puppets, and many were clearly following along, surprising the adults with the depth of their responses to the plot.

We were lucky to begin our creative journey with a 12-week immersion into a dedicated special education needs school with students with high support needs. There we developed an understanding of the value of multimodal communication approaches, combining our performance physicality with visual prompts, voice and key signs, as well as embracing rhyme and repetition.

During this first school immersion, we also explored preparing audiences for the show, creating a series of four bite-size workshops which introduced them to the environment, characters, themes and music. This model of preparatory workshops plus performance, inspired by Oily Cart's ideas of "embedding" (almost as a kind of Live Social Story), was, we believe, a best-practice model which resulted in a satisfying experience for just about everyone. However, this model relied on short school residencies and became difficult to fund and sustain, prompting us to come up with other ways to prepare audiences for our shows which were more viable for a theatre venue context.

In 2013 we started developing our next show, *Oddysea*, an under-the-sea adventure as a kinetic journey to the bottom of the ocean for audiences that included children who might not move independently or who navigate the world in highly individual ways. We wanted the audience to be potentially even more active within a dynamic story experience. Where possible, children came out of wheelchairs onto gold satin beanbag sand dunes or could "swim" through bubbles and have performers move around them, the set transforming as we all swam deeper. The ocean theme inspired an ebb and flow between presentational moments with the sea-creatures of the story and more individual experiential play moments such as beachcombing for real shells in real sand. The process of making the work in a host school taught us that trialling ideas with the children was key to challenging assumptions about what might work in the show. Observation while creating a show was as important as carefully observing children when performing in the finished show. We learnt to recognise subtle responses and that so-called "positive" responses might look very different for different audience members – inviting curiosity meant being prepared for children to each play in their own way. Eg: gentle water splashing in a touch pool with one child might turn into pouring a bucket over the performer for another!

As we toured *Oddysea* extensively over the next few years we explored different ways to "embed" the preparation for the show, trialling same-day pre-show sessions within theatres, outreach preparatory visits to schools and online filmed song and play sessions – all of which proved invaluable in enhancing audiences' experience of the shows. We found that preparation for the accompanying adults and seeking their partnership was almost as important as preparing the children and young people!

Our most recent show, *Whoosh!* developed in stages over three years from 2016, is an interactive space-mission where audiences actively take on co-piloting a spaceship to a mysterious planet. We were keen to extend the participation of the audience members (ages six and up) as co-protagonists in the story, inviting them to sign up as cadets to whoosh across the galaxy with our crew characters. Along with helping the cast fly the ship, they share an emergency landing with them and explore a second planet installation where they find a way to repair the ship together and make it back home.

In *Whoosh!* we wanted to explore ideas of free-agency and choice-making for our audiences. With an expanded artist team and budget that allowed us to use sensor-activated and wifi-operated "tech stations" with multiple outcomes on the spaceship, we provided a range of child-led "cause & effect" choices for individual audience members to take up throughout the story.

Set within a 360-degree geodesic dome spaceship, *Whoosh!* made us think clearly about one of the main tensions of interactive participatory work – the flow between interactions led by the participation of individual audience members and the more presentational performer-driven moments with the show. Using the soundscape, musical score and the lights and set itself to gently guide us, we alternated between the collective participatory moments and times when the audience are free to engage with the environment completely on their own individual terms. As always, it's a finely calibrated and highly individualised balancing act!

For *Whoosh!* we've tried a new way to encapsulate pre-show preparation for audiences with a digital app of songs, social story, games and clips for them to download and use before coming – which has proved very popular.

Having grown – in size, in reach and experience of a range of audiences – since our inception, Sensorium is committed to remaining connected to our target audiences by including them in the development of new works. Our next show will evolve out of a longer-term residency in a host school and include artists with disability amongst the devisors. Having most recently played with high-tech production values to create the large-scale *Whoosh!* we want to pare things back for the next show that we'll begin developing in 2021. Aiming for a simpler narrative and setting, we want to create enough "room" to keep investigating one of the guiding principles of our work – to invite curiosity.

37

Russia – Four Winds

Viktoria Violleau-Avdeeva, Producer of
Four Winds, **Writes**

Since 2014, I have been producing professional theatre projects with the participation of deafblind actors in Russia and abroad (*In Touch, Anima Chroma/Living Paintings*). These were the first theatre projects for people with multiple sensory disabilities as actors. But there were still no shows accessible for them as spectators. So, I started my search abroad.

I heard about Oily Cart during my *discovery trip* to the UK in April 2016. When I contacted Tim Webb, he immediately invited me to watch the preview of their new show *Mirror, Mirror* in a special school in the suburbs of London. It was the day when I witnessed a miracle. In the audience there was a boy with multiple disabilities, who could breathe only through a tube. He seemed to be absolutely disconnected from the here and now. I asked myself, *How is this boy going to understand? How is he going to participate?* (I had been told that the audience is involved in the action in Sensory Theatre.) *How can all this be possible?* Then a quarter of an hour later during the *magical beauty* section with clay the boy's fingers started to move to the rhythm of the music, while he was singing in his own special way (only sounds, but he was singing!). To me it was the answer – Sensory Theatre would be perfect for deafblind people as well. First of all, because it involves all the senses, including tactile, kinaesthetic and olfactory which are the most active for people who cannot see and hear. Secondly, the story is simple, and what is told or sung can be translated into other sensory systems. Finally, it is a close-up theatre, which allows a lot of personal contact with the spectators. As a producer, I appreciated other practical advantages of sensory shows: they are compact and can be played in just a room in specialised schools and centres, while the concept and language of Sensory Theatre can be used both by parents of children with disabilities and education specialists.

DOI: 10.4324/9781003091288-40

Our collaboration with Tim Webb developed very fast: a month after our first meeting, he presented Sensory Theatre and the Oily Cart method at a conference in Moscow. In June, he was invited to the summer camp for deafblind children and parents in Gelengzhik (Russian Federation) to do a laboratory with actors and educational specialists from all over Russia. Its effect inspired us so much that we decided to create a sensory performance for deafblind children in Moscow. The goal was to make a mobile, low-budget, but very artistic sensory show, which could then be showcased in various spaces such as schools, centres and children's theatres.

On the set and rehearsals, Tim worked with two associates Olga Sidorkevich and Albert Rudnitsky. Some of the production challenges were: lack of time for rehearsals with Tim, low budget (6000 euro), actors busy with other shows and not having experience in sensory storytelling. But most importantly, we had to find the ways to artistically communicate the visual, sound and verbal story to a deafblind audience. As we had not had long to plan in advance there was a lot to explore in the rehearsal process.

The first rehearsal week with Tim started with casting. Most of the performers came from children's theatres: though extremely nice and professional, they often forgot who their audience was, focusing on the narrative, on their own performance. As we needed to check our findings and the scenario with the audience, we invited four deafblind people of different ages and with different degrees of deafblindness to be our expert audience. It also helped the actors practice close-up performance before meeting the real audience.

Four Winds is a simple story of a girl whose toy is gone with the wind. And she sets off to look for it where the South, East, West and North Winds live. The audience meets different people and animals, explore different sensory experiences, like playing with sand and shells, walking on the moulded stones, a Siberian husky ride, sailing on a boat, riding a car, train journey etc. In order to see how inclusive audiences would accept the show, we played it for children both without and with sensory disabilities and, finally, made a version a little more visual and narrative.

After its premiere in April 2017 in the educational centre for deafblind children at Yasnaya Polyana (Moscow) *Four Winds* was played in various places like an orphanage for deafblind children (for children with different sensory disabilities, including totally deafblind), at a specialised school for the blind, at the conference dedicated to deafblindness (for educational specialists and deafblind actors) and at the inclusive children's festival, Galafest (for children with different disabilities).

The show worked very well for each kind of audience, especially for those with remaining hearing or sight. For totally deafblind or born deafblind it needed some changes. There are some observations on making an accessible sensory performance for people with severe complex sensory disabilities. The show must be slower than usual, more tactile and kinaesthetic with minimum or no text. If there is some text it is important to consider time for interpreting.

As deafblind people are usually accompanied by tactile sign language or finger spelling interpreters, they should be reminded to describe the space and actors before the beginning and interpret throughout the play, but without spoiling the magic. For example, while it was raining in the story, the grandmother of one of our spectators was making remarks like, "Now the actor is spraying some water on you from the atomizer." Such remarks probably would not enhance the spell of the show for the boy. Perhaps there should be a manual for the guides/interpreters on what and when it is necessary to describe and what should be trusted to the language of Sensory Theatre.

Four Winds was a wonderful experience for the audience, for the actors, and for those who work or live with deafblind children.

Unfortunately, the project did not continue further than the end of 2017 as I left Russia and there was no one to take it over.

With his workshops and work on *Four Winds*, Tim Webb planted a seed of inspiration and knowledge that will grow sometime soon into beautiful sensory performances.

Tim Webb Writes

I should like to add my own regrets that the *Four Winds* project stopped when Viktoria left Russia especially because she had assembled a very talented company who showed themselves most adept at Sensory Theatre. I also want to describe in more detail the summer camp project that we created in the week we spent together in Gelendzhik, a holiday resort town on the coast of the Black Sea.

The project was housed in a huge sanatorium built in the Soviet era. At the time I visited the sanatorium, it was given over to deafblind children and their families as well as specialists in working with the deafblind.

The sanatorium is situated in a beautiful, unspoiled beach area reminiscent of the Mediterranean back in the seventies with the sound of the cicadas and the scent of pine and thyme baking in the sun.

There were swimming and games sessions for the children and the families but little in the way of play equipment. Viktoria had suggested that I might like to arrange some form of multi-sensory entertainment with the children and for me the most interesting parts of the sanatorium were the grounds stretching down to the pebbly shore of the Black Sea.

So with the help of the deafblindness specialists we developed a trail, an outdoor site sympathetic piece that took a 30-strong band of deafblind children and their adult companions on a richly sensory journey through a warm Mediterranean pine forest, buzzing with a million insects, then down through a chill, damp echoing tunnel under the road that followed the coast and out onto the beach itself where the pebbles were almost too hot to walk on. There we paddled in the sea until King Neptune, draped in sea weed waded out of the waves to welcome us to his kingdom.

The range and the intensity of the sensory stimuli were wonderful. There were so many different odours, temperatures and textures for the hands and underfoot that it would have been impossible to recreate this richness in any kind of a *proper* theatre setting. The children were engrossed. Yet, strangely, the parents and some of the specialists found all this a revelation, and, actually, so did I. There were so many wonders to be found in that stroll through the garden and down to the sea.

38
UK – Frozen Light

The Isle of Brimsker toured 2018/19. Agata (played by Lucy Garland) shares a sound activated light up radio with an audience member. Devised by Frozen Light. Other performers Amber Onat Gregory/Sophie Coward, Composer and musician: Al Watts, Directed by Kate O'Connor, Set Design: Kat Heath, Props and Lighting: Dave Sherman.

Photo: JMA Photography.

Tim Webb Writes

In a relatively brief period, Frozen Light have not only pioneered a theatre for adult audiences with profound and multiple learning disabilities, but also established a touring circuit of theatres and art centres across the UK. With

DOI: 10.4324/9781003091288-41

a clearly thought through artistic strategy and consistently high production values, they have added a much-needed extra dimension to the field of Sensory Theatre.

Lucy Garland and Amber Onat Gregory, Co-Artistic Directors of Frozen Light, Write

Frozen Light creates and tours multi-sensory theatre for audiences with profound and multiple learning disabilities (PMLD) to theatre venues across the UK.

Frozen Light love the epic, awe and wonder of theatre, the celebration of life and the sharing of stories. We create bold, immersive worlds in which emotional narratives can unravel through an exploration of the senses. We use one-to-one sensory interactions, live music, engaging spatial design, collective sensory experiences, intensive interaction and signing, to create theatre that is accessible and engaging to audiences with PMLD.

The theatre we make is grounded in our fundamental belief that everyone has the right to access great art in their local community venues. It is rooted in a conviction that only when people are visible and included does the world move forward. We want to share joy through the power that art has to bring us together as a society, to share those experiences of what it means to be human.

Our focus on visibility and community has led to our commitment to tour exclusively to theatre venues and we tour extensively across the UK. Our 2018/19 tour of *The Isle of Brimsker* performed at 55 theatre venues and arts centres nationwide. We like to work closely with every venue to support them to reach new audiences. 56% of our audiences on our last tour had never been to the theatre before. This figure is even more shocking especially when you consider that most of our audience are aged over fourteen. Theatre venues (many receiving public subsidy) have a duty to reach their whole community, but people with PMLD often miss out. We also prioritise touring to areas that often have less access to the arts.

Our commitment to making work for adult audiences makes Frozen Light distinctive from other sensory theatre companies. The dramatic difference in opportunities for children, compared to adults with PMLD (and not just in terms of access to the arts), is widely documented. This was our core impetus for working with adults: to provide meaningful, engaging and entertaining experiences that people can share with their families and support staff.

We also ensure that the productions we devise acknowledge the lived experience of our adult audiences. We work with bold, yet universal themes, setting them in thrilling environments, against the backdrop of a striking score which takes the audience on an evocative and emotive journey. Adults with PMLD often have limited opportunity to display control over their lives and within the sensory moments in the productions we are able to provide that opportunity within the narrative of the work.

It can feel like a challenge making work for adult audiences in the sensory theatre sector. Most programmers who have a focus on "access" have children and family programming roles in venues. Conferences which include accessible sensory work often sit within a "younger audiences" focus. We hope to see the sensory theatre sector develop to include a wider breadth of work for adult audiences in the future, to ensure that individuals' needs are remembered beyond adolescence.

Frozen Light has a firm belief in the power of stories to bring people together, to help develop an understanding of self, emotions and the world in the broadest sense. Stories are *"opportunities for individuals to live beyond the often, life limiting restrictions of their disabled bodies, with the offer of some kind of shared meaning and purpose, a common identity that brought them together with others experiencing the same story and purpose – a sense of community perhaps."* Raising the bar through inclusive Theatre – A. Fergusson 2019. Story and narrative allows our sensory interactions to take on artistic significance and hold a greater sense of meaning.

As a company we take risks and push the boundaries of what theatre can look like for audiences with PMLD, whilst always acknowledging this is not a homogenous group, but one made up of a myriad of different individuals all with their own likes, dislikes and life experiences. We focus on creating a safe space at the beginning of our performances and only then, with great care, we guide audiences on an emotional journey. This allows us to gain trust so that as the story unfolds we can push the volume of the music (always a hit), experiment with bigger sensory experiences (giant floor fans, a 10m vibrating robe, collective sensory moments) and make the space darker (so we can use UV and play with drastic moments of darkness and light). All of this is so we can create a joyful, fun and engaging hour in which everyone has a great time together. There is no hierarchy of performer and audience, no space that the audience can't inhabit. Old, tired theatre convention is thrown out of the window, if the audience wants to dance all the way through the show in the centre of the stage they can totally go for it, if someone wants to scream with delight, that is embraced.

Ultimately a Frozen Light show is about fun, entertainment and bringing together people to share an experience. It is about giving the audience control and valuing what they need from performers and the performance in the moment. But most importantly, it is about an offer. An offer to access theatre in the same places that the rest of society does, in a way that is accessible and appropriate for the needs of people with PMLD. *"We are forgotten"* is the most common response we have heard when talking with carers about their experience of Covid-19 whilst supporting an individual with PMLD. The pandemic has exacerbated and highlighted the social isolation of people with PMLD and their families as well as the exhaustion experienced by carers. People with profound and multiple learning disabilities must be visible in our society, must have the opportunity to access the arts, and we must continue to develop and grow the sensory theatre sector to ensure that these offers exist.

39

USA – Trusty Sidekick

Phin Fogg (Spencer Lott) and an audience member tend a cloud in the 2015 premiere of *UP AND AWAY*, commissioned by Lincoln Center and created by Trusty Sidekick Theater Company. Environment Design by Nic Benacerraf, Lighting Design by Simon Harding, Costume Design by Natalie Loveland.

Photo by Alexis Buatti-Ramos. www.trustysidekick.org

Tim Webb Writes

In 2011, I was invited to be keynote speaker at the TYA-USA (the US branch of ASSITEJ) Congress in Seattle where I met Jonathan Shmidt Chapman who at that time was the Artistic Director of Trusty Sidekick,

DOI: 10.4324/9781003091288-42

an exceptionally imaginative and talented New York-based company making work for young audiences. After the keynote, we kept on talking about neglected audiences and different ways of making theatre, a dialogue that eventually led to the Oily Cart involvement in Lincoln Center Education's amazing production *Up and Away*.

Paul Brewster McGinley, Managing Director of Trusty Sidekick Theatre Company Writes

When Trusty Sidekick Theatre Company was commissioned by Lincoln Center Education in 2013 to create an immersive theatrical production for young people on the autism spectrum, our first outreach for mentorship was to Oily Cart and specifically Tim Webb and Claire de Loon. Our NYC-based company had been creating bold, original and often immersive works for young people for a few years, but this would be our first production created specifically to engage a neuro-divergent young audience and their families.

Our ensemble members were fortunate enough to engage in professional learning directly with Tim and Claire. Through a series of memorable and joyful workshops and interviews they imparted philosophies, skills and practical considerations that were incredibly influential to our two-year devising process.

The moniker *Trusty Sidekick* comes from the idea that the audience is the hero of every story we share. This manifests by centering audience participation in our productions and by involving our target audience in the devising process. We often partner with local schools, exploring salient ideas from the rehearsal room about a show's form and content with true experts, the kids themselves.

The resulting production, *Up and Away*, premiered in the fall of 2015. The audience joined the Fogg Family Balloon Society for their 1,000th hot air balloon flight through the clouds, caring for a *cloud seed* to be planted in the sky. A cast of ten (eight actors performing one on one plus two musicians) engaged an audience of eight young people, each with up to two accompanying audience members. For school shows we sometimes stretched to ten young people since there were fewer adults as chaperones rather than families. During the run we had four crew in the theater plus front of house staff. The full creative team was approximately 25 people.

One of our favorite and most humbling testimonials from a parent was *It can be hard for Sam to be entirely present for a performance. But we felt that in a beautiful reversal, your performance was present for him.* Through the creation process, our creative team synthesised all that was learned from Tim, Claire, school partners and additional research into eight "ingredients" for our process of creating theater for neuro-diverse audiences:

- Pre-Show Engagement for Comfort
- One-on-one Interaction and Adaptation
- 360-Degree Theatrical Design
- Episodic Story with Clear Schedule
- Multi-Sensory Communication
- Distinct Characters
- Repetition
- Zoom In/Zoom Out Structure (Inspired by Oily Cart's "jazz structure," a balance of prescribed, timed moments of audience as a community watching the full ensemble perform, along with more flexible moments of improvised one-to-one interaction between audience member and performer.)

Eager to continue serving this audience, *Campfire* premiered in 2017, positing *how can the great outdoors be brought inside?* Audience members joined the Dorothy Sanders Rangers in a large tent around a campfire to sing songs, share stories and hopefully catch a glimpse of the elusive white-tailed deer. *Campfire*'s huggable wildlife puppets and crooning *Hot Dog Man* puppet utilised the ingredient of *distinct characters* and affirmed the power and magic of puppetry for all audiences.

Audience capacity for *Campfire* was twelve young people with up to two accompanying audience members. A cast of ten (four leads, four secondary characters, and two supporting roles) experimented with more of a *Zone* approach to engagement: each pair of lead and secondary characters engaged three young people in a quadrant of the space. The supporting roles floated throughout the space.

Both Trusty Sidekick and Oily Cart were featured in Lincoln Center's Big Umbrella Festival in April 2018. We remounted *Up and Away*, Oily Cart presented *Light Show* and the Australian company, Sensorium Theatre, presented *Oddysea*. Beyond sharing the pieces with audiences, the festival proved to be an incredible opportunity for our artistic ensembles to observe each other's work and engage in passionate conversations about nuanced performing and engagement techniques.

While we originally had big plans for touring *Up and Away* and *Campfire*, the financials and logistics proved prohibitive. We are currently experimenting with a model of licensing a script for a theatre to do their own production and providing mentoring services, wherever helpful, to the theatre's creative team. In addition to the script and sheet music that would typically come in a play's license, we share producing resources and customise workshops to apply or adapt the ingredients of our process to the theatre's unique production.

In early 2020 we were applying lessons learned from *Campfire* and *Up and Away* to the devising process for a new production for neuro-diverse audiences that would be more mobile and tour NYC schools. COVID-19 interrupted that devising process and has inspired a reimagining of what post-COVID sensory theatre can be. When it is safe to resume our in-person work, we know the theatrical conventions will evolve to keep everyone physically safe, but the emotional connection between performing artists and audiences will endure with an even greater impact.

40
Sweden – Scen:se Project

Tim Webb Writes

I met Eva von Hofsten at an Oily Cart Summer School in 2015. Eva had come to find out more about theatre for the early years. In fact, the Summer School, which was being held in a school for people with profound and multiple learning disabilities, drew her attention to that sector. When she returned to Sweden, she embarked on the epic task of raising the profile of theatre and other cultural activities for young people with PMLD or on the spectrum and raising the funding to make it all possible. This became the wholly admirable Scen:se Project in which I was honoured to be involved as an artist. (See photo in Chapter 22: Staging a Show – Stranden).

Eva von Hofsten, Project Leader for the Scen:se Project Writes

The Scen:se project in Sweden is a three-year project where inclusive art experiences are created for children and young people with complex needs, profound and multiple learning disabilities or on the autistic spectrum.

The project started because there was a lack of work in Sweden, especially in the performing arts sector, for audiences with complex needs. The aim was to introduce this work and also to inspire other artists and art institutions to start working in similar ways.

The project is owned by Hudiksvall municipality but is in very close collaborations with the regional museum, Hälsinglands museum, and the regional theatre, Folkteatern Gävleborg. Since one of the aims of the project was to reach out to as many as possible during the three years it is also a collaboration with the national touring theatre, Riksteatern, and the major festival for children and youth, BIBU.

DOI: 10.4324/9781003091288-43

The artistic work and methods have been imported and made by artists from the UK, where there were skills, methods and long experience from artists working with this audience. The artwork includes one sensory, inclusive art exhibition and two inclusive performing arts productions. There have also been inclusive educational methods in drama developed in collaboration with a number of special needs schools in the region.

The exhibition *Sinnerligt* is a collaboration between visual artist Greta McMillan, sensory performance maker Ellie Griffiths and textile artist Laura Blake. It is a sensory and interactive exhibition which consists of installations that the visitors can explore and enjoy with all the senses.

The performance *Stranden* is made for a young audience with complex needs and profound and multiple learning disabilities. It was created and directed by Tim Webb, then the artistic director of Oily Cart. It is a multisensory, close-up, inclusive performance based on the poem *Dover Beach* by Matthew Arnold. It is performed by four actors. In the original cast they were Ulrika Beijer, Hanna Edh, Eva von Hofsten, Arabella Lyons and Richard Sseruwagi. Six audience members and their six companions are invited to a beach café where they are served a multisensory menu. The music is very central to the piece and accompanied by piano the actors sing the lyrics of the poem. There is also a screen with video projections of the seaside, waves, pebbles and stormy skies. In the end, the actors take the audience in their chairs into a whirling dance throughout a storm.

The performance, *Shakespeare's Heartbeat/Pericles*, is made for a young audience on the autism spectrum and is directed by Kelly Hunter from Flute Theatre, based on the Shakespeare play *Pericles*. It is performed by four actors and one musician and is created based on Kelly's method *The Hunter Heartbeat Method*. The audience of 10 young people sit on a mat together with the actors who perform pieces of the play that specifically focus on the moments in Shakespeare where characters emerge through seeing, thinking and feeling. These are then mixed with sensory drama games that the young audience does together with the actors.

The educational development work in special needs schools was led by the British theatre maker, teacher and researcher Dr. Gill Brigg. Apart from working with teachers and students, she also made an educational pack to be used by the schools after they have taken part in one of the shows. What has been really successful is also that before each performance of *Stranden*, a drama teacher from the project has visited each class and prepared them for the coming show.

The exhibition and the performances have toured all over Sweden, the performances in collaboration with the National touring theatre. They have all three been very well received and we can easily state that the need for this work in Sweden is enormously large. For example, the adults that accompanied the young people visiting the performance *Stranden* have after almost every show told the actors that *this is the first time that we have been invited to a performance that is actually created for our students.* Before they have often been invited to performances for toddlers, sometimes together with the toddlers. Also, the venues are relieved that they finally can offer something for young people with complex needs.

What has been most successful, apart from spreading the work and touring all over the country, is the interest and impact the project has made on the performing arts sector in Sweden. Many of the major performing arts institutions, especially the ones working with children and youth, have contacted us and are now either starting projects or planning performances on their own. During BIBU 2020, Scen:se was planning to collaborate and make a thematic program that would run during the whole festival, with performances, seminars and workshops all within the field of creating inclusive performing arts, but unfortunately Covid 19 has interrupted this and so many other beautiful projects.

The Scen:se Project is funded by Allmänna Arvsfonden (the Swedish Inheritance fund), Svenska Postkodstiftelsen (the Swedish lottery fund), Region Gävleborg and Kulturrådet (Swedish Arts Council).

41
National Theatre of Wales and Oily Cart

Splish Splash 2018 Oily Cart & National Theatre Wales co-production. Performer, Anni Dafydd in the water with mirror chest. Design: Jens Demant Cole.

Photo: Suzi Corker.

Tim Webb Writes

Splish Splash was a co-production by the Oily Cart with the National Theatre of Wales as part of their celebrations of the Seventieth Anniversary of the National Health Service. For most of the rehearsals and performances of *Splish Splash* that the company undertook in Wales, Francesca Picard, part

DOI: 10.4324/9781003091288-44

of the Emerging Director Scheme of the National Theatre of Wales, was assigned to the company and apart from doing an excellent job of looking after the team on the road, also maintained a blog with a thorough description of a touring hydro show.

Francesca Pickard, Francesca Pickard Writes

By the time I join Oily Cart, their pool-based show, *Splish Splash*, co-produced with National Theatre of Wales, has been in development for some time.

Director and writer, Tim Webb, hands me three sheets of laminated A4 paper, which act as the script, broken down into short episodes for three distinct audiences, ASC (Autism Spectrum), PMLD (Profound and Multiple Learning Disabilities) and those who are Deaf-Blind. I meet five performers, Anni Dafydd, Ruby Campbell, Hannah Kimpton, Kayleigh Cottam and George Panda, wearing an array of brightly coloured costumes with sponges, balls, musical instruments and even a scaled down ship attached to their heads.

The pool space is lit with underwater lights and three interactive boxes bob on the surface waiting to be discovered. The choreography has been learnt, the music scored, the narrative formed and the characters explored. In many ways, it seems as though most of the work has already taken place but, in fact, it is only now that the potential of the show can be realised. With the addition of its most crucial element – its audience participants.

Oily Cart has been making theatre for audiences with specific needs for 40 years and the attention to detail this work requires is staggering. The performers in the show need to be prepared for every eventuality in the pool, be that somebody surfing on their instruments, taking a bite out of their costume, making up their own song lyrics and dance moves or changing the structure of the piece entirely. The only way to be truly prepared and ready to react is to train . . . and for the next two weeks that is exactly what the extraordinarily committed cast do. Using a mixture of young people with a broad range of needs, their carers and a few willing adult volunteers, they explore the plethora of routes and pathways that the show could take, embracing each one as an opportunity to hone their responses and wring out every possibility for interaction, connection and feeling.

Tim is not satisfied until he has explored the sensory potential of every object in the room; what can a watering can do besides pour water? What happens if you use it under the water? Does it make an interesting sound and what sensations occur when the water is sucked in and pumped out through the top? Can an umbrella also be used as a fan to waft air over those in the pool or to make a soundproof bubble?

This innate curiosity and playfulness underpin all of the work taking place and each member of the team gets a chance to act as a participant and experience the sensory journey being created before it is shared with the far more discerning, real audience members. This, in itself, is revelatory. Much was discussed about the vibrations from the specially modified calabash *Saturn* drums, created for the show by Oily Cart's associate instrument maker, Jamie Linwood. However, it was not until I experienced the show as a visually impaired participant might, that about halfway through, my other senses metamorphosed and I understood what everyone was talking about. The surge I experienced in the water when the drumming began was incredible.

It is hard to explain how powerful this intimate work is but the impact it has on the children and the staff, who accompany them in the pool, is very moving. When one carer calls another over to see just how much a pupil with PMLD is smiling, or a boy who usually refuses to leave the safety rails decides to venture further into the pool to look at a box spewing bubbles, or children described as *nonverbal* expel all sorts of sounds and noises when hearing their name sung aloud; it feels like the show is offering a profound opportunity for self-expression, choice and play. For most of the first fortnight I well up during every performance and I ask the musical director, Max Reinhardt, when I will become more acclimatised to the proceedings. He says perhaps we should hope I never do, and he is probably right. I want to continue to be surprised and delighted by this exceptional work which can also make me laugh out loud in equal measure.

Despite the oppressive heat (the hydrotherapy pool rooms are a balmy 35 degrees), Tim watches every performance with hawk-eye focus, monitoring reactions and studying how the children and performers interact with one another and the watery wonderland around them. He then shares his observations with the cast, and they discuss how to incorporate the audiences' unpredictable offerings into the show even more, as well as the importance of pause and processing time. In tandem, Max continually refines the soaring harmonies and associate director, Debbie Bandara, fine tunes the choreography until the show is ready for its first proper previews.

We often acknowledge that no two theatre experiences are the same because of the nature of live performance and the energy and exchange between performers and their audience but this has never been more apparent to me than in *Splish Splash*. Each show is entirely different, moulded by a dedicated and sensitive cast to the individual requirements and personalities of the audience. Given the emphasis so often placed on what artists are trying to say or communicate, this totally audience-led approach is refreshing. Every decision in the pool is made with their needs and enjoyment as the primary concern.

Working with Oily Cart has expanded my ideas on theatre, audiences and disability. Creating work in a pool is not without its issues; stage manager and all-round super woman, Bea Galloway, is forever recharging batteries for the floating lights and working with production manager Will Aubrey Jones to replace or repair items that have suffered from the moisture or chemicals to which they they've been exposed.

The immersive environment, however, has opened my eyes to the possibilities of different spaces and how an audience might move or be moved within a performance. I have also been inspired by the generosity and care that the gifted, diligent actors have demonstrated. Most importantly of all though, what I thought I knew about disability has been challenged. Tim has talked about the use of categorisation and its potential to impose limitations or pigeon-hole those with special needs but as he points out, *they're just kids and they're all different.* He is, of course, absolutely right. They are also all equally deserving of space to play, the opportunity to make choices, to respond, share their joy and experience theatre, made just for them, by people who have dedicated their time and talent to crafting it in the best way possible, with and for their unique and brilliant audience.

July 17, 2018

42
What's Next for Oily Cart?

Tim Webb Writes

Ellie Griffiths originally joined the company as a performer in *Something in the Air*. She became a key member of the Oily team and contributed greatly to the success of many shows such as the three versions of *Tube*, *Light Show* and *The Bounce*. Ellie was appointed Artistic Director on my retirement in 2019.

This is transcribed from a questionnaire that I sent to Ellie and to which she provided some very illuminating answers.

Ellie Griffiths, Artistic Director of Oily Cart Writes: Why Did You Want to Work With Tim or Amanda, Max and Tim?

As a young performer/theatre maker I was told about a theatre company that flew its young disabled audience members up in the air! I had never heard of anything like it. Later, looking up the Oily Cart's website, I was blown away by the creativity of the company. They played so freely with form and experimented with different approaches to relate to their audiences. Oily Cart reconfigured and expanded my perception of theatre and what it could be and who it could be for. It opened up to a much broader palette of creative possibilities. The dignity of each audience member was clearly the priority of every show. I quickly realised that I didn't want to be part of theatre that was any other way. The combination of social purpose, with free artistic exploration and ambition is what makes their work so extraordinary.

This made me want to work with the company and learn from the creators. Tim, Amanda and Max blew apart any prejudices I had about work for young audiences being less ambitious, artistic or valuable than anything made for

DOI: 10.4324/9781003091288-45

adults. I learnt more from being part of Oily Cart rehearsal processes with the creative team then I did in my whole degree. I went from being a young performer who could never focus on anything long enough to finish it, to someone who stayed with the company and focused all my creative energy on their work for a very happy, stimulating and rewarding five years.

How Did the Audiences React to the Performances?

There were many varied responses and really anything could happen, which was exhilarating, fun and sometimes challenging.

Parents and observers were often very moved seeing the young people engaging with the work. Many parents would say things such as "I have never seen them do that." I remember performing closely with a very small boy who had limited movements. I was trying to pick up on his breath patterns to respond to him. Being honest, I wasn't certain that he knew that the theatre performance was happening or that I was there. I looked up and his two dads were crying. They said they had never seen him track someone with his gaze for this length of time (about 30 seconds I think). From him, this was a really significant response. All three of them as a family had clearly dressed up for the special event of the show. Seeing how much this meant to them really moved me. I still get a bit teary thinking about it.

There was another moment in *Tube*, where I looked around and every child was engaged and part of the same really soft atmosphere, but in completely different ways – one was lying on the floor in the middle of the stage area, one was licking water from an umbrella, someone else was watching intently from the safety of the corner, one had their back against the big tube instrument to feel maximum vibrations from the beautiful music. This felt like a perfect moment, but everyone shared an energy or atmosphere. I now judge the success of a show by its ability to achieve these fleeting moments where everyone shares a moment, in their different ways.

I always especially enjoyed moments when the young people hijacked the shows and themselves became the performers! We were primed to give their contributions equal status to anything we were doing. I remember one young woman dancing ferociously centre stage to her name song. She raised the roof! I also remember in *The Bounce*, one boy placing himself under my chin to feel the variation of my voice through the top of his head. We bounced gently together on the trampoline to the music – my arms under his, and he sung and vocalised in perfect harmony to what I was singing. It was a duet, and gave me goosebumps.

What Was Successful About the Performances?

The Sensory Aspects

This way of working brings everyone out of their head and into their body – which is so good for people, disabled and non-disabled. This has the ability to connect everyone equally and felt extremely successful for these young audiences. I can't imagine a show being accessible for young people labelled as having complex disabilities that isn't sensory. Sensory working is a good way of getting your ego out of the way – I used to be terrified of singing (bad drama school experiences). Working with Oily Cart I rediscovered my voice as an amazing source of vibration and gateway to connection.

Responsive

Using approaches like Intensive Interaction, and really listening and integrating the audience's responses into the performance was a really fundamental element to why Oily Cart's shows felt so successful with diverse young audiences.

Stillness and Breath

By giving space for processing, it felt like the shows provided open entry points for more people to engage than standard shows.

Close up

The use of touch in the shows was such a central, accessible performance language. Not shying away from touch and the close up, but really digging deep into this highly localised playing space seemed really effective for many young people who would be defined as very "hard to reach."

Not Prioritising Neurotypical Theatre Tropes

This one is hard to articulate, but it's something about working closely with groups of young people in the creative process, that meant that a neuro-divergent aesthetic and feel to the shows developed naturally and had great influence on the content. In this way, Oily Cart shows never felt like a group of neurotypical people telling their stories to a group of neuro-divergent young people . . . which I think is what can often happen. It felt like neuro-diversity was the dominant culture in the room. Neurotypical people had to shift their expectations and their ways of engaging in theatre, and that felt exciting in a world which always asks neuro-divergent individuals to fit into structures that don't suit them.

Balance of Structure and Chaos

The structure that left room for creative chaos and allowed for some healthy anarchy led to lots of comedy and fun and I think was quite liberating for many of the young people who are often told they're doing things wrong.

Music and Sound

The music held everyone together and relaxed and roused audiences – it feels like a naturally accessible form as even deaf young people could enjoy the vibrations of sound, which was always very popular. The compositions always respected non-tonal sounds as much as melody, which seemed really successful with many, particularly autistic young people who often themselves seek out and explore interesting sounds in their environments.

Framing

The core creative team were very good at framing moments of interesting sound or visuals. This kind of zooming in the focus on one really interesting sound – like water hitting a metal bowl, was always really successful with our audiences. It often led to some good comedy moments too, for example the three red balls dropping from the sky in Something in the Air.

What Didn't Work?

By the time I began working for Oily Cart as a performer, Tim, Amanda and Max were masters of making sensory theatre for these audiences, so there wasn't anything in the mix that felt like it didn't work, only more possibilities to keep playing with. I used to come up with "new" ideas for a sensory show. I would use Tim as a sounding board and quite often he would reply something similar to "ah yes, we did try that once in the nineties" . . . it's been a very tough act to follow!

The more sensory shows I make, the more I find that there is no such thing as a perfectly inclusive performance. Whatever format you pick, and whatever content you generate, it always creates barriers for someone. Fundamentally people are different and need different things. For example, one person may need close up, human interaction to be able to engage with a piece, while others might find the close-up work too socially intense. Maybe the biggest danger is to start generalising. I think Tim's highly responsive style is the best chance you have of avoiding this.

Were You Surprised by Any of the Audience Reactions or Other Feedback?

I was continually surprised by audience reactions and feedback throughout my time performing with Oily Cart. The real beauty of sensory theatre is that there are endless ways of engaging, and crucially, all are given equal value. This can range from an individual exploring the shoes of a performer with their mouth (my first performance for the company!) to someone wearing a washing basket on their head to view the show through (I assumed this was to diffuse the social intensity of the situation). In everyday life, we are so often socialised to mask our true feelings or needs (especially us Brits), that it was relaxing and energising to be in a space where this wasn't necessary or needed. I know this sounds a weird irony to describe acting in a show! But it felt like the theatre space, where you have control of the environmental elements, had the ability to reset and reshape a micro-world that suited many more different people. This is hugely powerful to witness and be part of.

I feel that this ethos and feeling rubbed off on us performers, we let our guards down too, and that is what would make the potential for proper connection, which led to some really moving atmospheres and spontaneous moments. Oily Cart has taught me so much about people, it's been like re-learning the world. I really value that.

This isn't to say that sometimes the hugely varied responses weren't challenging – we were often working with people who had very high anxiety, and some found the sensory aspects over-stimulating so needed to go to a quiet space to decompress. The atmosphere of the room could quickly go from feeling joyful, to chaotic, to challenging. You would apply the exact same approach and structure for two different crowds and they would react in opposite ways. This meant as a performer you had to be quite resilient and accept failure as part of the work. In an audience of six young people who are on the autistic spectrum, it's not unusual for one person to not make it into the room, or to leave during the show. Making it easy for someone to leave is part of respecting their autonomy.

I was sometimes surprised by the feedback of non-disabled adults who came to the shows. Sometimes (not often), it felt they didn't *get it* or would hold it up to set notions of theatre and what it *should* be. I think to really absorb the value of this work you have to be prepared to open yourself to the beauty of other ways of being.

Do You Think These Productions May Have an Effect on Your Future Work?

Ha Ha, Just a Little!

Tube for me was the happiest and most at home I had felt in my work to that point. It was a real turning point where I felt that for me everything came together and started to make sense. I loved that show like a pair of comfortable shoes that I liked the look of and fitted perfectly. We had so much space to play and improvise and respond within a really strong structure. This led to tours that were full of some of the most hilarious, connected and creative spontaneous moments. I have a photo of this show in my office to remind me why I do this work.

At various points in my career, I have been advised against pigeon-holing myself, or getting too specialised in one area. I have found that since focusing fully on sensory theatre, everything has built in a really organic, authentic way. As an area of work, it continues to open up and get richer and deeper. It's full of challenges and rewards in equal measure. Once you've really experienced it, it's not something you can ever turn away from.

What Are Your Hopes for the Future of This Work?

I hope that this work starts to feel less specialist. Sensory work is a universal way of making theatre that has the ability to level the playing field. The wider theatre sector has work to do to get to a point where audiences who have complex disabilities are always a consideration, or part of the conversation when every show is being made. Inclusion is everyone's responsibility. It's no longer acceptable for a whole part of society to be ignored or erased by the cultural sector.

I hope that more diverse artists feel inspired to make sensory theatre work. Oily Cart have found one way of making, but the creative possibilities are infinite. It's not enough to have one show for these audiences available every two years. Different styles and formats work for different people. I look forward to a point where our audiences can make more choices about the types of work they want to experience and the work they like. We need more artistic options so people can lead varied and active cultural lives as artists and audiences.

How Can an Interactive Close-up Methodology Survive Covid?

Sensory theatre makers have always worked within many parameters and seeming limitations, to engage people with different ways of being in the world. This situation has made us dig deeper and get more creative to figure out how to enable moments of joy, connection and play within these new parameters.

I have been experimenting with how we can get this connection without using touch. This has led us to some new formats. For example, we have been doing a Doorstep version of a music show we made last year. This is now being performed by three musicians in the garden or on the doorstep of the family. The family were sent a package of sensory items to support this in the post before the event. There is also an accompanying sensory video of ideas they can try at home to extend this work. I have been really encouraged by how intimate these mini gigs have felt, with all the room for listening and responding to the young person and family.

We also have a version of this on Zoom, which I was a bit resistant to in the beginning, questioning how we could make sensory theatre work on screen. Although it is totally different, what's been interesting is that we have reached young people through this format that we wouldn't have been able to in any other way. For example, we performed last week for a young boy who never leaves his bedroom due to the complexity of his disabilities. His family wrote us a message emphasising how special it had felt to have this show for their boy in a format they could access. I think that feeling of being acknowledged and celebrated is really powerful and doesn't wholly rely on touch. I think it's about the rigour and care and attention to detail you put into these experiences that makes them feel special.

In a different example, when we made a sensory exhibition that had no performers, we used recorded singing and voices in some platforms the visitors could lie on and feel the vibrations. I was amazed how intimate this felt, and this piece was the most popular of any of the other pieces of the exhibition.

I think that, particularly for people who have social disabilities, such as autism, it gave intimacy without social interaction, which can be valuable in itself. It's quite a neurotypical thing to always think that human connection is what makes everyone tick. So, in some ways, these new distanced formats may work just as well, or even better for some individuals.

Going into the future, we should fight for the value of positive touch. The young people we work with shouldn't be denied this for the next few years because they are seen as being high risk. We now need to find ways that the adults who are in their bubbles can be the translators of this work.

43

Can We Touch? Sensory Theatre in a Time of Covid

I began work on the first draft of this book in mid-March 2020, just as the first lock-down in England was imposed to prevent the spread of Covid 19. Everyone seemed to know that life would never be the same again. The chief ray of hope was that the virus did not appear to affect children.

But anyone involved in theatre or any other form of live performance could see that their jobs were particularly under threat. We were being told that. Well, we were being told many things – often different things from day to day and from week to week. If it was designed to keep us alarmed and confused, it certainly succeeded. We were told we should remain isolated in our homes as much as possible. Outside our homes, we should maintain a distance of 2 metres between us and any other person.

Even when the advice eased up towards the end of summer and we were encouraged to use pubs and restaurants, and limited outdoor sport was reintroduced, the theatres had to remain closed.

A good deal of ingenuity was applied by people involved in Sensory Theatre to maintain some sort of a presence – if only online. Oily Cart, in association with the Up Front Performance Network, produced a wonderful International Sensory Lab. This was a series of Zoom-based blogs from around the world, featuring artists such as Sensorium from Australia, Frozen Light from England, Hospital Theatre Project from Japan, Scen:se from Sweden, Joanna Grace and Gill Brigg, both from UK. Oily Cart had also been mounting a revival of *Jamboree*, a music-based show, in which the young audience with disabilities encountered characters on Zoom who they later met *live* on their own doorstep or in the playground of their school.

Japan's Hospital Theatre Project toured a show well into 2020 that made careful use of Perspex screens and transparent face masks to work at relatively close range to the audience.

DOI: 10.4324/9781003091288-46

These projects were widely welcomed by the audiences and strong links developed between some companies and the families with whom they had been working.

As the pandemic subsides further into the background of our lives and we come to treat Covid as something endemic but containable, like the flu, I believe that we should do more to consider the role of SEND school staff. It is the staff who have been the ones continuing to offer the fun proximity, the touch, the breath and the interactivity that is so vital to the young people. It is the staff who can fulfil the role that family members take when sensory work happens in the home. I would suggest that the Sensory Theatre companies develop strategies to engage, inform and inspire teachers and teaching assistants, who could continue doing close-up and face-to-face work with the young people, while the sensory artists and companies provide the research, the training and the fabulous resources online and everywhere as needed, without spending too much time physically moving in and out of the "bubbles" of vulnerable school communities.

Having said that, it seems to me that it is wonderful what the small, modestly-funded Sensory Theatre artists and companies have achieved in this time of Covid, both in terms of the quality of the work and the engagement of the audience.

As I write, Covid continues to threaten us all. I fear that many of the biggest players in the struggles for profile and funding, the national theatres, opera companies, orchestras and museums, have yet to exercise their sense of entitlement and claim that as standard bearers of British culture they must be saved no matter who else goes to the wall. There are so many smaller organisations, including Sensory Theatre organisations, who make their mark not by playing to thousands but by working with the accuracy and intensity that can engage the most complex audiences. This is theatre that must be performed close-up to its audience – or it will achieve nothing. But done properly, and properly funded, it will continue to produce remarkable results.

Part Four
Extras

SOCIAL STORY

The Cover of the Social Story for *Light Show* 2015 Oily Cart. Graphic designer: Jo Hill.

DOI: 10.4324/9781003091288-47

Appendix I
Books That I Have Found Especially Useful

Brown, M. (2012) *Oily Cart – All Sorts of Theatre for All Sorts of Kids*. Stoke on Trent, UK and Sterling, USA: Trentham Books

Caldwell, P. (2007) with Horwood, J. *From Isolation to Intimacy*. London: Jessica Kingsley

Caldwell, P. (2008) with Horwood J. *Using Intensive Interaction and Sensory Integration*. London: Jessica Kingsley

Caldwell, P. (2010) Hoghton, M. and Mytton, P., *Autism and Intensive Interaction*. DVD and booklet London: Jessica Kingsley

Davies, C. (2011) *Creating Multi-Sensory Environments*. Abingdon: Routledge

Grandin, T. (1996) *Thinking in Pictures*. New York: Viking Books

Grandin, T. (2005) with Margaret Scariano. *Emergence – Labeled Autistic*. New York: Warner Books

Grandin, T. (2006) with Catherine Johnson. *Animals in Translation*. London: Bloomsbury Publishing

Gray, C. (2000) *The New Social Story Book*. Arlington, Tx: Future Horizons, Inc.

Grace, J. (2020) *Multiple Multisensory Rooms: Myth Busting the Magic*. Abingdon: Routledge

Hewett, D. (2012) Firth, G., Barber, M. and Harrison T. *The Intensive Interaction Handbook*. London: SAGE publications

Higashida, N. (2013), translation Mitchell, D. and Yoshida, KA. *The Reason I Jump*. London: Hodder and Stoughton

Howlin, P. (1999) Baron-Cohen, S. & Hadwin, J. *Teaching Children with Autism to Mind-Read*. Chichester: Wiley

Hulsegge, J. (1986) & Verheul, A. *Snoezelen Another World*. London: Rompa

Kranowitz, C. (1998) *The Out-Of-Sync Child*. New York: Perigee Book

Pagliano, P. (2012) *The Multisensory Handbook*. Abingdon: Routledge

Silberman, S. (2015) *Neurotribes*, London: Allen & Unwin

Spaggiari, S. (1996) & Rinaldi, C. *The Hundred Languages of Children*. Reggio Emilia, Italy: Reggio Children

Williams, D. (1999) *Nobody Nowhere*, London: Jessica Kingsley

Appendix 2
A List of the Shows Written/ Directed by Tim Webb

Date	Show	Audience	Company Oily Cart unless stated otherwise
1981	Out of Their Tree	Under 5's	
1982	Grease	Park show	
1982	Bus Stop	Under 5's	
1982	The Exploding Punch & Judy	Park show	
1982	Prehistoric Playtime	5–9	
1982	Bats in Their Belfry	5–7	
1983	Rainbow Robbers	Under 5's	
1983	Bedtime Story	Under 5's	
1983	Beam Me Up Spotty	7–11	
1983	Down the Plughole	5–7	
1984	Parrots of Penzance	7–11	
1984	Seaside	Under 5's	
1985	Picnic	Under 5's	
1985	Tibet or Not Tibet	7–11	
1985	Soap Suds	Under 5's	
1986	Slipped Disco	7–11	
1986	Up on the Roof	Under 5's	
1987	Curse of the Mummy's Sphinx	7–11	
1987	Box of Tricks	Under 5's	
1987	Bermuda Rectangle	7–11	

Date	Show	Audience	Company *Oily Cart unless stated otherwise*
1988	*Box of Socks*	SLD one day	
1988	*Playhouse*	Under 5's	
1989	*Chest of Drawers*	Under 5's	
1989	*Pleasuredome*	SLD one day	
1990	*Colour Me, Colour You*	SLD one day	
1990	*Will It Hurt?*	5–7	
1990	*Ocean Notion*	7–11 (Hearing impaired)	
1990	*Red Lorry, Yellow Lorry*	Under 5's	
1991	*Funky Philharmonic*	SLD one day	
1991	*Off the Wall*	Under 5's	
1991	*It Crept from the Crypt*	7–11	
1992	*Gobble and Gook*	5–9	
1992	*Dinnerladies from Outer Space*	SLD one day	
1992	*Greenfingers*	Under 5's	
1993	*Euro Broadbent*	SLD two day	
1993	*A Bit Missing*	Under 5's	
1993	*Fishing for Pigs*	5–9	
1994	*Georgie Goes to Hollywood*	SLD two day	
1994	*A Peck of Pickled Pepper*	Under 5's	
1995	*George After a Fashion*	SLD two day	
1995	*Perfect Present*	Under 5's	
1996	*The Roly Poly Pudding*	Under 5's	
1996	*George Sells Out*	SLD two day	
1996	*Tickled Pink*	PMLD one day	
1997	*Garratt Fair*	Smallwood Primary School project	
1997	*Bubbles*	PMLD – r&d water show	
1997	*Over the Moon*	PMLD one day	

Date	Show	Audience	Company Oily Cart unless stated otherwise
1998	Hunky Dory	PMLD one day	
1998	Pass the Parcel	Under 5's	
1999	Big Splash	PMLD – water show	
1999	Playhouse	Under 5's	
2000	Knock Knock! Who's There?	Under 5's	
2000	Dreams and Secrets	PMLD & ASC – water show	
2001	Waving	PMLD – water show	
2001	Under Your Hat	Under 6's two-day & installations at Southbank & Lyric	
2002	Boing!	PMLD – trampoline show	
2002	Tonic Water	PMLD – water show	Giant Productions, Glasgow
2002	Jumping Beans	Under 5's & baby show	
2003	Baking Time	Under 5's	Co-production with Carousel Players, Canada
2003	Moving Pictures	PMLD – trampoline show	
2004	Hippity Hop	Under 5's & baby show	Co-production with Lyric, Hammersmith
2004	The Ship of Gold & the Genie's Lamp	Under 5's – outdoor fountains event	Co-production with Somerset House
2004	Conference of the Birds	PMLD & ASC	
2005	King Neptune & the Pirate Queen	Under 5's – Fountains event	Co-production with Somerset House
2005	If All the World Were Paper	Under 5's	
2006	Big Balloon	Under 5's	

Date	Show	Audience	Company Oily Cart unless stated otherwise
2006	Blue	PMLD & ASC	
2006	Baby Balloon	Baby show	Co-production with Pantalone, Brussels
2007	Blue – embedded characters	PMLD & ASC	Co-production with Manchester International Festival
2008	How Long Is a Piece of String?	Under 5's	
2008	Pool Piece	PMLD – water show	Co-production with Snakes & Ladders and Theatre Is . . .
2009	Red Kite, Blue Moon	ASC	Chicago Children's Theatre, USA
2009	Christmas Baking Time	Under 5's	Co-production with the Lyric, Hammersmith
2009	Something in the Air	PMLD & ASC	Co-production with Ockham's Razor and Manchester International Festival
2010	Mole in the Hole	Under 5's	Co-production with Unicorn
2010	Drum	Under 11's PMLD & ASC & baby shows	
2011	Ring A Ding Ding	Under 5's	
2011	Gorgeous	PMLD & ASC	Co-production with Manchester International Festival
2011	Llechan Lan	PMLD	Galeri, Wales
2012	In a Pickle	Under 5's	Co-production with the Royal Shakespeare Company
2013	Tube	Under 11's PMLD & ASC	
2013	Baby Tube	baby show	

Date	Show	Audience	Company *Oily Cart unless stated otherwise*
2013	Mr. and Mrs. Moon	Under 5's	
2014	*The Bounce*	PMLD & ASC – trampoline show	
2014	*There Was an Old Woman*	Under 5's	
2015	*Light Show*	PMLD & ASC	
2015	*Land of Lights*	Under 5's & enhanced performances	
2016	*Mirror Mirror*	PMLD & ASC	
2016	*Four Winds Project*	PMLD/ASC/MSI	So-Edinenie, Russia
2016	*In a Pickle*	Under 5's & enhanced performances	
2017	*Kubla Khan*	PMLD/ASC/MSI	
2017	*Pop-Up Picnic*	PMLD	Helium, Ireland
2017	*Hush-A-Bye*	Under 5's / babies & enhanced performances	
2018	*Splish Splash*	PMLD/ASC/MSI – water show	Co-production with National Theatre of Wales
2018	*Stranden*	PMLD & ASC	Scen:se, Sweden

Key

SLD one day	One day-long event in Severe Learning Disability School
SLD two day	Two day-long event in Severe Learning Disability School
PMLD	Profound and Multiple Learning Disability audience
ASC	Autistic Spectrum Condition audience
MSI	Multiple Sensory Impairment audience

Appendix 3
How Philosophy and Theatre Can Help Us Value Profoundly Disabled People

EXTRACT OF IOE BLOG BY JOHN VORHAUS

PROFESSOR OF MORAL AND EDUCATIONAL PHILOSOPHY, INSTITUTE OF EDUCATION, UNIVERSITY COLLEGE, LONDON AND EDITOR OF IOE BLOG

Splish Splash 2018 Oily Cart & National Theatre Wales co-production. Performer, Anni Dafydd in the water with a young participant. Design: Jens Demant Cole.

Photo: Suzi Corker.

Tim Webb Writes

I first met John Vorhaus when I was visiting one of my Oily Cart productions in a London Special School. John was there as part of his study of the moral and educational basis of work with profoundly disabled people. This led to him taking an interest in our theatre productions in these settings. He invited me to talk to his students on several occasions. In 2018, he and a colleague, Sarah Richmond, produced a short film as part of their research into the experience of theatre for children with Profound and Multiple Learning Disabilities which looked at the development of the Oily Cart hydropool production, *Splish Splash*. (Link to **The Work of Oily Cart: Bringing Theatre to Children with PMLD – 2018** on YouTube https://youtu.be/BPlzoF3Modw).

I have enjoyed discussing the value of Sensory Theatre with John. It has been very useful to see the work from a different perspective. John edits the IOE blog at University College London: Expert opinion from academics at IOE, UCL's Faculty of Education and Society. I thought that it would be worthwhile including an extract of a piece that he wrote in April 2014.

John Vorhaus Writes

A series of philosophical questions arise from reflection on profound disability and dependency, with implications not only for profoundly disabled people, but for all of us at some stage in our lives. A few thoughts about our moral status will illustrate the point, with help from the world of theatre.

What does our moral status depend upon? A common response is the capacity for autonomy and rationality. But not all human beings have much of either. What about the importance of human relations and relationships? But where would that leave the lonely or unloved? Belonging to the same species? For some this is just a matter of biological taxonomy, yet for others it is of the utmost moral significance, a reminder that we are all *fellow creatures*.

Philosophers think about these features of humanity in strikingly different ways. Some explore the meaning of a human life and the language we employ to understand it. Others emphasise empirical enquiry, looking especially in the direction of the neuro- and cognitive sciences. People with profound and multiple learning difficulties and disabilities (PMLD) present a challenge. What exactly is *their* moral status? They lack what many see as the hallmark of moral agency – a capacity for rational autonomy.

When thinking about these questions it can help to get one's head out of a book and spend time with parents, carers, teachers, interpreters, therapists – and theatre directors. **Tim Webb** first set up Oily Cart over 30 years ago, producing *all sorts of theatre for all sorts of kids*. His company offers interactive, multisensory theatre to profoundly disabled children, and what it provides is not only *theatre* as you or I might understand this, but an experience of smelling, hearing, touching and feeling a rush of fanned air against your face. It's a world in which, as Lyn Gardner of The Guardian described one performance, *soundscape, sensory diversions, colour and water come together in a liquid world of enchantment.*

The work of Oily Cart – what they bestow on the children, and what they succeed in bringing out of them – whether a smile, stilled attentiveness or chuckling pleasure – is a wonderful thing to behold: magical, sensitive, clever, pretty, thoughtful, imaginative and – above all – a world which reaches inside the children, exciting their senses and imagination, and making an intimate connection with a group of human beings who number amongst the most dependent and hard to reach on earth.

Possibilities abound: how theatre might reveal what someone is capable of that might otherwise be thought impossible (adults watching on sometimes cannot believe their eyes); how the subtlest enticing of the senses might draw out and enliven a previously inert and *unreachable* child. And while these children may never participate in politics or anything like it, they might succeed in contributing to a theatrical event, becoming – if only momentarily – members of a group sharing in a common human endeavour.

These possibilities are open to ridicule as the product of sentimental wishful thinking. But the thoughts inspired by theatrical work of this kind are not to be dismissed out of hand. We are shown how a human being may surprise herself, and us, when brought alive by something captivating, becoming part of something beautiful that she will not see for herself, but which she is yet contributing to and representing. Thoughts of this nature, prompted by remarkable theatre, and a remarkable and exceptionally vulnerable group of human beings, are worth reflecting on when thinking about the contours of their moral status, and ours.

This is a link to the full article: https://blogs.ucl.ac.uk/ioe/2014/04/17/how-philosophy-and-theatre-can-help-us-value-profoundly-disabled-people/

Appendix 4
Links to Oily Cart Show Videos on YouTube

Baby Balloon **PtI (2006)**

Performance for babies at Pantalone Art House, Brussels
Ernst Reijseger on cello

> YouTube link: https://youtu.be/z21RaH2o9-E

Baby Balloon **Pt2 (2006)**

> YouTube link: https://youtu.be/Z4tI-MF2hVc

Blue **(2006)**

Edited version from two performances for young people with Profound and Multiple Learning Disabilities or an Autistic Spectrum Condition.

> YouTube link: https://youtu.be/SyshdtT_4BY

Something in the Air Trailer **(2009)**

Oily Cart and Ockham's Razor present *Something in the Air* at the Contact Theatre Manchester, as part of the Manchester International Festival.

> YouTube link: https://youtu.be/3_QtmvWZaEw

Oily Cart Performance. Manchester Evening News. Something in the Air **(2009)**

A unique performance by Oily Cart & Ockham's Razor at the Contact Theatre commissioned by Manchester International Festival.

> YouTube link: https://youtu.be/MXUh4p3R8_4

Tim Webb on Ring A Ding Ding (2012)

Tim Webb, Artistic Director of Oily Cart, reflects on *Ring A Ding Ding*, a new show for ages 3–5, playing at The New Victory Theater.

YouTube link: https://youtu.be/C7GkRCKBMJw

Ring A Ding Ding From Oily Cart (2012)

Short trailer for the show at The New Victory Theater in New York. A tabletop set turns "round and round" as Alice and her friends search left and right, high and low for her runaway pet in this colorful and creative piece of participatory theater.

YouTube link: https://youtu.be/j2IYqMkKzKE

In a Pickle: Royal Shakespeare Festival Documentary (2012)

The making of . . . includes clips of *Mole in a Hole* and *How Long Is a Piece of String?*

YouTube link: https://youtu.be/xAs7jjXlMs0

In a Pickle, an Oily Cart Production for 3–5 Year Olds (2012)

An Oily Cart production first commissioned by the RSC. This is total theatre experience for children aged 3 to 5, their families and friends inspired by *The Winter's Tale*. Our young audience join us on a voyage of discovery through the landscapes of Shakespeare's imagination and the music of his language.

YouTube link: https://youtu.be/kJ0rHc-vId8

There Was an Old Woman Trailer (2014)

Trailer for *There Was an Old Woman*, Oily Cart's new show for 3–5 years olds, opening at Southbank Centre on 13th Dec 2014.

YouTube link: https://youtu.be/FR927YSj2EI

All About the Bounce (2014)

Instructional video on how best to get on and off the trampolines for *The Bounce*, Oily Cart's new complex disability show.

YouTube link: https://youtu.be/hsLsgRsulNg

The Bounce: Teacher Interviews (2015)

Oily Cart's complex needs production *The Bounce* toured the UK in 2014 and 2015. We interviewed some teachers about their thoughts and observations about *The Bounce* experience while we were resident at their schools.

YouTube link: https://youtu.be/uoHojg8gxlQ

The Art of the Cart: Oily Cart Design Exhibition (2015)

YouTube link: https://youtu.be/bfDvy9Hrees

Land of Lights Trailer (2015)

Oily Cart presents a brand new immersive show for 3–5 year olds and their families, jam-packed with live music, puppets and a medley of wonderlands, all leading us to a sparkling finish. *Land of Lights* tours to artsdepot, London from 15 Dec 2015–3 Jan 2016, Theatr Clwyd, Mold from 12–23.

YouTube link: https://youtu.be/GDjzHAN2_q0

Mirror, Mirror: Teacher Interviews (2017)

Oily Cart's complex needs production *Mirror, Mirror* toured the UK in 2016 and 2017. In this video, teachers share thoughts and observations about their *Mirror, Mirror* experience while we were resident at their school.

YouTube link: https://youtu.be/btwJU8JPO3w

Hush-a-Bye Trailer (2017)

YouTube link: https://youtu.be/TEaig9uZC1c

Kubla Khan & Splish Splash: Creating the Shows (2018)

"There aren't any limits – you just have to make sure you realise that when you embark on any voyage."

YouTube link: https://youtu.be/96ErgdyzFUo

Kubla Khan & Splish Splash: Creating Tailored Theatre for Different Needs (2018)

"We need to make sure that we're equipping everybody with the biggest, the best toolkit to draw upon, in order to create the best experience." Hear from the team behind our recent shows *Kubla Khan* and *Splish Splash*.

YouTube link: https://youtu.be/fmSm6n0iE9c

The Work of Oily Cart: Bringing Theatre to Children With PMLD (2018)

In 2018, John Vorhaus and Sarah Richmond, two philosophers from University College London, commissioned this short film as part of their research into the experience of theatre for children with Profound and Multiple Learning Disabilities (PMLD). It follows the development of *Splish Splash*.

YouTube link: https://youtu.be/BPlzoF3Modw

Oily Cart: Reimagining Theatre for Young Audiences to Make It More Accessible (2019)

YouTube link: https://youtu.be/ENx-DLoOSIE

Index

Note: Page numbers in italics indicate a figure on the corresponding page.